# The Midwife–Mother Relationship

# The Midwife–Mother Relationship

Edited by

MAVIS KIRKHAM

palgrave

Published by
PALGRAVE MACMILLAN
Houndmills, Basingstoke, Hampshire RG21 6XS and
175 Fifth Avenue, New York, N. Y. 10010
Companies and representatives throughout the world

PALGRAVE MACMILLAN is the global academic imprint of the Palgrave
Macmillan division of St. Martin's Press, LLC and of Palgrave Macmillan Ltd.
Macmillan® is a registered trademark in the United States, United Kingdom
and other countries. Palgrave is a registered trademark in the European
Union and other countries.

ISBN 0–333–76053–0

This book is printed on paper suitable for recycling and
made from fully managed and sustained forest sources.

A catalogue record for this book is available from the British Library.

10   9   8   7   6   5   4
10   09   08   07   06   05   04

Editing and origination by
Aardvark Editorial, Mendham, Suffolk
Printed in China

# Contents

# Contents

# Notes on Contributors

**Tricia Anderson** *Lecturer in Midwifery Studies, Institute of Health and Community Studies, Bournemouth University, and Independent Midwife*
Tricia Anderson trained as a midwife in Dorset where she worked in both community and hospital settings before commencing independent midwifery practice in 1997. She was formerly Editor of the *MIDIRS Midwifery Digest*, Co-Editor of the *Informed Choice Initiative* and Associate Editor of *The Practising Midwife*. At Bournemouth University she has pioneered student midwife caseload-holding as a model for midwifery education. Her research interests include the second stage of labour and breastfeeding peer support.

**Chris Bewley** *Senior Lecturer in Midwifery, Middlesex University*
Chris Bewley's research interests include domestic abuse and its effects on pregnancy, communication between health professionals and their clients, interpersonal relationships, emotional needs of women having twins and other higher order births and support for midwives returning to work after pregnancy loss. Her other interests include developing effective pre- and post-registration education programmes for midwives.

**Margaret Chesney** *Senior Midwife Lecturer, University of Salford*
Margaret Chesney is a graduate of the University of Huddersfield and Surrey University. She is currently undertaking a PhD at the University of Sheffield, studying birth for some women in Pakistan. She began nursing in 1974 and has been a midwife since 1980. She has made eight working trips to Pakistan to work in a Red Crescent Maternity Hospital in Sahiwal. Her current role in the University of Salford is as a Senior Midwife Lecturer in the Directorate of Midwifery and Associate Head of the School of Health Professions (Research). She is on the British Journal of Midwifery Editorial Board and the RCM Council. Her clinical background is in community midwifery, as a midwife then a manager. Since 1991 she has

carried a small caseload of women with students, providing continuity. Her special interest is with the care of childbearing women.

**Mary Cronk** *Independent Midwife*
Mary Cronk is a mature but hopefully up-to-date and forward looking
midwife, who tries to combine experience of the past with a vision for
the future. Almost all of her professional career has been as a clinical
midwife. For over 30 years she was an NHS employed midwife in
both community and hospital practice. From 1991 onwards she has
practised independently. Since 1983 she has been involved in the
work of the statutory bodies regulating midwifery as a member of the
ENB and the UKCC. She presently sits on Professional Conduct
Committees and the Midwifery Committee of the UKCC. She is a
member of the Council of the Royal College of Midwives and of the
midwifery forum of Unison.

**Jean Davies** *Regional Officer for the Royal College of Midwives in
the north east*
Before taking up her present position Jean Davies was a community
midwife in Cowgate, Newcastle upon Tyne over a 10 year period. She
initiated the Community Midwifery Care Project giving enhanced
care to women with low incomes and also studied their family
networks for her MSc dissertation. She was the research midwife for
the prospective Northern Region Home Birth study in 1993. She is a
Trustee of the Iolanthe Trust, the funds of which go to research into
improving care for mothers, babies and their families.

**Nadine Pilley Edwards** *Researcher*
Birth activist and researcher, Nadine Pilley Edwards joined the Association for Improvements in the Maternity Services (AIMS) in 1980
and is currently the joint Vice Chair. She trained as a birth teacher
through the former London Birth Centre in 1982 and has run antenatal classes in Edinburgh since 1985. She and Lyssa Clayton set up
the Scottish Birth Teachers Association in 1991 to provide a training
course for birth teachers in Scotland and, with Andrea McLaughlin,
she founded the Birth Resource Centre in Edinburgh which runs a
variety of pre and postnatal events for women and families. Nadine
was the AIMS representative on the Lothian Maternity Services
Liaison Committee for three years. She is completing a PhD on

women's experiences of planning homebirths in Scotland, initially through Edinburgh University and currently through the University of Sheffield.

**Valerie Fleming** *Reader in Midwifery, Glasgow Caledonian University*
Previously involved in midwifery practice and research in New Zealand, Valerie Fleming later joined the academic staff of Massey University, New Zealand. Her research interests are in the area of women's health and more specifically in the practice of midwifery.

**Mavis Kirkham** *Professor of Midwifery, University of Sheffield*
Mavis Kirkham has 30 years' experience as a practising midwife and researcher. Her current research centres on informed choice and the culture of practice. She combines her academic commitment with work in a rural midwives unit and home deliveries in Sheffield.

**Nicky Leap** *Senior Lecturer in the Faculty of Nursing and Midwifery and Health at the University of Technology, Sydney (UTS) and Senior Research Fellow in Midwifery at Flinders University, Adelaide*
Since 1997, Nicky Leap has lived in Australia where she is involved in midwifery research, education and organisational change. Her main research interest is the development of midwifery theory regarding aspects of woman-centred practice, in particular midwifery perspectives on being with women in pain in labour and moving from classes to groups. She is a regular contributor to international conferences and workshops. She is currently enrolled in the Professional Doctorate in Midwifery at UTS.

**Sally Pairman** *Programme Leader (Midwifery), Otago Polytechnic, New Zealand*
Sally Pairman has been a practising midwife for 17 years, working in a variety of settings from fragmented care in hospital to independent midwifery practice with continuity of care in the community. She is committed to promoting midwifery as a strong, independent profession and to maintaining choices for women in childbirth services. Sally has a strong interest in midwifery education and is the immediate past President of the New Zealand College of Midwives.

**Ruth Wilkins** *Associate specialising in Health Care PFI projects at Beachcroft Wansbrough, Solicitors, London*
Ruth Wilkins experienced midwifery care firsthand when she had her own children and became interested in the distinctive contribution of the midwife to maternity care. She completed a PhD at the University of Surrey examining sociology aspects of the mother–community midwife relationship and subsequently worked at the Centre for Midwifery Practice, Queen Charlottes and Chelsea Hospital evaluating one-to-one midwifery care and undertook other women and children health research.

# Introduction

When I first had the idea of this edited volume, I was immediately amazed that such a book did not already exist. This feeling has stayed with me throughout its production. If midwifery is conducted in and through the relationship between the woman and the midwife, it is strange that this is, to my knowledge, the first book on that relationship. However, as one reads the book and considers the issues, it becomes clear that the organisational context of midwifery care has served to divert midwives from this fundamental relationship. This book seeks to refocus our attention.

After much thought, the book has been called *The Midwife–Mother Relationship*. There are cogent arguments for speaking of the midwife–woman relationship, as many of the contributors do. Yet historically and usually today, the midwife is also a woman, and this is a relationship developed and defined as one between women. Both women relate in their roles, as childbearing woman or as woman providing professional care during childbearing. So it seems odd to refer to one of those concerned as if her role were simply that of woman, or as if she were the only woman in the duo. Not all women in midwives' care go on to mother their children, yet all go through the transition of becoming a mother. Motherhood is so important in the relationship that it influences how both partners see each other (see Chapter 8). Midwives do not relate only to mothers. They relate to babies, partners, fathers, grandparents, whole families and many, varyingly significant others. Sometimes they relate to isolated women and help them to build the support networks so vital to mothers. Midwives relate to the mother–baby unit, both before and after birth. The baby is the mother's, as is the relationship with the professional. Childbearing women are the centre of the midwife's work: 'they are seen as themselves and their concerns are validated' (see Chapter 10). For all these reasons, the title has been chosen.

It has been a great pleasure to work on this book with ten women who are deeply concerned with the nature of the midwife–mother relationship. Eight of the contributors are midwives, as I am myself. Two, Nadine Edwards and Ruth Wilkins, report research on the experience of childbearing women, research that arose from a wish to understand their own and other women's experience. All but one of the chapters report research on varying aspects of the midwife–mother relationship. Mary Cronk's chapter is the exception, being a reflection upon that relationship from her uniquely rich and long clinical experience as a community midwife and now as an independent midwife. We synthesise, in our writing here, many areas of our experience, as midwives, mothers or supporters of childbearing women, with our research upon this relationship.

In Chapter 1, Nicky Leap reflects upon the philosophy of 'the less you do, the more you give' as a midwife. She sees midwives as being 'alongside women', embracing uncertainty together as women 'take up the power that will enable them to lead fulfilling lives as individuals and mothers' and motivating the woman's friendship group to be there for her. In Chapter 2, Mary Cronk describes her role as that of a 'professional servant'. This prevents the midwife from presuming 'a power that we had no right to presume' and from using 'that power to control women'. She relates how we got into the sorry state of obeying hospital policies and relaying them to women as orders. Again, changing the power base in the relationship is seen as necessary to enable 'women to feel more confident, more responsible, more in charge'.

Chapters 3 and 4 focus on the childbearing women's experience. Both look at their relationship with NHS community midwives. Nadine Edwards looks at how women planning homebirths see their relationships with midwives. This minority group's relationships with midwives, and their midwives' relationship with the women's dissident views on place of birth, raise many issues of wider significance. Issues of control, safety and trust are here seen from the perspective of women who are aware of tensions experienced by their midwives. The women negotiate their relationship with the midwife, and their trust in her, in the context of that midwife's professional values and commitments. Ruth Wilkins describes the 'professional paradigm' and its 'profound lack of fit' with the mothers' viewpoint and the way in which the dominance of that paradigm alienates midwives from their own experience. Nevertheless, her sample of mothers describes a special, personal relationship with their community midwives.

Tricia Anderson analyses a key point in the relationship: the second stage of labour. The tensions of trust and control are sharply focused in the chapter title: 'Feeling safe enough to let go'. The midwife's power to support or undermine is central and has an important influence upon the woman's relationship with her body.

Chapters 6 and 7 look at the relationship in circumstances where the cultural gap between midwife and mother is particularly wide. Jean Davies' research concerns women who are economically deprived and shows what can be achieved when efforts are made to bridge the divide between professional and client, and women claim 'their' midwife. She speaks of the challenge in adapting a more open way of working and acknowledges that 'it is easier to hide within a structure that is safe and can be closely defined and confined into a task-orientated approach'. This is the same phenomenon described in Nadine Edward's study, where women saw midwives hiding behind their need to 'check' and to carry out proscribed professional tasks rather than listening to women.

Margaret Chesney's work is with Pakistani women and therefore involves a 'three-way relationship' that includes an interpreter. In her remarkably honest reflections on practice, she recalls 'bad care days' when the rush to the Tuesday clinic prevented her listening, a phenomenon seen in many other settings. She also speaks of the need for a common philosophy and shared aims and understanding if midwife and interpreter are to give good care together.

Similar conclusions are drawn in several chapters on the need for shared values and aims between the midwife and mother. Margaret Chesney also speaks of an interpreter ordering women about, an acting out of pressures upon her that many midwives feel upon themselves, but which Margaret was trying to resist on behalf of her clients. Chapters 6 and 7 describe cultural differences and growing understanding. Both studies demonstrate what can be achieved when midwives and interpreters develop the understanding and confidence to stop hiding behind organisational defences.

Chris Bewley looks at a minority group within midwifery, midwives without children, and how their personal lack of experience of the transition to motherhood influences their relationship with women in their care during that transition. In examining this, she highlights important aspects of the personal nature of the midwife–mother relationship, which is explored in several chapters in differing contexts.

Chapters 9 and 10 concern the New Zealand model of partnership between midwife and mother. This model of a one-to-one relationship, with the conscious aim of balancing the power of the midwife and the mother, is seen as important to midwives in many other countries. Valerie Fleming introduces this partnership on a political level and explains how it came about. Sally Pairman examines this 'new kind of professional relationship', with its 'emancipatory outcomes as new knowledge of childbirth and midwifery is generated'.

Context is clearly important to this, as to any relationship. The tension between the midwife's relationship with an individual client and with her profession and her employer is a recurring theme throughout this book. It is not surprising that most of the contributors have chosen to examine situations where there is an opportunity for that relationship to develop. While the relationship can be profoundly important on one occasion, especially if that is the birth, a considerable degree of continuity of carer is fundamental to the development of this relationship over time. The development of the relationship is also more likely to be grounded in the experience of the mother if it takes place in her context rather than the professional context of the hospital.

The organisational context of birth has changed in recent years. In some places, such as New Zealand, change has favoured individual relationships between midwives and mothers, with a deliberate movement of power towards mothers. In other contexts, maternity services continue to be centralised and the needs of individuals, mothers or midwives, can go unheard. In many places, more midwifery care takes place in the community than happened in the recent past. Some of the contexts described in this book may be far from the experience of some midwife readers. They provide evidence of what can be done and stimulate us to think of what needs to be done at an individual and a political level.

In Chapter 11, I attempt to draw some conclusions.

I hope that what is offered here will serve as the opening of a growing literature on a subject fundamental to our practice as midwives.

MAVIS KIRKHAM
*University of Sheffield*

# Chapter 1

# 'The Less We Do, the More We Give'

*Nicky Leap*

## Introduction

In this chapter, I shall use the first person in order to acknowledge and own the subjectivity of the ideas I shall be exploring. Feminists such as Christine Webb (1992) have advocated this technique when presenting a personal evaluation or critique. The thoughts expressed in this chapter have arisen from my 20 years in midwifery practice and are not necessarily based on standard 'research-based evidence'. The chapter therefore contributes to a growing body of opinion arguing that authoritative knowledge should not be discounted in the drive to develop evidence-based practice, particularly around decision-making regarding individualised care (Sackett *et al.* 1997).

Although I am a mother, I am writing this chapter from the perspective of a midwife. Therefore, when I use the collective pronoun, it will usually be in order to generalise about how we, as midwives, engage with women. This is not to deny the important contribution to my thinking that several midwives played in my life on the occasions when I became a new mother, or the insights that arise from being on the other side of the midwife–mother partnership.

## The concept of 'the less we do, the more we give'

In life, there is the potential to stumble across a phrase that pulls us up short, often a simple truth that will resonate through our core beliefs and values, heralding a profound impact on how we approach life thereafter. So it was for me when I was a newly qualified midwife and Hazel Smith (independent midwife) said, in an almost throw-away aside, 'You know, in midwifery, it's often true that the less we do, the more we give.' At that time, these words may have reflected Hazel's interest in Zen Buddhism or her passion for reflecting on life and midwifery, but for me it was a gift. It altered the way I practised and became part of a midwifery philosophy at the very heart of how I see the role of the midwife.

During my midwifery training, I had learnt a lot about 'doing things'. I had learnt that when you are thrown together with a labouring woman whom you have never met before, you work hard at building rapport and gaining her trust. This would involve a lot of talking, finding common ground, jokes, massage, eye contact, loving attention, sitting beside her throughout labour, encouraging her with the sponge and iced water constantly poised. This is what I thought being 'with woman' was all about.

Midwives like Hazel Smith started showing me another way. I saw these midwives checking that all was well when a woman was labouring at home and then going to lie down in another room – or even going home if the woman was happy with that arrangement. I saw them sitting in a corner of a room in watchful anticipation during labour, but on the whole they were very quiet and non-directive. I saw women who were undisturbed withdraw into the state of consciousness that is associated with the release of endogenous opiates. I saw that where women were asking for physical support, the people doing all the eye contact, massage and loving attention were the people the woman had chosen to be there for her. The people who would have the ongoing relationship with the woman and her baby were the key players, not the midwives who would move on after the first month or so of the baby's life.

Slowly, over the years, a different underlying philosophy of care emerged as I had the privilege of working in the relatively untrammelled world of independent practice. I learnt about the potential for the empowerment of women through an approach that:

- minimises disturbance, direction, authority and intervention
- maximises the potential for physiology, common sense and instinctive behaviour to prevail
- places trust in the expertise of the childbearing woman
- shifts power towards the woman.

I am not saying that this approach does not happen in hospital situations, only that it is easier to develop in community-based practice where midwives and women have a chance to get to know each other.

The concept of 'the less we do, the more we give' is directly related to the feminist notion of empowerment. The word 'empowerment' is bandied around liberally, and I often hear midwives talk about how 'we need to empower women'. There is an inherent contradiction in such a statement. None of us can 'empower' another person or indeed give women power. By its very nature, power is not given but taken. At every stage of our interactions with childbearing women, as midwives, we should be adopting behaviours ensuring that women can take up the power that will enable them to lead fulfilling lives as individuals and as mothers. This process of empowerment may have far-reaching consequences in terms of women's feelings of self-worth and confidence.

In this chapter, I shall explore some examples of how the philosophy of enabling women to take their power relates to midwifery practice. In particular, I shall draw on personal experience in considering how midwives can engage with women in ways that avoid dependency and maximise the potential for women to learn from each other and build supportive networks in the community. First, it may be useful to consider the overall nature of the midwifery relationship that we refer to as being 'with woman,' the term derived from the Anglo-Saxon 'mid wyf'.

## The particular nature of the 'with woman' relationship

> The relationship that develops between the woman and the midwife is at the core of human caring and may provide the basis of the professional body of knowledge that encapsulates midwifery. (Siddiqui 1999:111)

As has been articulated so well by midwifery leaders in New Zealand (Guilliland and Pairman 1995), the relationship between a woman and her midwife is based on mutual respect, trust and the potential for both parties to learn from each other as they engage in partnership. Through their interactions, there is the potential for both the woman and her midwife to be enriched by exploring the inherent possibilities that are within the self (Guilliland and Pairman 1995, Siddiqui 1999). Much has been written about midwives facilitating the empowerment of women through their experience of childbirth, but this midwifery skill depends on the midwife being self-aware and 'in touch' with herself (Siddiqui 1999). Furthermore, it cannot happen where midwives themselves are disempowered (Jamieson 1994).

Within the concept of continuity of carer, this relationship is different from any other relationship that involves health care workers. Having a baby can be seen as a rite of passage. In many situations throughout the world, there is the potential for a woman to engage a 'midwife' to be alongside her as she explores how the experience of childbirth impacts on all elements of her life. This includes the physical, intellectual, social and spiritual challenges and ramifications of childbirth. The midwife maintains the 'midwifery overview', ensuring that all these interwoven elements of the woman's life are kept in relief, whatever the events that unfold. The midwife works with the woman and her community, collaborating with other health professionals if necessary, to ensure that everything is done to ensure a safe and supported transition to new motherhood, taking into consideration the woman's individual circumstances and wishes.

With occasional exceptions to be found in the field of palliative care, there is no other example of people engaging a health care worker to be alongside them in this way throughout a life event or 'episode of care' (a reductionist term often used by health care economists). The midwifery relationship is therefore intrinsically different from the relationships with clients that develop in, for example, nursing and medicine. This is not to deny the important and potentially emancipatory nature of other health professionals' relationships with clients. Old-fashioned rhetoric about midwifery being different from nursing and medicine because it adopts a 'wellness', holistic approach is no longer useful in a culture where primary health care philosophy and politics have permeated the education and working environment of all health care workers. It is therefore important to articulate how the unique nature of midwifery is based on the relationship between the midwife and the woman.

## Embracing uncertainty together

One of the essential elements of the midwifery process of being 'with woman' can be seen as the embracing of uncertainty together. The uncomfortable fact is that no amount of screening and information giving can give pregnant women and new parents the complete certainty they seek or indeed the ability to make 'the right choice'.

The question marks of pregnancy are the beginning of a process of grappling with the uncertainty and decision-making that will persist throughout the experience of raising a child. In the early days of this process, engaging with uncertainty involves profound learning for each individual woman and her midwife in a way that is reciprocal and unique. However, to describe the relationship between the two as one of 'equals' denies an inherent power imbalance. Women ask midwives to join with them in order to draw on our expertise, our experience and our knowledge. They are asking us to provide them with a safety net, a point of reference that they can choose to use as a resource in a world where there are more questions than answers.

Recognising and owning our midwifery expertise is an important step in understanding the power dynamics of this situation. Equally important is an understanding of the limitations of our expertise. There is a fragile element within the notion we call 'informed choice'. Apart from the potential for decision-making that is biased by the person who is doing the informing, there are many situations in which no amount of information will clarify the decision process for women. Instead of giving women lists of possibilities and options to choose from, a 'wait and see – keep your options open' policy is arguably more useful. In antenatal groups and with individual women, I have found that, in many situations, raising the notion of 'uncertainty' has led to more fruitful discussion than has pursuing the idea of 'informed choice'. Embracing uncertainty sometimes brings a sense of calm, a sense that what will be, will be. This is not about engendering a passive fatalism but more about enabling women to learn to trust that they will cope with whatever comes their way. Working through these issues is particularly important in a culture that privileges the notions of 'choice' and 'control' (Department of Health 1993).

## Believing in women

Our expertise as midwives rests in our ability to watch, to listen and to respond to any given situation with all of our senses. This will include the conscious and subconscious 'knowing' that has been generated from our experience and learning. It also involves a 'clue-fullness' as we respond to the overt and covert clues from women and their worlds. The skill lies in knowing when to inform, suggest, act, seek help and, most importantly, be still or withdraw and remove ourselves. Our belief in a woman's inherent ability to be her own and her baby's expert should underpin all of these responses.

If we believe that women have within themselves everything that is needed for the physiological processes of childbirth, we are bound to ask questions about the need to employ 'complementary therapies' as a matter of course. The very act of suggesting their use in a normal process can suggest that we think women cannot manage without them or that women's bodies are in some way deficient. If, at the end of the day, after an uncomplicated pregnancy and labour, a woman feels that she could not have managed without the aid of (for example) homeopathy, acupuncture, aromatherapy, or indeed the midwife, she is at some level giving away her power. She has invested in something outside herself, and this can perhaps subtly diminish her sense of achievement and triumph.

Ever since the wealth of publications from the alternative birth movement of 1970s North America, there has been a tendency for midwives to feel that, in the tradition of 'wise women', they should work out the deep psychological processes affecting the women they care for. The message within this literature was that midwives should engage in psychotherapeutic interventions; in other words, they should identify and help women get rid of the 'baggage' that might impede the process of childbirth. Anne Oakley (1980) has identified and questioned a process in which physiological problems of childbirth are sometimes identified as psychosomatic defences and psychological maladjustments.

Diane Gosden and Ann Saul (1999) have recently expressed concern about the potentially disempowering effects that can arise if there is a shift in the midwife's role 'from empathetic listener to a more interventionist psychological role'. Drawing on interviews with women conducted in the course of a research study on homebirth in Australia (Gosden 1996), they describe the sense of intrusion and loss of autonomy in determining their own pace of personal growth felt by women when midwives openly engage in this form of 'psychotherapy'. They cite, for example, a woman's feelings of vulnerability, self-blame and low self-esteem when the midwife suggested that she was holding onto her baby in an 'overdue' pregnancy because she was too scared to give birth (Gosden 1996:150).

In my own study regarding midwives' attitudes to being with women in pain during labour (Leap 1996a), midwives discussed the fallacy of predicting how women would 'be' in labour. They described a culture in which midwives still tend to make these predictions in private based on ill-founded 'psychological' value judgements and in spite of the apparent unreliability of such predictions. The place of psychotherapy philosophies in midwifery practice needs further exploration, especially in terms of the implications for power dynamics and the relationships between women and midwives.

As midwives, we need to believe in women even when, or maybe especially when, it seems as though the psychosocial odds are stacked against them. This means being clear that we have confidence in their potential to be able to:

- monitor their baby's development and wellbeing in pregnancy
- find a way through pain in labour
- give birth in spite of any fears or previous traumas in their life
- nurture their baby and monitor the baby's wellbeing and development
- listen to their baby's needs and respond appropriately according to instinct and common sense
- make wise decisions in the face of uncertainty, upheaval and exhaustion.

This process of inspiring confidence in women by our confidence in their abilities is often based more on questions than on giving answers. Asking women how their baby has been moving – and making it clear that there is no clinical value in our routinely listening in to the baby's heart in pregnancy (Sharif and Whitle 1993) – makes it clear that we recognise the supremacy of their expertise in monitoring their baby's wellbeing. Thus we can encourage women's awareness and sense of independence and responsibility. We can also avoid the 'separation from self' and enforced dependency described by Emily Martin (1984:1202):

> My doctor gave me the heartbeat. It's like he took it away from me because he said, 'Here's the heartbeat...' and I sort of felt like, well this is my baby's heartbeat but I can't hear it unless he does it for me... I felt funny about the fact we had to rely on him.

Similarly in the postnatal period, asking the woman how her baby 'is' rests in a far more empowering model of care than 'strip-searching' her baby. The same applies to tasks that were once routine with respect to the woman's body in the postnatal period. The process of 'top-to-toe' checking, with the undignified 'checking the pad and the perineum', is no longer being advocated as a routine procedure in midwifery education. Midwives are now being taught to listen to women and only perform such tasks at the invitation of a woman if she has expressed concern (Leap and Heptinstall 1997).

Putting our faith in women gives them powerful messages, especially during labour where the quiet 'midwifery muttering' – 'You can do it' – when a woman is saying words to the contrary is often all it takes to get women through the aptly named 'transition' phase of labour. These are the 'whispered words of wisdom' of 'letting it be' (Lennon and McCartney 1970). Sheila Kitzinger (1988:18) has described the skill of helping a woman in labour to have confidence in herself and the 'power of her uterus' in terms of 'patience and the willingness to wait for the unfolding of life'.

The key to this skill of patience is the ability to be with women in pain and resist the urge to try to take away the pain. Many midwives recognise the important role that pain can play in labour (Leap 1996a). This is not just in terms of its place within the interrelated hormonal cascades that enable a physiological process to occur and at the same time stimulate the release of the woman's endogenous opiates. Experienced midwives will hold back from offering the 'pain relief menu' in a normal labour, knowing that, where women give birth without having pain taken away from them, their sense of triumph may have far-reaching consequences (Robertson 1994, Leap 1996a). However, the notion of triumph does not only belong to the realm of 'normal' birth. Where women need to give birth with all the support of modern technology and surgical intervention, our expressed appreciation of the woman's courage and endurance may play an important role in the potentially empowering process of active reflection in the early postnatal period.

## The fourth 'C': community

In the 1990s, maternity care policy has concentrated on placing women at the centre of care by addressing the three 'Cs' – 'Choice, Control and Continuity' (Department of Health 1993). In the South East London Midwifery Group Practice (SELMGP) – a group of self-employed midwives who worked within the NHS with predominantly disadvantaged women – we came to believe that the three 'Cs' should hinge on a fourth 'C': 'Community'. We developed a 'philosophy in action' that concentrates on motivating the pregnant woman's own friendship group to be there for her, putting her in touch with other pregnant women and new mothers who will become her life-line in the early months of her baby's life. The friendships thus formed often endure for many years – 'I think it's most probably friends you'll have for life really' (Leap 1992).

The SELMGP has now become the Albany Midwifery Group Practice and is one of several midwifery group practices that have been developed within Kings Health Care, a large London teaching hospital. The midwives in this practice continue to work within this 'philosophy in action' from community-based premises. Women, their families and friends are given clear messages that reinforce their own role in taking responsibility and control with regard to their experience of childbirth. Conversely, the midwives minimise their own role. They recognise that they are invited guests in people's lives for a short while and do not delude themselves that they can change the underlying social conditions that often make life so difficult for women and their families. However, the aim is to instill the confidence and sense of independence that can change lives. The bottom line has to be 'You can do this.' Although the midwives end up spending more time with women where medical problems arise, they still in this situation attempt to activate the main source of support within the community.

As midwives, we are with women over such a tiny span of their lives. I would not want to diminish in any way the extraordinary repercussions of our input at this crisis time in a woman's life. However, we are potentially in danger of creating mutual dependencies if continuity of care leads to exclusive, special relationships between individual women and their midwives. There is something very worrying if a situation of 'friendship' or 'companionship' between a woman and her midwife leads to a scenario in which, at a last visit, the two sit having a final cup of tea feeling overwhelmed by a sense of loss because the relationship has to end there. Luckily, this does not happen that often because most women are so absorbed by their new relationship with their baby that the strong ties with the midwife that can develop in pregnancy are already loosened into realistic proportions.

There will always be some enduring friendships that emerge between women and midwives. In my experience, such friendships are responsible for most of the effective political action that changes the system in the interests of childbearing women. It is, however, possible that our most important contribution to the long-term well-being of women and their children lies in our role in activating support and networks within the woman's community. In supporting this notion, Soo Downe (1997:43) writes:

> Perhaps in the end the best model for women is one in which the midwife's role is not, to paraphrase a Christian Aid slogan to 'give a woman support in childbirth and she'll be happy for a day' but 'teach a woman and her family how to tap into support systems and they'll be happy for life'.

Since social support has been shown to be the single most effective 'intervention' in modern obstetrics in terms of labour outcome (Hodnett 1995) and long-term health gain (Oakley *et al.* 1996), there is good evidence to encourage us to develop strategies to enable community support. As Jane Sandall (1996:621) points out:

> When you combine continuity of care with social support from other women, you have a powerful recipe for improving physical and psychosocial outcomes during pregnancy and childbirth for women, children and their partners.

Midwives in the SELMGP recognised that strategies to promote community support and minimise dependency also contribute to the avoidance of 'burn out' (Leap 1996b, Sandall 1997). We were increasingly motivated to address these issues as we moved from the independent midwifery model that some of us had come from, into a public health service (NHS) model with its incumbent pressures of increased caseload. Two important strategies that we developed within our 'philosophy in action' were the development of the 36-week home visit with the woman's supporters, and the antenatal and postnatal groups. These groups became the nucleus of the midwifery group practice.

### Moving from classes to groups

The basic structures of the antenatal group are simple and can be summarised as follows:

- Women can come to the antenatal group at any stage of their pregnancy.
- The group is there every week and is facilitated by a midwife.

- There is no fixed agenda: it evolves during the course of each session.

- Each week the facilitator co-ordinates a round in which the group members in turn say their name, when their baby is due, where they are having their baby, whether or not it is their first baby, where they live, and anything else they may wish to say or ask about.

- Each week somebody returns to the group with a new baby and tells her birth story. This forms a trigger for discussion and information-sharing, and is a rich source of learning and support.

The original postnatal group grew out of a situation in which women kept coming back to the antenatal group after they had had their babies. The midwives concerned hired another room and started running a postnatal group with the same structure of starting with a round so that everyone was introduced and had a chance to say something. Again, responding to requests from women, another antenatal group was set up in the evening so that men could attend as well as women who worked during the day. The women asked for the women-only group to continue in the afternoon as they identified that the discussion and support had a different quality at that session.

'Helping you to make your own decisions: antenatal and postnatal groups in Deptford, South East London' (Leap 1992) is a video that was made by women who felt passionately that they wanted to tell people about how important the groups had been to their lives:

> The group has been absolutely crucial to my pregnancy.

> It means that you're not there as an island trying to cope on your own with a new baby. You can ring someone up and say 'I'm feeling like throwing the baby over the balcony. Have you ever felt like that?' And they'll say, 'Right what you need to do is this'... And it might not work but that doesn't matter, it's just the fact that you've been able to have a conversation with someone in the middle of the night. You know that you're not the only one.

> I would have been very isolated otherwise. Like a lot of West Indian women who work, I didn't know many women in the area.

The model for running these groups is very simple. Although we ran our groups in a community centre for many years, the model has been adapted to several settings such as:

- health centres, GPs' surgeries and midwifery group practice premises
- hospital clinics
- a maternity hospital ward for inpatients and women attending a risk assessment unit
- midwives' own homes
- a swimming pool following aquanatal swimming sessions.

The groups are not run on a 'drop-in' basis: they start and finish at a set time. We therefore found it essential to offer a crèche to those women who had toddlers in tow. The groups run for about an hour and a half, and consideration needs to be given to the timing so that the group finishes before women have to collect other children from school.

The women are able to learn from each other in a way that is relevant to their lives. The midwife is not setting the agenda. She is not the central focus of the group since the bulk of the learning comes from the sharing of ideas and experiences by women in the group:

> We were all seen as having our own expertise really. It wasn't like, 'Experts–Novices... Midwives–Us'. We were all seen as having a valuable contribution to make. That meant we took more risks, we shared more and we formed really deep friendships.

> It wasn't abstract information that you were getting. It stayed in my head because it was attached to real people. Therefore it got absorbed differently. Information came up in a sort of organic way. So that, as a woman was telling about the birth she's had last week and how the baby got stuck, the midwife picked up a pelvis and baby [doll] and showed how that happened.

One woman in the video compares the group to the antenatal classes offered in the local health centre:

> Clinic classes, the ones I went to, you were taught at a certain level which wasn't a very high level so it was rather patronising. This group deals with the more social aspects of things. It's made me feel more comfortable with the whole attitude of being pregnant.

The advantages for midwives in working in this way are manifold. Once the structure has been set up, there is never the uncomfortable first session of a new group in which the midwife has to worry about 'breaking the ice' and getting the group established. Women who have been coming for many weeks are relaxed, set the tone for newcomers and explain to them how the group operates. Since the women set the agenda for the topics that are discussed each week (usually triggered by somebody's story about birth and new motherhood), the midwife does not need to prepare information as she would if she were running classes. The answers to any questions that arise lie within the group and the midwife's facilitation can ensure that this happens by deflecting back to the group, for example: 'What do the rest of you think about this?' or 'Has anyone else had this experience?' The midwife is not expected to have all the answers. If she does not know the answer to a complex clinical question, her response can be, 'Shall we look up what the latest thinking is about that?' – either with appropriate resources to hand or with a promise to return next week with the information.

For midwives, the group provides an illuminating forum for listening to women's stories of their experiences. Hearing them tell other women lends a different quality to the reflection that happens postnatally between a woman and her midwife. It is the best situation that I know of to learn from women. There are also practical advantages in organisation around continuity of carer. Where midwives work in group practices with individual caseloads, women can be invited to attend other midwives' groups if they feel that it is important to them to meet the other midwives in the practice. Thus, the onus is on the woman, and antenatal care does not have to be fragmented in order to 'meet the other midwives'.

The philosophical base for this way of providing community-based education and support for women – groups rather than classes – is in line with the theory about adult learning (Knowles 1978), which includes the following principles:

- An adult learner's self-concept moves from dependency to self-direction.
- Life experiences are an increasing resource for learning.
- Readiness to learn is orientated to developmental tasks and social roles.
- Learning is problem centred.
- Adults respond to a friendly, informal environment.
- The process of learning is a shared experience between teacher and learner.

## The 36-week home visit

Another important strategy to promote community support developed
by the SELMGP midwives is the 36-week home visit. Although it
became known as the 'birth talk', this session in the woman's home
brings together anyone in the woman's family and friendship group
who may be involved in supporting her in the early postnatal period as
well as during labour. Where the woman has no support, the midwife
will draw on her contacts within the community, often women who
have been through the group. The purpose of this meeting can be
outlined thus:

● It provides an opportunity for the midwives to explore various
  choices that the woman might like to make concerning her labour.
  Details are discussed such as whether she wants photographs, what
  she wants to do with her placenta, and whether she has any particular wishes that are dictated by her culture of religion or beliefs.

● Child care for other children can be explored, and if the children
  are likely to be involved during the labour, appropriate arrangements can be made for their support.

● The woman's friends can meet the midwives, determine their perspectives and be reassured that they are not going to have to negotiate on the woman's behalf 'against' the midwives. Where people
  meet for the first time when a woman is in labour, much energy can
  be wasted in building up the trust that does not come easily on first
  acquaintance.

● Everyone has a chance to be clear about his or her role. The midwives can explain that they will be there at appropriate times during
  the labour as a 'safety net' but that they will not be the people providing all the tender loving care. That is the job of the people who
  will have the ongoing relationship with the woman and her child.

● Birth photographs provide an excellent resource for talking about
  what to expect, particularly in terms of noise and pain. The midwives can explain that they are not being cruel if they are not
  offering 'pain relief' and can explain the purpose and nature of
  pain in labour.

● Discussion can occur over the place of birth. Many women and
  their supporters need to be reassured that the option to make a final

decision in labour and stay at home if all is well is a safe option where midwives carry full emergency equipment with them at all times.

- The midwives can reassure everyone that, should someone else be their midwife during labour, all the midwives in the practice have the same philosophy of care.

- Practical support in the early weeks following birth can be arranged. Rotas can be suggested for visiting friends to take responsibility for one prearranged evening each during which they will come in and cook, clean, shop or take away washing.

During this meeting, particular attention can be given to talking through the concept of 'pre-labour', also known as the 'latent phase of labour'. This can lead to realistic expectations, particularly if it is a first baby, as well as the avoidance of early hospitalisation. The support group can have confidence in their ability to support the woman and (unless they are worried) not telephone the midwife until labour is well established. Discussion also includes the clarification of what to do if the baby arrives before the midwife. Bullet points in the maternity notes can reinforce these messages by listing situations that warrant calling the midwife, as well as a simple list of instructions detailing what to do if the baby is arriving in a hurry.

## The midwife–woman relationship: a metaphor

When considering the 'the less we do, the more we give' philosophy, it may be useful to think in terms of a metaphor. Pregnancy, birth and the early weeks of a baby's life can be seen as a journey. The midwife provides a map for the woman if she needs one, warning her at the same time that the journey includes uncharted landscapes for which there can be no planning. She points out the signposts for various alternative routes and warns of hazards to avoid or obstacles that can be circumvented or surmounted. Most importantly, she puts the woman in touch with other women who have recently explored the same terrain, as well as those who will be making similar journeys and may wish to share resources and support each other along the way.

The midwife may be there for a part of the journey if it is particularly rocky, for she usually knows the terrain well. When she does not, she makes sure that the woman is put in touch with those who will

consider the safety issues involved by offering their technical expertise and specialist knowledge of complicated landscapes. The
midwife knows that, for most of the journey, the woman will manage
with the support of her chosen travelling companions, so she gives
these people various tools that may be useful along the way. The
midwife will have prepared them all to keep an open mind about the
many unforeseeable adventures they may have ahead. She will have
been at pains to instill confidence and to give them the message that
she believes them all to have the stamina and courage to handle
anything that comes their way.

At the end of the journey, the midwife will enjoy celebrating the
woman's sense of triumph and achievement as she sets off with her
friends on her next journey. The midwife says goodbye and enjoys a
quiet satisfaction. She knows that the woman has discovered her independence. Whatever the unplanned events of the next phase of her
life, the woman will be able to rely on her inner strengths, her new
knowledge, her common sense and her instinctive responses. A new-
found awareness of these skills will get her through all the crucial
decisions and responses she will have to make in this next stage.

## Conclusion

The words of the *Tao Te Ching*, written over 2,500 years ago (in
Heider 1986), summarise the concepts that have been explored in this
chapter:

> The wise leader does not intervene unnecessarily. The leader's presence is
> felt, but often the group runs itself.
>
> Remember that you are facilitating another person's process. It is not your
> process. Do not intrude. Do not control. Do not force your own needs and
> insights into the foreground.
>
> If you do not trust a person's process, that person will not trust you.
>
> Imagine that you are a midwife: you are assisting at someone else's birth.
> Do good without show or fuss. Facilitate what is happening rather than
> what you think ought to be happening. If you must take the lead, lead so
> that the mother is helped, yet still free and in charge.
>
> When the baby is born, the mother will rightly say, 'We did it ourselves!'

## References

Department of Health (1993) *Changing Childbirth: The Report of the Expert Maternity Group*. London: HMSO.

Downe S (1997) The less we do, the more we give. *British Journal of Midwifery* 5(1): 43.

Gosden D (1996) Dissenting Voices: Conflict and Complexity in the Home Birth Movement in Australia. MA Honours thesis, Anthropology Department, Maquarie University, NSW, Australia.

Gosden D and Saul A (1999) Reflections on the use of psychotherapy in midwifery. *British Journal of Midwifery* 7(9): 543–6.

Guilliland K and Pairman S (1995) *The Midwifery Partnership: A Model for Practice*. New Zealand: Victoria University of Wellington.

Heider J (1986) *The Tao of Leadership*. Aldershot: Wildwood House.

Hodnett ED (1995) Support from caregivers in childbirth. In: Enkin MW, Keirse MJNC, Renfrew MJ and Neilson JP (eds) *Pregnancy and Childbirth Module of the Cochrane Database of Systematic Reviews*. London: BMJ Publishing Group.

Jamieson L (1994) Midwife empowerment through education. *British Journal of Midwifery* 12(2): 47–8.

Kitzinger S (1988) *The Midwife Challenge*. London: Pandora.

Knowles M (1978) *The Adult Learner: A Neglected Species*. London: Gulf.

Leap N (1992) *Helping You To Make Your Own Decisions – Antenatal and Postnatal Groups in Deptford SE London* (video), available from ACE Graphics, Sevenoaks, Kent and Sydney, Australia..

Leap N (1996a) A Midwifery Perspective on Pain in Labour. Unpublished Master's dissertation, South Bank University, London.

Leap N (1996b) Caseload practice: a recipe for burnout? *British Journal of Midwifery* 4(6): 329–30.

Leap N and Heptinstall T (1997) The Midwife Working in the Community. In: Sweet B (ed.) *Mayes Midwifery: A Textbook for Midwives,* 12th edn. London: Baillière Tindall.

Lennon J and McCartney P (1970) *Let it be* (lyrics). London: Northern Songs.

Martin E (1984) Pregnancy, labor and body image in the United States. *Science and Medicine* 19(11): 1201–6.

Oakley A (1980) *Women Confined: Towards a Sociology of Childbirth*. Oxford: Martin Robertson.

Oakley A, Hickey D, Rajan L and Rigby A (1996) Social support in pregnancy: does it have long-term effects? *Journal of Reproductive and Infant Psychology* 141: 7–22.

Robertson A (1994) *Empowering Women: Teaching Active Birth in the 90s*. Sydney : ACE Graphics.

Sackett D, Richardson W, Rosenberg W and Hayes R (1997) *Evidence-based Medicine: How To Practice and Teach*. Sydney: Churchill Livingstone.

Sandall J (1996) Moving towards caseload practice: what evidence do we have? *British Journal of Midwifery* **4**: 12.

Sandall J (1997) Midwives, burnout and continuity of care. *British Journal of Midwifery* **5**: 2.

Sharif K and Whittle M (1993) Routine antenatal fetal heart auscultation: is it necessary? *British Journal of Obstetrics and Gynaecology* **13**: 111–13.

Siddiqui J (1999) The therapeutic relationship in midwifery. *British Journal of Midwifery* **7**(2):111–14.

Webb C (1992) The use of the first person in academic writing: objectivity, language and gatekeeping. *Journal of Advanced Nursing* **17**: 747–52.

# Chapter 2

# The Midwife: A Professional Servant?

*Mary Cronk*

Throughout life, human beings make relationships with each other. The mother–father–baby–child relationship is probably the first one we form after our births and is arguably one of the most important relationships in our lives (Winnicott 1987, Raphael-Leff 1991). As we grow and mature, we form the relationships of childhood and adolescence with everybody we meet and come into contact with. Many of these involvements are transitory, short, superficial and seemingly unimportant, but I feel that each relationship we make with another throughout our lives contributes to how we mature and grow as people. It seems to me that the duration of the relationship is not always in direct ratio to its depth. Many people will remember a person met briefly in childhood and the results of that meeting having an enormous effect on their emotional growth in terms of both positive and negative effect. As we go through life, we are constantly learning and growing from the relationships we make. Let us consider a few of these.

First, family relationships. We learn so much from our family environment and our first human contacts. The parent–child relationship is initially one of almost total dependence, for our survival, for physical and emotional needs. Whether that first relationship is good or bad, strong or weak, it is vital to our development through childhood, adolescence and towards maturity (Richards 1974, Winnicott 1988, Raphael-Leff 1991, Niven 1992). Siblings, grandparents, aunts, uncles and cousins all contribute to the family dynamic (Winnicott 1965). During childhood, links are formed with others outside the family, perhaps child-carers, playgroup leaders, teachers, neighbours, family friends and other children. Other pupils and students share our

school or college days. We negotiate our friendships, our space
(Richards 1974).

Employment brings another set of people together – direct
employers, managers, fellow workers. We learn to negotiate our
contacts, our boundaries, and the depth and intensity of our involvement with our fellows.

Then there are sexual relationships, boys and girls maturing,
becoming men and women, growing, maturing, mating, looking for
a mate for life. In writing this, I realise that all these relationships are
interrelated. An early happy family relationship may lead a person to
seek a mate for life with confidence, and from a position of strength,
whereas poor early family experiences may have a person seek from
a partner someone to fill the gaps in their emotions that were unful-
filled in childhood (Steiner 1974).

The power base in relationships develops as we mature. When we
are children, adults have power, our carers have power, our teachers
have power; as we grow, that power base changes to a more equal
relationship with other adults and to assuming power over those who
are our juniors, or whom we assume we should control.

We make acquaintances, friends and enemies; we identify our peer
group. The relationships have a form – equal relationships and others
in which the power in the relationship is unequal. Relationships can
be loving, caring, formal, informal, welcome, unwelcome, construc-
tive, destructive, supportive, dependent, tentative, provisional.

As adults, we make relationships with people from whom we
purchase goods or services. We choose the shops we use, the person
who does our hair. We choose the plumber, the window cleaner, the
solicitor, the dentist. With all these people we form a relationship. The
power balance with people we employ to provide us with services is
different from that of friendship or kinship.

So what factors are we looking at when we consider the optimum
relationship between midwives and the people they serve? I was
about to write 'women' instead of 'people' but then I thought: 'It's
not just women midwives care for; it's their babies and the babies'
fathers and sometimes siblings as well', as we hopefully nurture the
families we are involved with as we provide maternity services as
professional midwives.

The midwife is providing a service either as an employee of a
health service Trust that has a contract to supply midwifery services
or as an independent midwife directly employed by a woman to
provide her with maternity services. Anyone providing a service is a

servant. The midwife is a member of a profession, which surely means that she is providing professional services. The *Oxford Concise Dictionary* says that a servant is 'a person who has undertaken usually in return for stipulated pay to carry out the orders of an individual or corporate employer'. It further says a servant is 'one who serves another'; a professional is 'one belonging to or connected with a profession', and a profession is said to be 'a vocation, calling, especially one that involves some branch of learning or science'. These definitions fit very nicely into what I believe a midwife should be – a professional servant. In modern usage, there is some tension between these words, for 'learning' and 'science' carry status and power, while a servant role does not.

I have some old doctors' bills presented to my parents by their doctor, and by the midwife who attended my birth, before the NHS came into being. The doctor and the midwife were professionals; my father was a Clydeside shipyard worker. The bill says 'to professional *services*'. My father had great difficulty paying doctors' and midwives' bills and welcomed the NHS. I have often wondered what he would have thought about the changes in the relationships between professionals and their clients since its inception.

It may be difficult for many of us to think of ourselves as a woman's servant, albeit a professional servant, but that is really what we are. I practise independently and therefore provide my professional services directly to people who employ me, and I think of myself as their professional servant, but is that not the relationship that all midwives should have with the people they serve? Yet many of us presume we have a power over the people we serve, the people for whose benefit we practise. A power 'to allow'.

I am unclear how the power base between women and midwives changed, how it came about that we assumed a power that we do not have. How was it that we started 'allowing' women to eat, drink, walk, get out of bed, go to the loo, and so on; 'letting' women have a companion in labour, feed their babies when they wanted to, even pick their babies up; 'giving' women permission to make a noise, or telling them not to make a noise? I puzzle over what happened to that employee–employer relationship that existed between women and their midwives. A change took place that enabled us to presume a power we had no right to presume, and use that power to control women.

I feel that the first Midwives Act, yes our beloved 1902 Act in England and 1915 in Scotland, started the power shift. 'Ladies' became midwives. The bona fide midwife, who had cared for women who paid her, often in kind, was still around, but frequently she was not a 'lady' and she had not really thought of herself as a professional, even though she had been helping women in childbirth for a very long time. The new 1902 professional registered midwife was very conscious of her status and her subservient role in relation to the medical practitioners by whose grace and favour she practised (Heagerty 1997). It should be remembered there was no requirement for a midwife to sit on those first Midwives Boards, and early editions of the *Midwives Rules* had a great deal to say about the need for implicit obedience to the doctor's orders. If one has to obey orders concerning one's 'patients', one gives orders to one's 'patients'; if these 'patients' are of a lower social order, this is not difficult. The midwife employed and paid for by a Nursing Association or a Jubilee Midwife could and did give orders to the women for whom she was caring (Leap and Hunter 1993). The bona fide midwife had been controlled not by doctors but by the people who employed her, but she was literally dying out. The private midwife was in a different position: she was directly employed and could be dismissed if she failed to give satisfaction. Ordering one's employer about rarely leads to a satisfactory relationship.

The new registered midwife employed by a Nursing Association was required to wear a uniform. Uniforms are associated with military discipline, orders and hierarchy. The arrival of the NHS in 1948 removed from most woman–midwife relationships the remaining direct payment by the woman to the midwife. Again, our assumption of power grew. Midwives practising 'on the district', employed by the local authority and attending women in their own homes gave their orders, but the woman in her own home often ignored orders that she did not want to obey, could not obey or saw no need to obey (Llewelyn Davies 1977).

In 1976 the reorganisation of the NHS brought district midwives under the same employer as the hospital-based midwife. They were now expected to obey 'hospital policies'. Homebirths were almost completely phased out by the power of the employers of midwives, and the midwife obeying hospital policies relayed them to the woman as orders. The midwife–woman relationship power dynamic had almost entirely changed, except for the few of us who practised independently and were employed by our clients.

The servant bit of the professional servant status became almost forgotten. The various government reports – *Changing Childbirth* (Department of Health 1993) in England and *Maternity Care Matters* (Scottish Programme for Clinical Effectiveness in Reproductive

Health 1998) in Scotland – did attempt to change the power base, but in practice not much has changed. Women still perceive themselves as being 'allowed' to go over their dates, 'allowed' to refuse routine interventions, 'given' choices.

So where do we go from here? Would it be a good thing if we remembered our professional servant status? I believe it would. I believe that, for mothers and their partners in parenting, to reclaim their rights with our support will enhance their parenting. With rights go responsibilities. And parents are responsible for their children, aren't they?

One of the problems of professional status is the assumption that the expert knows best and that power is inherent in expert knowledge and opinion. In the present climate, when a woman becomes pregnant, it is perceived that the midwife knows best; if she does not, well the GP knows best, and the obstetrician certainly knows best how this pregnancy should be managed. After the birth (managed by those who know what is best), the midwife on the postnatal ward and the midwife who visits after the transfer home know what is the best way to feed, clean, hold, change and comfort the baby. After the midwife departs, along comes the health visitor. She knows best about lots of things: feeding, clothing, sleeping, potty training, immunisations; after all, she is a professional, so of course she knows best. Then off to school. And who knows best there? Teacher knows best, and the local education authority certainly knows best, what school little Darren or Ellie should attend.

Then, all of a sudden, it seems that the little darling is 16 or so and, as 16-year-olds are prone to do, does something antisocial, if not downright diabolical. What does society say? Who is to blame? Why, the parents of course. 'No sense of responsibility.' 'Parents must take responsibility for their offspring', says society. 'Fine these irresponsible parents', scream the tabloids. But it's a bit late isn't it? I believe that our assumption of power over the women for whose benefit we practise at the beginning of their parenting can begin their disempowerment as parents and take from them the feeling of responsibility for their children on which good parenting depends. Our input in terms of nurturing, enhancing and respecting the development of feelings of parental responsibility will, I believe, benefit society.

If we want to do this, how can we set about encouraging the young mother to take and accept responsibility for herself and her offspring? How do we stop ourselves telling her what to do and taking responsibility? Would it be a good thing if we balanced the assumption of power in our professional expertise by remembering the servant aspect of our relationship with the people for whose benefit we practise? How could we start to do this? We would have to remember to give professional advice rather than orders. We would have to learn to cope with sometimes having our advice rejected. We would have to almost recondition women to feel more confident, more responsible, more in charge. I believe that changing the power basis in the relationship between midwives and women would enhance all the qualities that contribute to parents becoming competent, confident and responsible.

So how can this power balance be changed? Perhaps one of the main ways in which parents could feel that theirs were the responsibilities would be to change the way in which maternity care was provided so that choice of midwife, continuity of care and control over their care could be returned to women. It is my hope that future maternity care will be a partnership model with the woman choosing her professional attendants. But can we change within the structures we now have in the NHS, which do not by and large empower parents?

Let us consider:

• The words we use
• The tones of voice we use.

We would have to watch our language – no more 'allowing', no more 'giving' of choice, no more 'having' to do as we, or Mr Hyanmytee, have ordered. It is difficult to remember to say, 'Could we consider', or 'I advise', or 'I strongly advise', or 'It is recommended', or 'The evidence shows that', instead of 'You must', or 'You have to', or 'Mr Bloggs allows', or does not allow. I have been practising independently for nine years now, having been a district midwife and an NHS-employed midwife. I have worn a frilly nurse's hat, given my orders and thought I had authority to tell women what to do because I was a midwife, and of course I knew what was best. I may have been a professional, but I had forgotten that my relationship with my clients was that of professional servant.

Actually, when I think of all the things I knew best about over the years, I cringe. A few to reflect on include: mandatory shaving (in hospital; we did not do it on the district), mandatory enemas, mandatory episiotomies (Mr Hyanmytee liked them), telling all women how to push, they being too stupid to know how, forbidding women to get out of bed, ordering men to leave the room (as I knew the women did not really want them there), forbidding women to eat or drink, taking their babies to the nursery, without even thinking to ask if that was what the woman wanted. I wonder if in ten years' time, I will think the same about the things I think I know best about now?

If the woman is young, disadvantaged and unused to having her opinions sought, let alone valued, it needs to be remembered that she may find NOT being told what to do quite threatening, and it will require sensitivity on the part of her midwife to gently empower her, perhaps increasing her decision-making as the pregnancy progresses.

In transactional analysis terms (Berne 1961, 1964), personality encompasses three major aspects, which are defined as parent, adult, child, and which are reflected in the way in which we relate to one another (Figure 2.1). We want, surely, to have our clients relate to us as adults.

**Figure 2.1**  The midwife–mother relationship
in transactional analysis terms

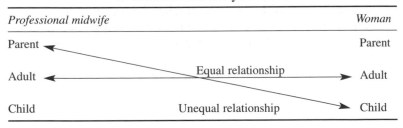

| Professional midwife | | Woman |
|---|---|---|
| Parent | | Parent |
| Adult | Equal relationship | Adult |
| Child | Unequal relationship | Child |

When the midwife says to the woman, 'You are 41 weeks now so if you haven't had the baby before Monday, you have to come in to be started off', she is speaking in the parent-to-child mode. If the woman responds by saying, 'Thank you for your advice, I will think about it and let you know', she is converting the relationship to one of adult to adult and cutting across the relationship the midwife has presumed they have. We should welcome this.

There are many other examples of where a midwife assumes the parent role. One may in the early antenatal period have said something like: 'We do a routine ultrasound scan here at X, Y and Z weeks, so that makes your first one on Wednesday week at 2.30 at the clinic on the first floor with a full bladder please.' If we were changing to professional servant or adult-to-adult mode, we might say something like: 'We offer ultrasound scanning checks here because it enables us to check that your baby is... How do you feel about this? Would you like to know more about ultrasound before you decide whether to have these scans?' Then, following a discussion, we would check that the woman has understood that we are advising and offering the service. 'Would you like to book your first appointment for next Wednesday? It is done in the antenatal assessment clinic on the first floor and we get a much better picture if your bladder is full.' Or with respect to something as ordinary, to us, as urinalysis: 'Have you brought a specimen? Well, dear, didn't you know you have to bring a specimen? You have to bring one every time you come; don't forget again, its important.' The 'routine' blood tests, the abdominal palpation – there are all sorts of these scenarios in which reflection can help us to see opportunities we can use to empower the parents, to help them feel responsible adults, and there are times when it is all to easy to affirm childbearing women in the subservient child role that they may feel it appropriate to assume.

The tone of voice we use should be similar to that which we would expect to be used to us by our solicitor, builder, hairdresser, optician, accountant, the people we engage to provide us with services. Are we likely to be addressed by them as 'dear' or 'honey bunch' or 'lovey' or 'duckey'?

Few of us would prick a baby's heel for the Guthrie test without informed consent from the mother, but it is also necessary to remember to ask: 'May I pick up, examine, check your baby? Is it all right if the doctor has a look at your baby?' All these phrases reinforce and affirm that this is *her* baby and we care for the baby with *her* permission because she is the responsible parent. Each time we pick up a baby without asking, we are missing an opportunity for promoting responsible parenting. New mothers are so vulnerable, and we have such power. Let us use it to empower them.

Perhaps it would help if we thought to ourselves, 'Would this couple choose to have me as their midwife if they had the choice? If they could dismiss me and engage someone else, I wonder if they would do so? Would I speak to them as I have just done if they had that power?' It makes you think, doesn't it? As thinking professionals, we do not demean ourselves as professionals by fostering an adult-to-adult relationship between us and the people for whose benefit we practise and by whom we are paid, directly or indirectly, to give a professional service. The most powerful thing we can do as professionals is to empower the parents of the babies at whose births we assist.

## References

Berne E (1961) *Transactional Analysis in Psychotherapy*. New York: Grove Press.

Berne E (1964) *Games People Play*. New York: Grove Press.

Department of Health (1993) *Changing Childbirth: The Report of the Expert Maternity Group*. London: HMSO.

Heagerty BV (1997) Willing Handmaidens of Science. The Struggle Over the New Midwifery in Early Twentieth-century England. In: Kirkham MJ and Perkins ER (eds) *Reflections on Midwifery*. London: Baillière Tindall.

Leap N and Hunter B (1993) *The Midwife's Tale: An Oral History from Handywoman to Professional Midwife*. London: Scarlett Press.

Llewelyn Davies M (ed.) (1977) *Life as We Have Known it: By Co-operative Working Women*. London: Virago.

Niven CA (1992) *Psychological Care for Families, Before, During and After Birth*. Oxford: Butterworth Heinemann.

Raphael-Leff J (1991) *Psychological Processes of Childbearing*. London: Chapman & Hall.

Richards M (1974) *The Integration of a Child into a Social World*. Cambridge: Cambridge University Press.

Scottish Programme for Clinical Effectiveness in Reproductive Health (1998) *Maternity Care Matters*. Aberdeen: Dugald Baird Centre for Research on Women's Health.

Steiner CM (1974) *Scripts People Live*. New York: Bantam Books.

Winnicott DW (1965) *The Family and Individual Development*. London: Tavistock.

Winnicott DW (1987) *Babies and their Mothers*. New York: Addison-Wesley.

Winnicott DW (1988) *Human Nature*. London: Free Association Press.

# Chapter 3

# Poor Relations: The Paucity of the Professional Paradigm

*Ruth Wilkins*

## Introduction

Why is one woman still aware of her community midwife's working hours a year after she last had need to know? Why does another claim to love her? Why did a third 'really mourn' the end of their relationship? Why does a fourth think her 'a saint', a fifth want her to be 'a friend'? Why is a sixth disappointed not to know her 'as a person', a seventh upset by her brusqueness, an eighth by her indifference? What on earth is going on?

I became interested in midwifery as one of the women referred to above. From my own experiences and discussions with other mothers, I became aware that the mother–community midwife relationship has a significance over and above its 'professional' functions. The mother–midwife relationship is often described as 'special' (Flint 1987, Page 1988, Cronk and Flint 1989). I wanted to know what was 'special' and distinctive about it in the community setting.

I decided to research the mother–community midwife relationship from a sociological perspective for my PhD thesis. The research was a longitudinal study involving in-depth interviews with a group of 43 mothers and their principal community midwives about community midwifery in general and their relationship in particular. The study was preceded by a pilot study and supplemented by an observational study of community midwifery in the same district in the south east of England, a substudy of some self-selected 'special' relationships (involving seven of the 43 mothers) and a review of the relevant midwifery research literature (Wilkins 1993).[1]

At an early stage in the research, I became aware of a profound lack of 'fit' between the viewpoint of the mothers and midwives I interviewed and the 'professional paradigm' that dominated the midwifery literature. The clash of perspectives was so fundamental that there seemed to be no way of incorporating what mothers told me was important or 'special' with prevailing conceptualisations of midwifery practice and the mother–midwife relationship. Consequently, I also become interested in the processes by which knowledge is constructed in academic and professional discourse.

In the first half of this chapter, I explore the paradox I had encountered and some reasons underlying it. I suggest that a 'professional' outlook is conceptually blind to the processes that make the relationship 'special' to mothers. It thereby overlooks important ways in which community midwives are (or can be) supportive of mothers. This, I shall suggest, is part of a wider incapacity to consider human relationships, emotions and biographical experiences as integral aspects of midwifery practice. This oversight is in turn explicable in terms of the assumptions concerning knowledge and meaning that support a professional perspective. A 'professional' outlook divorces mothers from midwives and midwives from themselves. For reasons I shall explore later, there was virtually no clue in the research literature to what mothers or midwives themselves hold to be special about the relationship, this despite the recognition that a 'special' relationship does, or can, exist.

In the second half of the chapter, I draw on findings from my research and suggest that the distinctive aspects of community midwifery practice lie in the three 'R's: relationship, role and real social context:

- *Relationship*: The 'special relationship' of which so many women speak is a personal one in which they are emotionally engaged and each party becomes known to the other; placing the other within a personal and biographical, rather than a narrowly professional, context. This in turn requires continuity of carer.

- *Role*: The 'role' of the community midwife (compared with medical practitioners and health visitors) is woman centred and psychosocially orientated.

- *Real social context*: The 'real' social context of the community, and in particular the home, facilitates the development of relationship and role, making available those social, emotional and biographi-

cal aspects that underpin the distinctive role of the midwife as supporter, carer and clinician to childbearing women.

## Outline of the professional paradigm

Although one can distinguish a profession, a professional, professional practice and the professional–client relationship, each is
informed by the same underlying assumptions. A profession is:

> A superior type of occupation... that requires advanced education and
> training. It thus has a specific and exclusively owned body of knowledge
> and expertise. A profession organises and, to some extent, controls itself by
> establishing standards of ethics, knowledge and skill for its licenced prac-
> titioners. (Oakley 1984:27)

Professional knowledge is exclusive, formal, discrete and cerebral.
A professional is a person in possession of specialist abstract knowledge who thereby stands in privileged relation to his or her clients.
Professional practice is the application of professional knowledge in
an object-orientated relationship of domination and control, whether
of a body, a mind or a situation.

In these ways, the professional paradigm (or worldview) enshrines
and prefers concepts of rationality, objectivity, formal knowledge,
culture and control (themselves associated with masculinity) in opposition to those of emotion, subjectivity, experience, nature and caring
(which are in turn associated with femininity). These preferences are
underwritten by ontological distinctions between object/subject,
rational/emotional, knowledge/experience, mind/matter and culture/
nature (Wagner 1986, Oakley 1992). Thus, the professional paradigm
exemplifies 'normative dualism', a process in which:

> Things that may be complementary or even inseparable [are conceptu-
> alised] in terms of exclusive disjunctions (either–or but not both)... They
> then value one disjunct more highly than the other. (Garry and Pearsall
> 1989:xii)

In the professional paradigm, facts, reason, knowledge and science
are actively pulled together, concertina fashion, along an epistemological drawstring called objectivity. The professional paradigm recog-
nises only one, 'professional', way of knowing. It prefers rational,

formal knowledge, which it homogenises and then monopolises. It prioritises professional practice (the active application of expert knowledge) and in so doing gives pre-eminence to the professional as the 'doer', overlooks the agency of the client and obscures other sources of knowledge. It also situates professional and client in wholly different 'planes of being' (or social dimensions), thus precluding any analysis of their relationship to each other and their similarities.

As Oakley (1984) notes, some sociologists, acknowledging the contradictions that this poses for a female professional, have labelled professions with a predominantly female workforce 'semi-professions' (Etzioni 1969). Other sociologists, recognising the masculinist normative preferences inherent in 'professionalisation', have questioned whether women should strive to become professionals at all. Addressing the nursing profession, Oakley (1984:27) suggests:

> If a profession is by definition male dominated, then nurses might as well give up. Alternatively, nurses might ask the truly radical question as to what is so wonderful about being a professional anyway... the current crisis of confidence in medical care should tell us that professionalisation is not the only answer.

## The professional paradigm and midwifery research

The implications of this argument have not been fully articulated in relation to the developments taking place in midwifery. Midwives are beginning to redefine the role, policy and practice of the midwife as distinct from that of medical practitioners. One aspect of this has been the assimilation of 'caring' as a professional objective. But this reversal of the 'care versus control' dichotomy in the medical professional model has led to neither a critique of related dichotomies or, more radically, a critique of the normative dualisms on which the professional paradigm (and science) depend. Accordingly, midwifery continues to be articulated in a language appropriate to medicine rather than midwifery. For example:

> The midwife has a central place in the provision of care in pregnancy and childbirth, as it is in her role in particular that the main elements of maternity care – clinical assessment and monitoring and the provision of advice and support – are combined. (Robinson 1989a:162)

The incorporation of the professional paradigm gives rise to a persistent tendency to conceptualise midwifery care in a conventional, object-orientated way in a manner that denies points of connection between professional and client and appropriates power and control to the 'expert'. There are three particular difficulties, as described below.

### *Location of mother and midwife in different planes of being*

The professional paradigm situates mothers and midwives in different planes of being (or social dimensions). This gives rise to two particular shortcomings. First, it denies the validity and relevance of the midwife's biographical self to professional practice. That is, it alienates the midwife from herself, constructing her 'personal' and 'professional' selves as entirely separate. This is part of a larger failure to incorporate a subjective viewpoint. It denies the social self (and thus the possibility of sensitising biographical experiences) and the psychological self, the midwife's culturally acquired 'ways of knowing' and 'conscious subjectivity' (Garry and Pearsall 1989, Stanley 1990).

Second, it denies points of connection between women. Mothers and midwives are conceptualised as if they inhabit mutually exclusive social spaces. The paradigm cannot accommodate the social and psychological identities that inscribe relationships between women in general, so cannot appreciate the gendered basis of the mother–community midwife relationship in particular. That is, it eclipses something of profound importance to women. It cannot explain many of the most emphatic statements they themselves have made, for example the importance of their community midwife being a woman and the desirability of her being a mother.

The paradigm is inadequate to the analysis of the mother–community midwife relationship. It is conceptually blind to the relationship as a dyad on the one hand and the points of connection within it on the other. It separates mothers from midwives and midwives from themselves.

### *Overemphasis on the professional*

The professional paradigm prioritises professional activity and professional knowledge and encourages an object-orientated perception of clients or patients. Emphasis is given to the activity and concerns of the professional. The professional paradigm invites practitioners to atomise the professional relationship and to fashion instead the entity 'professional practice', a discrete body of knowledge and expertise divorced from the social and relational context of its application. If the relationship is considered at all, as in some analyses of the 'midwifery process', it is instrumental to the professional objective, as for example with 'the provision of advice and support' (Robinson 1989a), rather than being conceptualised in its own right.

The relationship is, however, often of value to mothers in and of itself, not instrumental to the provision of advice and support but an instance or expression of it. That is, it is the human relationship rather than merely the service or skill that is valued. It is not a package but a process, and the professional paradigm cannot see this. In order to understand the value of the relationship as it is lived, in order more fully to appreciate how midwifery is part of the social network, an aspect of social support, a real human relationship between two people, the professional paradigm has to be relinquished.

## *Alienation of women from their own experiences*

The language of the professional does not articulate women's experiences. It is unable to accommodate what mothers value about their relationships with their community midwives and thus 'alienates them from their own experiences' (Smith 1988:86). It is the language of disinformation. It denies the need for a 'relationship' except for purely instrumental purposes and undermines women's own feelings. Women can be heard wanting a close personal relationship with their midwives:

> I'm hoping that a midwife will be almost like a friend's relationship with you. (Mother; Wilkins 1993:59)

yet recognising these as 'outlaw emotions' (Jaggar 1989:145):

> But apparently that's unprofessional... you don't bring yourself, your own experiences, into that sort of thing... that's what I've heard... but I don't know whether I agree. (Mother; Wilkins 1993:59)

There are other, derivative, difficulties. For example, the professional paradigm constructs and prefers 'knowledge' over 'experience',
so that research, rationality and training are preferred over individual
experience, whether professional or personal. The midwifery profession itself appears to be stratifying along these lines. Bodies and minds
are also dichotomised, robbing mothers of their minds and midwives
of their bodies. This approach also de-emphasises and undervalues the
practical basis of many professional skills.

In short, the professional paradigm is a way of constructing knowledge and human activity, one which relies on a series of dichotomies
that polarise professionals and clients, midwives and mothers in turn.
It is an ontology without a subjective viewpoint, ill disposed to relational analysis of any sort and capable of articulating relationships in
only an instrumental and object-orientated manner. It is conceptually
blind to subjective relationships since there is no point of connection
between expert and subject and therefore no way of understanding the
emotionally connected and biographically grounded relationship that
many women seek from their community midwife. It also prevents
midwives perceiving that relationship in anything other than an
object-orientated way.

This leaves midwifery conceptually impoverished. There is, for
example, no way of differentiating the role of the midwife from that
of the medical practitioner, except as a matter of emphasis. Furthermore, in failing to challenge professionalism's normative dualisms,
the entire edifice remains intact. On this construction, 'care' will
always remain less central to professional practice than 'clinical
assessment', 'monitoring' and the 'provision of advice'.

### Consequences of the professional paradigm in midwifery research

If we turn now to consider how the mother–community midwife relationship has been understood in the academic and practitioner-based
literature reviewed, we find an almost total silence. The relationship
between a childbearing woman and her midwife has been almost
entirely neglected. This is an oversight all the more surprising when
one considers that midwives are women's primary professional maternity care-givers, that midwifery is increasingly community orientated,
that increased research attention is being paid to the psychosocial
aspects of maternity care, and that midwives are re-establishing a

distinctive professional role, practice and research tradition, a central tenet of which is the provision of care that is supportive of and 'sensitive' to the needs of the mother (Adams 1987, Flint 1987, Flint and Poulengeris 1988, Kirkham 1989, Methven 1989).

If the relationship is recognised at all, it is characterised as an orthodox, if caring, professional–client relationship (Ball 1989, Laryea 1989, Methven 1989, Robinson 1989a, 1989b). It is recognised that the relationship is, or can be, 'special' (Flint 1987, Page 1988, Cronk and Flint 1989), but there has been no attempt to specify how or why. This is part of a wider failing to incorporate the concept of human relationships into midwifery practice.

In addition, notwithstanding policy statements in favour of community-based midwifery care (Association of Radical Midwives 1986, Royal College of Midwives 1987), there has been no attempt to specify what is distinctive about the mother–midwife relationship in the community. With very few exceptions, the studies emphasise hospital rather than community midwifery and distinguish these for pragmatic or organisational rather than conceptual reasons (Wilkins 1993).

It is in 'scientific' research that the contradictions implicit in midwifery research (those arising from the incorporation of the normative dualisms of science and professionalism such as object/subject, rational/emotional and knowledge/experience) are most acutely posed. In obstetric clinical research, the randomised controlled trial (RCT) has been vigorously advocated (Chalmers and Richards 1977, Enkin and Chalmers 1982, Chalmers *et al.* 1989). A direct opposition is asserted between 'experience' and 'knowledge'. For example, Enkin and Chalmers refer to the 'shaky foundations of authority and clinical experience' and caution 'conscientious clinicians' to base their clinical practice on the results of scientific evaluation arising from the conduct of 'appropriately designed research' (Enkin and Chalmers 1982:278). Although they acknowledge that 'many things that really count cannot be counted' (ibid:285), there is no way of reconciling that sentiment with the putative superiority of scientific over other kinds of knowledge.

This approach has profoundly influenced the design and methodology of much midwifery research[1] and has three particular consequences. First, it undermines and deflects attention away from the midwife-researcher's biographical experiences as a source of professional knowledge, as well as from the skill and knowledge arising from that experience. Second, it denies the possibility of learning through identification with the client because it asserts an epistemic distinction between lay and professional knowledge corresponding to 'objective' and 'subjective' states (knowledge and experience respectively). In so doing, it implicitly (and erroneously) asserts the epistemic purity of scientific research through a sole reliance on 'objective' knowledge, methodologies and practice (Knorr-Cetina 1981). Third, it seeks to confine 'subjectivity' to specific discrete and manipulable variables (and to research subjects), whereby subjectivity becomes divorced from other indices or outcome measures (for example, the degree of medical intervention during labour and delivery) and from the research process itself.

As noted earlier, this entirely fails to fit the central conclusions of my own research, which suggested that the importance of the mother–community midwife relationship lies precisely in those sources of 'knowledge' which the empirical scientist denies: the midwife's skill and experience on the one hand and her personal and cultural qualifications on the other. The personal, emotional and relational aspects of midwifery practice are crucial to both mother and midwife. Flint's *Sensitive Midwifery* (1987) abounds with examples of the importance of biographical experience and empathic identification to midwifery practice. Personal, emotional and biographical experiences are crucial aspects of the professional process, but this insight is denied by the perspectives of 'professionalism' and science. These perspectives denude the mother–midwife relationship and deny its richness and complexity. Moreover, since neither is able to appreciate the distinctive contribution of the midwife to maternity care, the midwife's contribution is indistinguishable from that of any other clinical provider.

## Research findings: distinctive aspects of the mother–midwife relationship

In the following section are presented findings from my own research, grounded in a viewpoint that relinquishes the normative dualisms of the professional paradigm, which reveals values and priorities that are not visible from a 'professional' perspective and that confirm the role of the midwife as distinct from that of other clinical carers of child-bearing women.[1]

The best insights into what Cronk and Flint call 'that special relationship... on which so much depends' (1989:9) come from direct experience rather than formal knowledge:

Mothers and midwives are intertwined, whatever affects women affects midwives and vice versa – we are interrelated and interwoven... To be a midwife is to be with women (the meaning of the Anglo-Saxon word) – sharing their travail and their suffering, their joys and their delights. (Flint 1987:viii, 1)

This implies two related aspects of the 'special' character of the relationship: a personal relationship between women and an emotional connectedness across the professional–client divide. This echoes the findings of my own research, which indicated in addition the rooting of the relationship in mothers' 'real' vital concerns. My research suggests the community midwife's distinctive contribution lies in what I have termed the '3 Rs': the relationship, the role and the real social context respectively.

## The relationship

The relationship was 'special' to the women interviewed to the extent that it was a *personal* relationship, akin but not identical to friendship. Mothers frequently expressed the wish to know, or the pleasure of knowing, their midwife 'as a person'. Moreover, for the women interviewed, it was indissolubly a relationship between women. They stressed the importance of a confiding, trusting, close relationship that held them, their emotions, experiences and concerns at its heart. Pregnancy and childbirth is in this sense a process of self-exploration shared with their community midwives. Such women want their midwife to be 'like a friend' to them. As the relationship deepens emotionally, so it expands socially; one mark of a developing relationship is the extent to which the social dimension extends into the 'clinical' encounter.

## The role

The subjective, psychosocially orientated role of the community midwife concentrates on feelings and experiences. It also engages the midwife's culturally acquired 'ways of being' and 'ways of knowing'. This combination of professional role and cultural capability is a powerful and valued one. It is an important basis for the personal relationship referred to above. In addition, it places mothers and midwives in the same 'plane of being' and thus engages the midwife's personal as well as professional resources.

Many mothers valued the midwife's 'cultural qualifications'. Some valued the fact that she was a woman, others that she was a mother. If she was a mother, this was an important basis for sharing experiences and drawing the relationship closer. To many women, these cultural qualifications were important sources of professional expertise, encouraging empathy and social and emotional awareness. For these women, mother and midwife were drawn together through their mutual grounding in shared identities and experiences.

The role also enables mothers, through the medium of their midwives, to gain access to other women's experiences of childbirth. Here, midwives are valued for their rich and detailed knowledge of women's experiences of childbearing and the social and emotional transitions accompanying it, made possible by an empathic and supportive role and a sensitive and sentient attunement within it. It is an intensely subjective conceptualisation of midwifery. Midwives are the embodiment of women's experiences of childbearing, an invaluable and unique resource.

### *The 'real' social context*

The community context is the appropriate context for the role, rooting it within the psychosocial context it serves. In the community, midwifery is interwoven into the fabric of women's real, vital, immediate, practical and emotional concerns. Mothers usually feel more relaxed in their own homes and experience greater intimacy and personal connection in that setting. These visits also tend to be more leisurely. On this construction, the community context is both permissive (of the relationship) and a more appropriate venue to appreciate women's own concerns and priorities.

In the following pages, I explore each of these aspects (relationship, role and real social context) in more detail.

### **The mother–community midwife relationship**

Midwives and mothers belong in the same 'plane of being', on the same 'side', in the context of an emotionally and practically important and supportive relationship. On this construction, what is 'special' is the *human relationship* within which midwives' skills and knowledge are embedded. What they value as 'special' and distinctive is an emotionally connected supportive relationship that both draws upon and expresses women's culturally acquired skills and experiences, one that is embedded in women's 'real' concerns and situations.

Bonds are formed from the sharing of intimate emotional experiences. So it is with childbirth. The deepest bonds are formed between mothers and community midwives who have shared an emotionally intense experience, be it the joy of birth or the trauma of bereavement. Birth, as one woman noted, is 'a very intimate experience to share with somebody'. Bonds may be formed unilaterally, but it is more usual for them to be mutual (although not symmetrical):

> I think if you're not prepared to reveal something of yourself you can't expect to get something back from somebody else. It's got to be a two way thing. You can't keep yourself aloof at the same time as expecting someone else to reveal their vulnerability. It's just not on. (Laura, midwife)

As this occurs, so the social dimension of the relationship is redefined. The emphasis switches from a role-based to a personally based relationship, with the consequent inclusion of social and biographical elements as the midwife is taken in by the mother from a personal perspective. These three elements – emotionality, mutuality and familiarity – are the core constituents of a close personal relationship:

*Mother (Amanda):* I wanted a community midwife, yes, I did. Given the choice I had hoped it would be. Given the choice I had hoped it would be Anna as well.

*Recorder:* And was it what you hoped it would be.

*M:* It was what I hoped it would be and an awful lot more. It was an amazing experience… totally because of Anna. Yes, it was totally different from Paula and its what every woman's experience should be I think… but, yes, she just made it really.

*R:* What did she do; can you identify it?

*M:* Well first of all, I think it was just her reassuring manner, that everything was going as it should be and she helped me feel that I was in control of it, whereas when Paula was born it was very high tech – you know, she was monitored and forceps and epidural and everything. And it was just so totally different. I think just the reassurance that she gave that I was doing all right: even when I was sort of getting to the end and I remember hearing myself saying, 'No I can't do it any more, I can't.' And you know she said, 'Yes, you can and you've got to because that's the only way the baby's going to come.' And its the continual reassurance that the baby's doing all right; and yes it was just her whole professional manner really...

She was very good as far as Mike was concerned as well [involving him]. It was real sort of shared experience. There was no point that we felt she was sort of the medical person present; she was part of the whole situation, she was one of the active people involved in it all... We were both totally overwhelmed about what had happened and how she had made the experience for us. And she said it had been an experience for her as well, which was lovely.

And we were just given so much more time. I remember when Paula was born, we were very quickly whipped out of the delivery room and up to the ward. Here, we were left together for ages. And she brought a telephone into the room, it was all little things like that that just made it; and no rush to get out and into the system or anything... Absolutely marvellous, it really was...

R:  Did that make it hard to say goodbye to her?

M:  Very, yes it did, very very hard. Because in a funny way, it's almost like a sort of initial bonding when the baby's born, that then just bonds you with them. And you know the initial bonding you have when the baby's born, there's also that sort of feeling with the person who's delivered your baby. And yes, it was very very hard, very hard.

R:  Did you have that feeling with the person who delivered Paula?

M:  Um, no, not to the same extent, although she was lovely. But I was just one of a number. I mean I still am to all intents and purposes, but you were just made to feel very individual, I think that was the difference. I mean, yes, we were very grateful to the midwife who delivered Paula but it was a different... Right at the very end, that moment just before he was born, I was thinking, 'I really can't push any more, I've pushed all I can', and Anna suddenly said to me, 'Come on, say a prayer, you can do it.' And it really sort of brought me up and kept me going, and he was born within the next couple of minutes. It was amazing.

R:  Did you get her a gift?

M:  Well we did buy her something. We bought her a picture. It was one of those things where I knew what I wanted but couldn't go into a shop and say, 'I want this'; I knew it immediately I saw it. We both agreed that that's what we were going to do. But as you say, it was only a very, very small token of all that we'd had.

*R:*  Have you got any plans to keep in touch with her?

*M:*  Well yes, we have actually. She said to me before she went... she wants me to go up there... which would be lovely. She's such a lovely person. And it really did make the experience. That's not to say that Suzy [another midwife] is any lesser qualified because I'm sure the experience also would have been a wonderful one, but I think Anna was right for us... It's to be treasured really. It's not something you could write down; it's just something that I'll keep... It's what every community delivery should be. It's certainly what every woman should feel...

*R:*  Did it make a difference as well when she came round afterwards; what difference did it make that she'd been there... did you talk it through or did it deepen the relationship?

*M:*  Yes, it did... it was nice to have her reassurance, you know, the person that has actually delivered him and everything that he was going to be all right; I think it was just the reassurance of having Anna coming back every day, and not losing her, not letting go of her.

*R:*  Did you talk over the birth?

*M:*  I kept on saying what an experience it was, and I mean it was Anna who said that it was what every woman should experience and that was how they saw their role, but it was just a question really of man/womanpower and of the actual logistics of it all... A friend of mine who's expecting in June who I know is very apprehensive about it, she had a bad experience... I mean if I could sell it to her that it needn't be like that. Gosh, yes, if you could bottle it and sell it, you'd make a fortune. But I mean that is how it actually feels... It made me want to go and tell everybody, it really did.

## The community midwife's role

Women seek an emotionally supportive personal relationship with their community midwife, one that is woman centred and pyschosocially orientated. This is the critical difference between the role of the midwife (particularly in the community) and that of other professional care-givers. The community midwife's role is empathically woman centred. Her role is to be 'with woman'. She therefore takes on the concerns of the woman, and it is this which gives her role its distinctive psychosocial orientation. The roles of GPs and health visitors, on the other hand, are not experienced by the mothers in such terms. The GP's role is seen as more objective and medically orientated, the health visitor's more bureaucratic, advisory and interventionist. This places both GP and health visitor in a different plane of being from the mother and largely precludes an empathic, supportive, woman-centred role orientation.

This is not to deny that GPs and health visitors can be supportive, or that community midwives can be unsupportive: individuals may have a role orientation or personal disposition that departs from this, just as there is variability between midwives (Wilkins 1993). It does, however, identify an important source of difference in mothers' experiences of their respective roles. These differences make it more difficult for a GP, for example, to be as socially supportive as a community midwife, whatever her or his personal outlook.

I was able to identify four distinguishing features of the midwife's role compared with that of the GP. First, the relationship is more personal and subjectively orientated. Women refer to the relationship with the community midwife as being more supportive, personal, intimate, friendly, informal, enjoyable and continuous.

Second, the role is psychosocially orientated. Her role involves greater intimacy between mother and midwife, in particular, a more personal, caring, intimate and supportive orientation, more extensive and intimate contact with the mother's body and more contact with her in her own home. The lines of communication are more open between mothers and midwives. In particular, they feel more able to confide and to ask about 'little things' that they may feel are too trivial to mention to the doctor.

Third, the midwife is seen as the more appropriate professional, associated with childbearing in a way that medical practitioners are not. Midwives make more time, and there is greater continuity of care. The midwife 'sees you through' the whole experience, antenatally, intranatally and postnatally, in a way that the GP does not. These relational and role differences give rise to concrete differences of practice style. Women refer to midwives as better informed, as more thorough in the care they provide, and as providing better explanations. I observed that the style of consultation is more informal and the seating arrangements less confrontational with community midwives. Midwives and mothers are connected in a way that mothers and doctors are not.

An instrumental and clinical orientation defeats the expressive and psychosocial aspects that are such a crucial part of midwifery. In general, the relationship with the GP was described by the mothers as professional rather than personal. Essentially they felt the GP to be out of touch with women. Notwithstanding the need to foster a relationship for the purposes of subsequent contacts after the pregnancy, the GP was felt to be less interested in, and less sympathetic to, 'minor' or emotional aspects of care, and to have less understanding of women's needs and concerns. The mothers suggest there is less personal interest in the women themselves, and where interest is expressed, it is somehow less attuned to women's own feelings. The GPs resort to the notes, the computer, or the midwives to avail themselves of details that community midwives grasp and retain informally.

Finally, women describe ways in which doctors are socially more remote than midwives. At one level, this reflects class and status differences, but the distinctions they describe are sown into the fabric of the relationship in subtle ways that reinforce the dissociations inherent in the professional paradigm. The use of titles rather than first names reinforces social distance. Status distinctions underwrite social distance when women are called by their first name and doctors by their title. Doctors are very much 'that side of the desk', and women are summoned to consult them by a buzzer, in contrast to the practice of most midwives of going to greet and accompany the mother from the waiting room. There is less time, the GP is more busy (or mothers feel them to be), and they are conscious of the queues of people waiting behind them. The atmosphere is less relaxed and more formal. It is not an environment conducive to sharing and support.

There are superficial similarities between midwives and health visitors. Each is a health professional and almost invariably female. Each has contact with the mother in her own home. Each is concerned with facilitating the wellbeing of the family unit. Each is (usually) a trained nurse. Each has an advisory aspect to her role, and each is involved in a key life event.

The mothers' experiences and depictions, however, suggest the two roles are very different and mark something of a culture shock for the mothers. First, the health visitor has a more advisory role. Second, this lacks the supportive and intimate orientation of the community midwife. The relationship is less personal, less satisfying, less involved and less easy. Mothers often say that there is no sense of a relationship at all. Third, the health visitor's remit is seen as the baby rather than the woman, and the woman may feel on trial as a mother.

Fourth, it is a more dissociated, bureaucratised relationship marked by the mores of formal knowledge including clinical measurement and textbook advice. Correspondingly, there is less emphasis, investment and immersion in experiential knowledge. Finally, mothers perceive a potential conflict of interest between themselves and the health visitor. The alliance between mother and community midwife is gone, replaced by the advisory, surveillance role of the health visitor.

With few exceptions, mothers painted a picture of mild antagonism towards the health visitor, who was variously perceived as unhelpful, out of touch or an inconvenience, there to instruct or test rather than support and befriend the mother. There were some positive comments, for example that she was involved, highly trained, gave good advice and was practical. Another woman whose child was physically challenged had major needs of the health visitor, was emotionally more invested and thus developed a stronger relationship. One health visitor in particular had a supportive orientation and was well integrated into the community. She tended to be appreciated in terms similar to those used for community midwives, but there was no suggestion of the 'special' relationship characteristic of community midwifery. Nonetheless, even some of these appreciative women still clearly distinguished the role of community midwife and health visitor along the lines indicated above:

*M:*  Yeah, she played quite an important part. She was brilliant... She just knows everything. Yes, she was very good, very helpful, very positive person and I just think you need somebody like that...

*R:*  Were there any differences from the midwife's role?

*M:*  Well yeah, you know that the midwife is there to support you and help you through your labour, and there again it's attention on you; whereas the health visitor I used to think was just looking at the baby, she was just making sure that he was OK, nothing really about myself, whereas the midwife is as concerned for me as she is for my baby. (Lydia, mother)

In these ways, the roles of both GP and health visitor operate within the confines of the professional rather than the personal paradigm. In addition, the specific roles of the GP and health visitor differ significantly from that of the community midwife, in a way that detracts from the supportive, intimate, woman-centred relationship that mothers themselves value.

## The 'real' social context

I have suggested that the distinctive character of community midwifery rests on three key features: the relationship, the role and the real social context. The relationship is an intimate, personal one. The role is a psychosocial one, supportive of and centred on the mother. This leaves the third aspect, the real social context. The *context* of care fundamentally affects its character, creating some possibilities, precluding others. The community is the appropriate context for midwifery care, complementary to both role and relationship. It enables the personal and psychosocial aspects of midwifery care to be realised more fully. It does this by anchoring midwifery within the mother's social context, making visible and emphasising her psychosocial needs and concerns.

This has four consequences for midwifery. First, it improves empathic understanding, which facilitates both role and relationship. The midwife has access at an experiential level to feelings, knowledge, relationships, environments and priorities that would not be apparent in the hospital. Second, it enhances the psychosocial dimension of midwifery care, which is central to the community midwife's role. Childbearing is as much a psychosocial as a biological event, and it is lived in the community. This is therefore the most appropriate site for the provision of psychosocial support. Mother and midwife experience the vivid realities of motherhood at the centre of the appropriate stage. Third, it enables the midwife to give more appropriate practical advice because, as noted, she has more direct access and exposure to the mother's environment. Conversely, the hospital setting is culturally discontinuous with the social and domestic context within which parenting occurs. This diminishes its practical utility. Finally, the community context facilitates the intimate and personal relationship. In the home context in particular, women typically feel more relaxed and more powerful, and this means that the relationship is more equal and open.

Both mothers and midwives indicate that it is easier to know and understand women in the community context as their circumstances and viewpoint become more visible. It is more the mother's domain, whereas the hospital is more the domain of professional experts. These are not absolute distinctions but they are key distinctions for midwifery because the community setting provides information, experiences and understanding that would be unavailable to even the most sensitive midwife in the hospital setting. Compared to the hospital setting, women feel they enjoy better care and better relationships in the community, and midwives feel that they gain a better understanding and appreciation of the women for whom they care. It is more personal, relaxed and humane, less clinical, medicalised, bureaucratic and rushed.

On the other hand, women experience the hospital as 'an institution': cold, impersonal and clinical. Mothers and midwives draw attention to three particular aspects of the hospital environment. First, it depersonalises. Within such an environment, mothers and midwives are dissociated, care is stripped of its emotional aspect, and women become tongue tied, anxious and angry. In hospital, you are 'just a number', anonymous, stripped of personal identity. You are redefined as a 'patient'; sanitised, passive and helpless:

> What do we do? We bring you in, we put you in a white gown and we put... a label on you. You're a patient, I'm a nurse. It's terrible... I feel it, every time I put a bracelet on a patient, on one of the women; now you're a patient. And they're not really. They're just in there because the facilities are there for them to have a baby. They're no different to me. (Joanna, midwife)

Second, the parties do not know each other, despite the existence of a team midwifery scheme. The interaction is more superficial, less grounded, less meaningful. In these circumstances:

> I guess the answer you give is quite a stat answer. You just answer their question. It's not a meaningful one, it's not [like]... when they asked a question [in the community setting]. We did have some women that used to come up quite regularly and that was great: 'Oh a face I've seen before!' And they would latch on to you too. But yes, it is different [in the hospital]. You're just a midwife... there's not that personal contact... I was still myself but I just didn't feel I knew the person... I was desperately missing my women. (Joanna, midwife)

When Joanna returned to the community after an absence of three years, she had to re-establish the rebuilding of relationships with the women.

> You just don't know any of the women... And I also feel it when they come in and say, 'Oh another face'. ...there's nothing I like nicer than walking out into the waiting room and spotting the woman who's next on the list, calling her by her Christian name and saying, 'Hi, how are you?'

rather than going out there not knowing who's who, and just going out there and calling their name... And I missed the hands on... And you're looking at the most non-maternal person. (Joanna, midwife)

The community midwife aspect of it, what makes it special has just got to be this continuity of care, and the fact that you do get to know the woman that you're looking after; and if you manage to stay in the same job for a while and they start coming back the second time around, that is lovely. (Elizabeth, midwife)

Third, hospital is seen by many as an irrelevance, a waste of time. For them, impersonal care is impoverished care. With the exception of the scan, the clinical care offered in the hospital is seen as similar to that in the community but the setting is less congenial and considerably more inconvenient:

You... go into a hospital and it's just so impersonal. As I say, although it's in my notes, I haven't even bothered to make an appointment to go up to the hospital because to me it's just a waste of time. I'm a number to them and they'll have my file but they won't know anything about me. Whereas I know at this stage if I've got a problem, I'll go down to see Anna or Suzy or Dr Peters and be dealt with in a much better, more humane way. And it won't take two and a half hours... That's something else, they will come back to you if there's a problem... I really don't see the point of [going to the hospital]. I mean, they look after you so well [in the community]; why go and sit up there and have exactly the same thing done to you that Anna can do? (Amanda, mother)

You don't know people. You go into a room cold. You've got minutes to get a rapport with that person... You can do it but it's not as satisfying. I can't remember their names, for instance. I can remember the incidents. It's not as satisfying as going into somebody's house that you know, is it? (Anna, midwife)

The second of these extracts tells its own story. In a hospital context, the midwife noted for her intimate orientation forgets the personal details, remembering simply the 'incidents', abstracted away from their contexts. She remembers incidents rather than people. Her recollection is fragmented, decontextualised and depersonalised.

It may be suggested that these distinctions reflect not the social setting *per se* but the organisation of care, which in the hospital setting is typically more fragmented. According to this argument, if there were continuity in the hospital setting, the same relationships could be formed. But even if one could overcome the medicalised, bureaucratised and hierarchical culture of the hospital setting, and even if continuity, familiarity and sensitivity were fostered, the relationships would differ for the reasons indicated earlier: the woman's social context would be invisible, the relationship would be less personal and less psychosocially orientated, and the possibilities for realistic social support would be severely diminished because it would be enacted within an inappropriate environment, that of the expert rather than the client.

> Looking back on the time in hospital, when somebody comes in you put them in a nightie; that person's in a nightie. With the best will in the world, that person's still in a nightie. You've got no idea of their social background or their emotional needs. (Carol, midwife)

So the community provides a context within which midwives can most appropriately be 'with woman' and supportive, incorporated within a personal paradigm. The midwife becomes an aspect of the community, part of the social network and the family unit; not 'facilitating' or manipulating it but immersed in it, part of it, orientated to both in a way the hospital context prevents:

> I think you just feel that she's done this so many times before, and living round here she's delivered so many babies round here that she's sort of part of the whole – part of the area really. And you see all these people waving to her in the car. Everybody feels the same about community midwives I think; I mean, they're really part of their life really. They remember when their birthdays are and all that sort of thing... in a way I'd like to go and have these babies in a country where the midwife is really part of the village atmosphere, never far away... It's a very special job, very special... I don't know how emotionally they cope with being part of each little unit. Because I mean I almost cried when she left after 10 days... And I was thinking, 'I wish she could come every other day or something'; it would be nice if it almost was weaned off. I think it's quite sad... I remember feeling, 'It's like losing a member of your family really', as she was going... Do you know what I mean? She's gone... I'd have liked her to pop in... I really did feel very upset and bought her a present. (Virginia, mother)

I conclude this section by dealing briefly with the suggestion that what has been depicted as distinctive in community midwifery amounts in practice to 'being there' at a major emotional experience, that of childbirth. If this were true, mothers would feel similarly towards all principal care-givers present at the delivery. Certainly, when women describe their labours, it is not unusual for them to speak of strong feelings of affection and gratitude for their immediate care-givers, whether or not they had prior contact with them. Moreover, Klaus *et al.* (1986) refer to the socially supportive effects of *doulas*, or specialist lay attendants, who attend and support the mother during labour, with a statistically significant reduction in the number of perinatal complications in the general sample and a shorter labour in women requiring no intervention.

It is clear that 'just being there' is in itself not enough. Mothers often refer to the unimportance of GPs or students during labour. It is the principal care-giver who is likely to have a major impact, be it positive or negative. It is also well established that women do benefit from continuous emotional support during labour, although the nature of their requirements may vary.

Beyond this, two points can be noted. The first is that women's depictions of the delivery experience differ where the midwife is unknown, or relatively unknown, compared with the principal community midwife, even if the experience with hospital midwives has been emotionally intense and positive. Many women describe their hospital midwife as 'nice', 'friendly', 'lovely' and 'caring'. They may also describe social and biographical exchanges more typical of established relationships. But what is missing from their accounts is the relational element: the depth of relationship on the one hand and the sense of shared experience on the other. This manifests itself only in relation to community deliveries. Even if the most intense emotional attachment was with the unknown hospital midwife at delivery, the community midwife, as the one who 'knows you and has seen you through it', remains an enduring association.

In addition, the picture that emerges of *medical* care in hospital is the familiar one of a depersonalised, controlling service involving the elevation of the expert, and expert knowledge, within the professional paradigm. The 'patient' is overlooked, her insights are dismissed, and her body is taken over. She becomes the object of professional practice: stripped of knowledge, emotional needs, social location and responsibilities, fragmented, dislocated and objectified. This echoes the difficulties that women encountered in their dealings with GPs,

but in the hospital context, anonymity, fragmentation and decontextu-
alisation compound these difficulties. The best endeavours of some
medical practitioners cannot overcome structural obstacles to open
and empathic communication.

## Conclusion

For the past three centuries, midwives have had increasingly to
compete with medical men for the privilege of delivering women's
babies. To be a 'midwife' is to be 'with woman'. Until the sixteenth
century, midwives had almost always been women. Symbolically,
they were both feared and revered, representing women's powerful
sexual and creative energies. The church took trouble to control them.
For better or worse, midwives' skills were empirical, pragmatic and
acquired through experience and apprenticeship. The rise of medicine
and the invention of forceps, however, gave men both the power and
the means to overcome this fearful female monopoly, to establish
male supremacy and control (Oakley 1977, Donnison 1988). In
essence, battle has been drawn along these lines ever since. On the
one hand, there is woman, experience, intuition and allegiance. On the
other, there is intervention, difference, medical/professional control
and abstract knowledge.

But battle wages not just between midwives and medical men, but
also, more subtly, between mothers and midwives. On the platform of
protests against medicalised childbirth, midwifery has begun to
reassert itself and has gained in power and influence. As part of these
developments, it has reclaimed its ideological heritage as comprising
care-givers 'with woman', supportive of and allied with childbearing
women. Midwives have taken their distance from the medical model
of childbirth and begun to articulate a distinctive midwifery approach.
Midwives, however, have rejected the medical model without relinquishing the conceptual apparatus, the professional paradigm, which
supports it and which precludes an understanding of the important and
unique contribution of the midwife.

During my research, I identified three broad tendencies in
midwifery research. The first was a disaffection with and movement
away from obstetric supremacy, reorientating the field of enquiry
towards the nature and quality of the care provided by the principal
care-giver, the midwife, and institutional/interprofessional impedi-
ments to appropriate and autonomous midwifery practice. The

second, related tendency was an attempt to redefine the role, policy and practice of midwifery so orientated. This involved a critical reappraisal of medical procedures in midwifery practice, the ideological recognition of midwives as practitioners 'with woman' and a corresponding conceputalisation of childbearing as 'an altered state of health' inextricably embedded in and influenced by psychosocial factors. The provision of continuity of care, and the development of team midwifery and the 'midwifery process' were central to this reorientation. Finally, as part of a broader tendency within obstetric and epidemiological research in the maternity services, there was a commitment to 'scientific' research practice. The dominant research orientation was evaluative, the dominant epistemology empiricist and the favoured method the RCT. There was an increased emphasis on the psychosocial aspects of care, but within an intellectual framework that located knowledge and control with the 'professional', whether a scientific researcher or a clinician. Consequently, midwifery ended up ideologically in conflict with itself, and the interests of both mother and midwife became articulated within a perspective that ultimately denied them.

The renaissance in midwifery therefore left it without a coherent paradigm on which to build a distinctive midwifery policy and practice. There remained a residual and unanalysed commitment to the professional perspective that underwrites medical practice on the one hand, and a related commitment to the research paradigms of epidemiologists on the other. In consequence, midwifery research developed on an uneven footing, its policies inclined in one direction and its paradigms in another. This tended to obliterate the insights and implications of the protests against medicalised childbirth and thus the possibility of recognising the distinctive contribution of the midwife to childbearing women.

What implications does this have for future research, policy and practice? It suggests that mothers and midwifery research are facing in different directions. If midwives want to be 'with woman', they will have to do it without the professional paradigm. This does not mean that their outlooks have to be identical or wholly subjective. But the orientation of a 'caring professional' is not thoroughgoing enough.

As Methven's work (1989) indicates, language and concepts are among the most powerful definers of situations. If midwives really wish to challenge the medical model in their own practice, they have to address the professional paradigm that supports it. This is no small task, for ultimately it entails a critical re-evaluation of how we know what we know, who defines it for us, what goes on inside our own heads and hearts, and where we stand in relation to others. It restores mothers and midwives to the centre of the process, but in so doing it poses as many challenges as it meets. This is a challenge that other 'professionals' (among them sociologists, scientists and social workers) must also turn to face. Together we can find a voice.

## Note

1. See Wilkins (1993) for a detailed discussion of the metatheory, methodology and research methods used in the research and the literature review undertaken in connection with it.

## Acknowledgements

Three years is a long time to support somebody, and I would like to thank those who have supported me. I am grateful to the Economic and Social Research Council, without whom this research would not have been possible; to Ann Oakley and Jo Garcia for getting me started and to Sara Arber and Sarah Nettleton, my PhD supervisors, whose insights and encouragement enabled me freely to develop my ideas. My gratitude to them is open ended, as it is to the research subjects (mothers and midwives) who generously allowed me to share such an important time in their lives. To my family and friends, a humble and sheepish thank you, for 'taking it' when the tolls were high and the research absorbed me like a sponge, and for 'giving it' when you were so much needed. Without your love and support, I would have crumbled long ago. I hope it has been worth your efforts. Finally, my love and thanks to Rebecca and Rachel, my daughters, and Andrea, my midwife, for journeying with me through childbirth and teaching me so much about ways of knowing and growing in the world.

## References

Adams M (1987) Deliveries: Mothers or Midwives. A Study of Communication Styles in Midwifery. Unpublished MSc thesis, University of Surrey.
Association of Radical Midwives (1986) *The Vision*. Ormskirk: Association of Radical Midwives.
Ball J (1989) Postnatal Care and Adjustment to Motherhood. In: Robinson S and Thomson A (eds) *Midwives, Research and Childbirth*, Volume 1. London: Chapman & Hall.

Chalmers I and Richards M (1977) Intervention and Causal Inference in Obstetric Practice. In: Chard T and Richards M (eds) *Benefits and Hazards of the New Obstetrics*. London: Spastics International Medical Publications.

Chalmers I, Enkei M and Keirse M (eds) (1989) *Effective Care in Pregnancy and Childbirth*. Oxford: Oxford University Press.

Cronk M and Flint C (1989) *Community Midwifery*. Oxford: Heinemann.

Donnison J (1988) *Midwives and Medical Men*, 2nd edn. New Barnet: Historical Publications.

Enkin M and Chalmers I (1982) Effectiveness and Satisfaction in Antenatal Care. In: Enkin M and Chalmers I (eds) *Effectiveness and Satisfaction in Antenatal Care*. London: Heinemann.

Etzioni A (ed.) (1969) *The Semi-Professions and their Organisation*. London: Collier-Macmillan.

Flint C (1987) *Sensitive Midwifery*. London: Heinemann.

Flint C and Poulengeris P (1988) *The 'Know Your Midwife' Report*. Available from 49 Peckarman's Wood, Sydenham Hill, London SE26 6RZ.

Garry A and Pearsall M (1989) 'Introduction', and 'Introduction' to Parts 1–7. In: Garry A and Pearsall M (eds) *Women, Knowledge and Reality*. Boston: Unwin Hyman.

Jaggar A (1989) Love and Knowledge: Emotion in Feminist Epistemology. In: Garry A and Pearsall M (eds) *Women, Knowledge and Reality*. Boston: Unwin Hyman.

Kirkham M (1989) Midwives and Information-giving During Labour. In: Robinson S and Thomson A (eds) *Midwives, Research and Childbirth.*, Volume 1. London: Chapman & Hall.

Klaus M, Kennell J, Robertson S and Sosa R (1986) Effects of social support during parturition on maternal and infant morbidity. *British Medical Journal* **293**: 585–7.

Knorr-Cetina K (1981) *The Manufacture of Knowledge*. Oxford: Pergamon Press.

Laryea M (1989) Midwives' and Mothers' Perceptions of Motherhood. In: Robinson S and Thomson A (eds) *Midwives, Research and Childbirth*, Volume 1. London: Chapman & Hall.

Methven R (1989) Recording an Obstetric History or Relating to a Pregnant Woman? A Study of the Antenatal Booking Interview. In: Robinson S and Thomson A (eds) *Midwives, Research and Childbirth*, Volume 1. London: Chapman & Hall.

Oakley A (1977) Wisewoman and Medicine Man: Changes in the Management of Childbirth. In Mitchell J and Oakley A (eds) *The Rights and Wrongs of Women*. Harmondsworth: Penguin.

Oakley A (1984) The importance of being a nurse. *Nursing Times* December: 24–7.

Oakley A (1992) *Social Support and Motherhood*. Oxford: Basil Blackwell.

Page L (1988) The Midwife's Role in Modern Health Care. In: Kitzinger S (ed.) *The Midwife Challenge*. London: Pandora.

Robinson S (1989a) The Role of the Midwife: Opportunities and Constraints. In: Chalmers I, Enkei M and Keirse M (eds) *Effective Care in Pregnancy and Childbirth*, Volume 1. Oxford: Oxford University Press.

Robinson S (1989b) Caring for Childbearing Women: The Interrelationship Between Midwifery and Medical Responsibilities. In: Robinson S and Thomson A (eds) *Midwives, Research and Childbirth*, Volume 1. London: Chapman and Hall.

Robinson S and Thomson A (eds) (1989) *Midwives, Research and Childbirth*, Volume 1. London: Chapman & Hall.

Royal College of Midwives (1987) *Towards a Healthy Nation. A Policy for the Maternity Services*. London: Royal College of Midwives.

Smith D (1988) *The Everyday World as Problematic*. Milton Keynes: Open University Press.

Stanley L (ed.) (1990) *Feminist Praxis*. London: Routledge.

Wagner M (1986) The Medicalisation of Birth. In: Claxton R (ed.) *Birth Matters*. London: Unwin.

Wilkins R (1993) Sociological Aspects of the Mother–Community Midwife Relationship. Unpublished PhD thesis, University of Surrey.

# Chapter 4

# Women Planning Homebirths: Their own Views on their Relationships with Midwives

*Nadine Pilley Edwards*

## Introduction

This chapter focuses on how 30 women planning homebirths experienced their relationships with midwives. It is part of a more extensive piece of work to explore women's experiences of homebirths in Scotland. Unless otherwise specified, all the quotations in this chapter arise from women in the study.

The number of babies born at home has rapidly declined over the past three decades, to around 0.5 per cent in Scotland and 2 per cent in England and Wales (Macfarlane and Mugford 1984, Macfarlane and Campbell 1994, Tew 1998). Research shows planned homebirths as providing good outcomes for women and babies in Britain (Macfarlane and Campbell 1994, Davies *et al.* 1996, Northern Regional Perinatal Mortality Survey Coordinating Group 1996, Chamberlain *et al.* 1997 and Tew 1998) and elsewhere (van Alten *et al.* 1989, Tew and Damstra-Wijmenga 1991, Durand 1992, Berghs and Spanjaard 1988 quoted in Eskes and van Alten 1994, Ackermann-Liebrich *et al.* 1996, Wiegers *et al.* 1996). Restrictive government policies have been reversed (House of Commons Health Committee 1992, Expert Maternity Group 1993). A rhetoric of choice has been introduced, but negative attitudes to homebirth still prevail, it being tolerated as a marginal activity. In the words of one woman in this study:

> Your whole life is spent being told that you have babies in hospital.

On the surface, homebirth may seem to be of limited interest. There is, however, a growing awareness of 'difference' and the need to research the experiences of so-called minority groups in order to develop appropriate and sensitive services (see also Chapters 6 and 7). There is also evidence that suppressed groups on the margins of society have valuable insights, hidden to those in mainstream society (Harding 1993, McLennan 1995, Charles and Hughes-Freeland 1996). These expand our understanding of issues and benefit the wider community.[1]

There is a rich collection of individual homebirth accounts in midwifery and lay literature,[2] but relatively little in-depth research on women's experiences of homebirth from their own point of view. Qualitative research has usually been retrospective and typically based on single interviews or surveys (Damstra-Wijmenga 1984, Caplan and Madeley 1985, Alexander 1987, Spurrett 1988, North West Surrey CHC 1992, O'Connor 1992, Bastian 1993, Oswin 1993, Bortin *et al.* 1994, Ogden 1998). Research on women's experiences of homebirth, and birth in general, confirms that birth is a major life event, with lasting repercussions (Simpkin 1991, 1992, Ogden *et al.* 1997a, 1997c). While this research has raised pertinent issues, such methods do not allow a deeper understanding of the process or of why women may have difficulty in gaining support for homebirth (Ogden *et al.* 1997b). For these reasons, it seemed important to learn more about women's experiences as they moved through pregnancy, birth and the postnatal period.

This chapter describes briefly how I carried out the research, presents the relevant findings and provides an outline of the theoretical concepts I used. It discusses how these theoretical concepts enriched my understanding of women's experiences of the themes they raised, such as support, control and trust, and concludes with possible ways forward.

## Research methodology: talking to women

Women who booked for homebirths during the study period were given information and an invitation to join the study by their community midwives. The first 30 women to respond took part, 13 of whom were expecting their first babies. In most cases, I interviewed each woman twice before her baby's birth and twice following it. The final interviews were carried out 6–8 months after birth, so that each woman had an opportunity to process and reflect on her experience.[3]

Nearly all the interviews took place in the women's homes. They were usually an hour and a half to two hours in length, taped and transcribed. I used a qualitative software programme, NUDIST, to assist with the analysis. I asked women open-ended questions about their experiences and invited them to contribute their own comments, in the hope that between us we would gain a fuller picture of their concerns and experiences. I attempted to engage with women in a way that enabled them to talk and share their knowledge (Finch 1984, Belenky *et al.* 1986, Devault 1990, Anderson and Jack 1991, Minister 1991, Oakley 1993).[4]

One of the values of a series of in-depth interviews was that I was able to develop trusting relationships with the women. This enabled us to explore thoughts and feelings and engage with complex issues over the course of a number of interviews. The women developed their views on birth and talked about matters such as safety, continuity, support, trust, choice and control in ways not usually discussed in research published to date.

Issues of confidentiality were discussed, and I obtained Ethics Committee approval prior to commencing my study. Twenty-three of the women actually gave birth at home and seven in hospital.

### Themes from the data: what women said

All the women were aware of the contemporary cultural norms they transgressed when they planned homebirths. Most experienced implied or overt criticism from GPs, obstetricians, midwives, family, friends and colleagues:

> He [the doctor] said something like, did I want to end up with a dead baby?, when I was asking him about the homebirth.

On the basis of negative reactions, stories from friends and birth accounts in books, many women approached community midwives with both trepidation and hope: trepidation that they would side with the body of opinion that frowned on homebirths, and hope that they would respond positively to their decision to plan a homebirth and support them during pregnancy and birth to realise their ideals.

As I talked to women over an extended period of time, one of the themes that grew in strength was that of discord. All the women in the study were dedicated to the best possible outcome for their babies, themselves and their families. With few exceptions, they found that midwives were accepting of homebirth and dedicated to providing the best service they could. Paradoxically, this did not always translate into the supportive, trusting relationships the women had hoped for.

The women I interviewed expressed a spectrum of views on how supportive their midwives actually were, these polarities being evident across a wide range of issues. There was, for example, much discussion about normality and risk. The differences between women and midwives often focused on the issue of transferring to hospital care during labour. Very few of the 30 women felt confident that:

> If I end up in hospital, I know it's been for a good reason.

Most women's main concern was that their midwives would want them to transfer to hospital unnecessarily in their terms:

> I almost got the feeling that she was trying to tell me that, given the chance, any time they could transfer me, they would.

One felt that her midwife's greatest concern was that she would not transfer to hospital if advised to do so:

> I think [the midwife] is very frightened that I'll stand there saying, I'm not going into hospital, and I'm staying here, you know, and just be really uncooperative and put her in a really difficult situation of not knowing what to do so; yeh, I don't think she trusts me that way.

The women who seemed most committed to homebirth sometimes felt that their midwives emphasised transferring to hospital, by relating warning stories about other women who had held strong attachments to homebirths but had had hospital births, or by dwelling on complications:

> When we've talked to them, we tend to polarise with them; we tend to push them into being more hospital oriented than they might be, because we so much don't want to go to hospital, and you know, were I less vocal about that, they might be much more encouraging, and say, oh, it'll be easy, or, you know, it's very unlikely that we'll have to go into hospital, the sorts of things I'd like them to say [laughs]; they do tend to talk quite a lot about the possible complications rather than make the assumption that there are very unlikely to be complications.

Most felt that the best that could be achieved was that midwives would not advise transfer for spurious reasons, and would discuss their concerns with them:

> On the whole, I think, yeh, I think they know that I definitely want to have a homebirth and they're not just going to be flippant, you know; I don't think they'd use the smallest excuse for transferring me and I think they're all into talking and discussing it beforehand.

The same polarities were evident in terms of how supportive women thought their midwives would be. They expressed a range of views from:

> There'll be a sort of expectation that, yeh, we can do this together.

to:

> I'm not putting too much emphasis on the midwife.

They differed, however, in how far they were able to develop trusting relationships with the midwives from:

> I really trust her and I trust her judgement.

to:

> To be honest I didn't really trust the midwives very much.

The same sort of spectrum emerged again when women described how in control they felt, ranging from:

> I know that I truly was in control.

to:

> Even though you're in your own home, you still don't have a great deal of control.

Where there was dissonance, this was confusing and anxiety-provoking for some women:

> I just don't see why I should have to be assertive you know; I just feel that women should be given what they need.

Other women located the problem beyond the individual midwives:

She was pointing out the sort of dangerous side of it and I was getting into
a sort of argument with her... but then again, you see, I think she was just
doing her job [in relation to her employer].

From what the women told me, it seemed that most experienced their
relationships with the midwives as a complex intermingling of the
different axes: from supportive to unsupportive, trusting to mistrusting,
confidence inspiring to undermining and communicative to uncommu-
nicative, and from a partnership to individuals in opposition.

In order to keep in the foreground what women said and gain an
understanding about these polarities, I have employed the postmodern concept of knowledges and embedded power relations. I
have drawn extensively on work carried out by the midwife anthropologist Brigitte Jordan (Jordan 1993, 1997) and further developed
by the medical anthropologist Robbie Davis-Floyd (Davis-Floyd
1992, Davis-Floyd and Dumit 1997, Davis-Floyd and Sargent 1997,
Davis-Floyd and St John 1998).

## Theoretical framework

### *Postmodern concept of knowledges[5]*

The postmodern concept of knowledges includes the idea that there
are different knowledges or belief systems. It begins with the proposi-
tion that there are no 'truths' as such, but different belief systems that
have been given the status of knowledge. It has been suggested that
knowledge is relatively undetermined by facts as such but is socially
constructed to reflect the beliefs and values of any given society or
group (Kuhn 1970, Nelson 1993, Potter 1993). These concepts
provided me with a theoretical framework with which to make sense
of both the apparent conflict and the apparent congruence between
women and midwives.

Bodies of knowledge jostle for primacy. Some forms of knowledge
inevitably become more 'authoritative' than others, but they are not
necessarily more 'correct' than others (Jordan 1997). In this framework, the medical model is an example of authoritative knowledge:
its existence, however, does not preclude the existence and authority
of alternative philosophies and knowledges of birth.

The development of postmodernism has undermined any simplistic notion of knowledge and truth. This has been instrumental in enabling us to contrast different knowledge systems in a way that attempts not to privilege one over another. This allows for a more effective suspension of judgement, permitting a focus on different knowledges, and in this case developing a capacity to listen to women's experiences more closely. This in turn enabled me to understand more about the nature of any conflicts between women and midwives.

Different philosophies of birth each have their own internal logic, which generate their own definition of birth and appropriate birth practices. The medical model, as a dominant ideology, has imposed its own structures and policies to manage birth and govern the distribution of resources in maternity services in ways that profoundly affect relationships between women and midwives.

## *The medical model and holistic philosophies as belief systems[6]*

That birth and midwifery have indeed been medicalised by white, Western cultures is well documented in sociological, anthropological and gender studies, and midwifery literature (Oakley 1976, 1984, 1993, Roberts 1981, Rothman 1982, 1993, Towler and Bramall 1986, Donnison 1988, Garcia *et al.* 1990, Davis-Floyd 1992, Marland 1993, Davis-Floyd and Sargent 1997, Heagarty 1997). With notable exceptions, this medicalisation of birth is less well documented through the minds and hearts of women. The following section considers some of the key defining elements of the medical model and alternative philosophies of childbirth.

While belief systems are not necessarily fixed, discrete entities, Robbie Davis-Floyd (1992) makes a useful distinction between 'technocratic' and 'holistic' belief systems of childbearing as the opposite ends of a spectrum. In more recent work (Davis-Floyd and Dumit 1997, Davis-Floyd and St John 1998), she adopts a more postmodern approach acknowledging that the boundaries between systems are more fluid than her initial distinction suggested (see also Shildrick 1997). Within these two systems, Davis-Floyd suggests that there are certain core values and assumptions about childbearing, women and women's bodies, which define the role of women and their caregivers. The following descriptions of the two belief systems summarise the essence of each.

In the technocratic or medical view, the body is likened to a machine (Martin 1989, 1990). Under the influence of the hierarchical structure of Cartesian reasoning, the woman's body becomes a defective machine not to be trusted[7] (Turner 1987, 1991), in need of continuous monitoring and correcting through medical practices and technology. There is a strong distinction between professional and patient, the professional's knowledge being considered to be superior and authoritative and the patient's knowledge largely irrelevant. Thus, the professional role is one of decision-making and action, and the patient's role is one of passive acceptance (Davies-Floyd 1992, Jordan 1997, Shildrick 1997).

In contrast, the holistic philosophy of childbearing reunites body, mind and spirit, and focuses on the rhythms and processes of pregnancy and birth. The emphasis is on the woman's wellbeing and the relationship of trust between her and her care-givers, who support and facilitate the process through attentive nurturing. This view encompasses a trust in the woman's abilities to reproduce, sees the woman as an authoritative (expert) source of knowledge and brings into focus the social aspect of childbearing. Medical or technological assistance is considered to be damaging except when unavoidable.

The extremes of the North American technocratic approach to birth appear to be attenuated in Britain, and the diversities of holistic philosophies appear less developed than they are in the USA. While defining a technocratic and holistic view of birth is helpful in plotting the ends of a spectrum, I found that women often held varying degrees of both belief systems and experienced their midwives as doing the same.[8]

What impacted greatly on the relationships between women and midwives, however, was that many women held a more holistic view, while most midwives were experienced as holding a more technocratic view. Given the very different definitions of birth arising from these different belief systems, it is not surprising that conflict arose; this provided one explanation for the co-existence of dedication and discord referred to earlier.

Crucially, I will examine in more detail how women were confronted with the different meanings of childbearing through midwives' practices and policies, and how this limited or enhanced the relationships between them, defined the support they were able to give each other and ultimately affected the level of control that the women experienced.

## Looking below the surface: listening more closely

In the following section, I will illustrate in greater depth how these underlying differences in belief systems affected women's relationships with their midwives in the key areas of support, control, power and trust.

### *Support*

There appears to be a consensus that pregnant and birthing women need and benefit from support (Oakley 1989, Oakley *et al.* 1996), but there seems to be less agreement on what form that support should take and how it could be given. Through their talk, women identified different forms of support that they needed in order to move successfully through the significant life event of childbearing. They needed supportive midwifery practices that would enable them to focus on normality, decrease their fear and increase their trust and confidence in their ability to give birth. They wanted care that could support their spiritual and emotional as well as their physical needs. They wanted supportive qualities in their midwives, to listen to, respect and accept their ideals, and to give them clear information on which to base decisions and expand their own knowledge of birth. They wanted maternity care to be organised in ways that could facilitate all of the above by enabling them to get to know and trust their midwives.

### *Focusing on normality: risk versus potential*

> Policies and practices that are supposed to protect women from the risks of childbirth, have often created another set of risks to their physical and emotional well-being. (Aspinall *et al.* 1997:33)

Within the dominant belief system, risk and safety in childbirth have been defined in very particular ways. A safe outcome means that neither mother nor baby dies; this can be seen from the main body of research that has been carried out on place of birth. It originally focused exclusively on mortality and has latterly included morbidity as the death rate has decreased (Shearer 1985, Tew 1985, Treffers and Laan 1986, Wayne *et al.* 1987, Howe 1988, van Alten *et al.* 1989, Ford *et al.* 1991, Tyson 1991, Woodcock *et al.* 1994). This definition does not, however, consider the psychological, emotional or spiritual wellbeing of the woman and her family.

One of the core differences between the two belief systems is that the technocratic or medical model uses risk management as its main indicative tool. This defines risk and safety in its own absolute terms and provides a medically constructed, detached definition of normality that is embedded within its own practices and policies. This can translate into impersonal care based on statistical evidence. A more holistic philosophy uses normality as its main indicative tool. The meaning of normality is not defined in absolute terms but is closely aligned to the individual mother–baby unit. Blanket practices become less relevant, and there is more scope for individualised care and creative solutions drawing on other forms of knowledge, such as 'tricks of the trade' (the North American publication *Midwifery Today* exemplifying this approach) and intuition (Davis-Floyd and Davis 1997, Roncalli 1997).

The women in this study became aware of medical policies and practices based on risk rather than normality in different ways. For example, women planning homebirths who had had a previous post-partum haemorrhage or a caesarean section were initially advised that these constituted medical risks and were indications for hospital birth. In weighing up risk and safety in different ways, however, the women took the view that hospital birth itself posed physical and emotional risks because of the greater likelihood of invasive and damaging inter-ventions, or potential interference with the crucial bonding processes.

In the medical view, childbirth is an inherently risky business that frequently requires technological assistance and should therefore take place in a hospital where equipment and expertise are readily avail-able. There are, however, differing interpretations of risk. Anthony Giddens (1991) describes a risk society in which technology presents one of the greatest risks to humanity. His arguments focus on the risks themselves, and how to stop the technological 'juggernaut' causing mass destruction. A different critical analysis has been developed by Frank Furedi (1997), who asks us to consider why the concept of risk has become so prominent at this particular moment in history. He argues that risk has been pitted against potential and has led to a curtailment of human potential. In other words, we are attempting to reduce risk by deliberately minimising our activities and those of others. A good citizen becomes a passive citizen who abides by accepted norms and avoids risks.

The women themselves often saw birth in terms of its potential (in Furedi's terms), and technology as problematic (in Gidden's terms). Staying at home was a way of realising this potential and avoiding inappropriate interventions and interferences. Thus, most women assessed risk in very different ways from the usual tick-list of medical criteria (see also Stapleton 1997). Using these contrasting beliefs, it is possible to understand why midwives found it problematic to support women in certain circumstances. A crucial dichotomy emerged when some women planned homebirths. Women's attempts to decrease risk, by avoiding technology, unfamiliar surroundings and strangers, could be interpreted from the standpoint of medical ideology as increasing risk; it was sometimes misconstrued as women asking midwives to take risks.

Consequently, when definitions of risk and safety diverged in this way, women could not feel supported in their decisions and felt distanced from their midwives:

> She's not part of it with me... I feel quite alone in it really.

Women who held more fluid concepts of risk, safety and normality experienced the more rigid approach as an impersonal form of 'policing':

> They're only here to take a monitoring role.

It seemed that, on the issues of risk, safety and normality, women wanted midwives to focus on their individual circumstances but experienced their policies as measuring them against abstract norms, which could not relate to them as individuals.

A confounding factor in the relationship between women and midwives was the potentially contradictory rhetoric of choice based on women's rights, which supposedly overrides practices and policies. Again, where belief systems did not coincide, the woman had the confusing task of deciphering the midwife's advice, which was grounded in the medical model but superimposed by the rhetoric of choice. For example, one woman, describing her experience during labour, said:

> She [the midwife] was at the very most a foot away from me, she was being very directive and saying that, you know, we should be going to

hospital, bla, bla, bla, and then she said at the end of all that, of course, we would be very happy to stay here and deliver you at home.

In effect, the midwife had the 'schizophrenic' task of supporting institutional policies and women's choices that were in opposition to each other (Clarke 1995).[9] Often, when the woman and the midwife held different core values, the midwife could only give limited support. Some women were aware of this conflict and realised that they were asking midwives to side with their values when they had indicated the impossibility of this. Women were often seeking unconditional support for their belief systems, and midwives could only provide conditional support:

> She [the midwife] said, I'm always here to answer any of your queries, but I thought, my main query is, can you help me with coping with a system that is stacked against me?

In addition to conflicts arising from the different definitions of risk and normality already discussed, the marginalised position of homebirth in Scotland could undermine the support that midwives were able to provide. Women in the study looked to their midwives to provide positive, enthusiastic support for their initial decision to plan homebirths. Midwives who support homebirths are, however, equally marginalised and may risk reprisal if they are too supportive (Wagner 1995). Thus, even at the point of first contact, the midwife's support could be experienced as 'lukewarm', or lacking:

> I contacted the midwives and one of them came to see me…, that was my first *very* disappointing experience; I was very disappointed because prior to that I hadn't expected very much from my GP…, but I thought, right, this is one of the community midwives, this is someone who could deliver my baby, these are the people I need to speak to, this is my lifeline.

### Support for the whole process

> Bringing together the aspirations to create the reality. (Fleming 1999)

In addition to support for their decisions to have homebirths, women wanted support for their own particular meanings of childbirth and support to realise their hopes and ideals. Because of the beliefs embedded in a medical view of birth, and the organisation of care arising from this, the support that women needed and the support available did not always coincide.

The diversity of views expressed in this group of 30 women was striking. However, all the women were clear that, before relationships could be supportive, they needed to get to know the midwives, in order to have some common ground to build on. Unusually in this study, one woman received nearly all her care from one community midwife and could not imagine a satisfactory alternative:

> I think it is really important to have a relationship with your midwife and it's important to see the same one all the way through, otherwise you wouldn't have had a chance to build up that relationship.

However, while the women placed a great emphasis on relationships, the organisation of community maternity care, which has been developed more in line with the medical model of birth, places little emphasis on these. Women quickly experienced that the way in which their care was organised did not facilitate the development of relationships. Many women saw a different midwife at each antenatal visit in order to have met each of the 6–8 midwives assigned to them on at least one occasion. Most commented that 10–15 minutes would usually be allowed for visits. This resulted in:

> This kind of relationship thing isn't happening.

The next focus, then, is on how women described the content of these 10–15 minutes and how this exemplified the difference between the belief systems:

> What they did was checks, lots and lots of checks… which I didn't need; I felt like I was able to gauge my own health, and that I didn't need to be measured, weighed, checked so much, and I needed something else and there wasn't anything else; the medical check went under the guise of getting to know you, and you know, I just thought, actually this is all wrong, and I found that it made me feel very unattractive; I felt kind of sow-like, you know, just having my tummy measured, and if that's all that was going to happen, it was ignoring so much.

I have suggested that the medical approach to childbirth separates body, mind and spirit, and defines birth as an unreliable, mechanical, physical process. The core task of supportive care derived from this view is monitoring pregnancy and birth in order to detect problems that can then be 'corrected'. In contrast, an holistic approach attempts to integrate body, mind and spirit. The main task of supportive care derived from this view is to develop a trusting relationship between the woman and her midwife so that both can work together towards a successful outcome. Most women defined their need for support from a more holistic perspective but experienced receiving 'checks':

> It's like you're bombarded with things that you don't want, and not getting the things you do want.

It was not so much that women did not appreciate the care provided by their midwives but that it was not in the context of a relationship and other forms of holistic support. One woman who moved from more fragmented care to more holistic, one-to-one care was able to articulate the difference:

> The difference… is because I have time to get to know [the midwife], so what normally happens is that she comes round, we have a cup of tea, we have a chat, …then by the time she's been there for 45 minutes or an hour, we do the check, so she will do all these things, but it seems relevant; it's like somebody you know who's caring for you, checking that you're okay, so it feels different because you're not straight in the door and on the scales, or straight in the door lying on your back with your top up; you've actually engaged as an adult with somebody first.

However friendly and supportive individual midwives were, without this engagement they could be experienced as distant professionals and their approach as clinical – 'lovely' but 'strangers'.

Where a bond developed between women and midwives, and the relationship was based on shared values and trust, the woman saw the midwife as 'being on my side'. She was able to value both her own knowledge and that of her midwife. She saw her midwife as having the qualities of a friend and the competences of a professional. It was a personal relationship in terms of supporting her, and a professional one in terms of bringing additional knowledge and experience to bear on her individual circumstances:

> There won't be fear in the air, there'll be a sort of expectation of, yeh, we can do this together.

Another aspect of the medical model's hold over definitions of birth impinged on how women and midwives discussed support in labour in the limited time available. Conversations that did occur tended to focus on negotiating what the woman wanted to avoid, in terms of pharmaceutical pain relief, time limits, Syntometrine, vitamin K and so on.[10] Thus, support was mainly defined in negative terms in relation to the medicalisation of birth. There seemed to be little language to facilitate discussions about alternative forms of support:

> When people stay at home it's almost as if they're saying [to the midwives], well I don't need any of these things, I'm going to do it all on my own, but I'm trying to say, well in fact I do need a lot, I need all of those things but in a different way at home; not the drugs, I don't need drugs, and I don't need surgical instruments I hope, but what I really need is support.

Despite this, there were powerful examples of holistic support during labour. The following quote exemplifies this kind of non-technological, profoundly human contact between woman and midwife:

> There came a stage when I *really* wanted her to be absolutely with me, I just remember looking *really* hard into her eyes and she absolutely meeting that stare, and taking it in and giving me strength just through the way she looked at me, which is exactly what I needed.

## *Control*

> The social relationships between the childbearing woman and her carers are different when the birth occurs in the woman's home, where she is in control and her carers are guests. (Campbell 1997:4)

Most women in my study initially felt that staying at home to give birth would enable them to remain in control, and most commented how their midwives had asserted that this would be the case. As the women explored issues of control, however, a more complex picture emerged. They clearly had more control over their environments, but once again the level of congruence between women's and midwives' belief systems, and the predominance of a technocratic model with its practices and policies, shaped information exchange, on which decision-making and ultimately control were largely based.

## Information exchange

> The parameters of appropriate behavior are communicated in unequivocal
> terms... In exchanges with midwives, for example, it is made obvious that
> one should limit one's contributions according to *their* definitions of the
> subject at hand. Those regarded as irrelevant are cut short and questions,
> although handled efficiently are disposed of as briefly as possible.
> (Comaroff 1977:120)

Comaroff observed this over two decades ago. Since then, others have
also found information exchange to be problematic (Kirkham 1989).
The experience of many of the women in my study showed similarities with this previous research. Part of a woman being in control, or
being able to take an active role in defining her experience of birth,
was gathering information relevant to her unique circumstances in
such a way as to support her decision-making process.

Most women initially saw relating to midwives as a potential
source of valuable information, which would enable them to remain
central to the birthing process and enable them to make their own
decisions. For a number of reasons, this did not always appear to
materialise. As already described, when views on safety did not
concur, the midwives could not support the women unconditionally.
In addition, when time was short, continuity lacking and the focus of
antenatal visits on checks, conversations were limited and often
restricted to brief question and answer sessions:

> Within that setting, to try and bring up complex issues would feel quite
> wrong.

However, when I examined the role of information exchange, difficulties appeared to go beyond structural issues. Again, exploring the
different role of information in different knowledge systems shed
light on both accord and discord between women and midwives.

A dominant ideology, such as the medical approach to birth, assumes
a monopoly on knowledge. Within this belief system, information-
giving takes place through a hierarchical framework, in a one-way,
didactic transfer from professional to woman. In an holistic philosophy,
both woman and midwife are seen as sources of knowledge, and
information-giving becomes a mutually expansive activity, based on a
sharing of knowledge. Information exchange therefore has a very
different role within different belief systems.

While women and their experience of midwives did not conform to any simplistic version of one or other of these belief systems, the women often experienced a more technocratic response to requests for information. Some women, for example, wanted to clarify arrangements for the possibility of having a breech baby at home. None saw this as an absolute reason to abandon their plans for a homebirth. They were told by their midwives that, in the very unlikely case of their babies being breech at term, the birth would occur in hospital under the supervision of medical staff. Women found that they were unable to engage their midwives in any further dialogue on this issue. Their holistic perspective and the possible risks of a medical approach could not be discussed. They were therefore unable to weigh up possible advantages and disadvantages in order to make an informed decision and remain in control.

Women's experiences of information-gathering seemed to focus on two different aspects: clarifying their midwives' policies and practices, and complementing their own knowledge of birth.

*Information on the 'rules of the game'*

The values, practices and policies of the dominant ideology of birth are deeply embedded in both its practitioners and the wider culture. They become so taken for granted as to be rendered largely invisible and were therefore difficult for women to identify. One woman, discussing midwives' practices, said:

It almost seemed to be shrouded in mystery.

The onus was on women to identify these policies and practices, in order to make decisions, but many found that it was difficult to gain information:

Most of the questions that I had, I wouldn't get a satisfactory answer to, so I stopped bothering asking them and just found out myself really, although that does leave you with a lot of gaps, it means you're going in blind. I could find out a lot about the physiology of birth without asking a professional, but I can't find out about their procedures without asking them, and when they're not very forthcoming, I wouldn't say that they were deliberately vague, I don't know, somehow it all stayed vague, just like my questions, so I never felt like I was being told the truth about whether I would be transferred to hospital and things like that.

It often remained unclear which issues were appropriate to discuss:

> One minute you're a child who's being told to shut up and not raise diffi-
> cult issues and the next minute it's like, well, it's absolutely up to you,
> you're an adult, you decide what you want, …but it's very unclear which
> attitude applies to which issue.

By researching these issues through other sources, women were
able to identify many of the practices likely to be used and were able
to form a view on these. Isolated practices could then be challenged if
the women felt assertive and confident enough to negotiate this. Some
practices remained invisible, and women were only able to say after
giving birth that, had they known about certain practices, they would
have refused them, for example carrying out a vaginal examination in
order to decide when to call a second midwife, and using hands-on
techniques for assisting the birth of the baby's head.

In a more holistic approach, policies were less in evidence and
practices more flexible. The focus was on the woman's expectations
and her definitions of birth:

> Mostly she [the midwife] wouldn't give an opinion; she just helped me to
> make decisions myself about things.

## Information as complementary

Women often stated that they wanted themselves and their babies to
be in the foreground during the birth process. They wanted midwives
present in a background capacity, to support them to follow their
instinctual and intuitive knowledge and to provide a 'safety net' if an
emergency arose. This was complicated because women's knowledge
has been largely suppressed. Thus, although the women believed that
they should be listened to and be central to decision-making, they
were hesitant about their capacity to know in the face of the 'expert'.
A more technocratic approach further undermined the woman's
ability to know:

> Their focus was very much on fear, which I found completely disempow-
> ering, it made me think, well, maybe I can't deliver a baby… it felt like,
> you know, that all my grand ideas of being in control were just silly
> fantasies or something.

Other women felt that their knowledge and decision-making abilities were being questioned:

> You do assume that the people who have experience, know better, but I suppose that question of whether to have your baby at home or not is probably a very individual one, so in fact somebody else can't really know for you.

A more holistic approach appeared to support the woman's ability to know:

> By the time I got to know what her opinion really was, I'd already made up my mind, so she slowly built up my feeling that my intuitions were good.

Whether the woman was attempting to clarify her midwives' policies and practices, or attempting to develop her own body of information, acquiring information was problematic where the views of women were more holistic and those of their midwives experienced as more technocratic. In much the same way that Valerie Levy (1998) observed in her work on antenatal booking appointments, information was given in such a way as to steer women into making decisions that were more in line with their midwives' views. For example, the majority of women in the study did not wish to use Syntometrine to assist the delivery of the placenta but found that some of the midwives used it routinely. When this was the case, there was pressure to accept this practice:

> I've given in to that; I must admit, I've given in.

It could be argued that providing information generated by a specific knowledge system was used to engender realistic expectations of its values, policies and practices, and was experienced as a mechanism for control. In this sense, information given antenatally could be interpreted as a part of a socialising process that undermined women's knowledge and validated 'expert' knowledge, rather than a mechanism to empower through a sharing of knowledge that validates both the woman's and the midwife's knowledge.

## *Power*

> 'Of course we won't do anything without your consent'; well, what sort of
> consent are you going to be giving at that point [in labour] and that's not
> ever frankly discussed.

The supposedly woman-centred rhetoric of choice and informed
consent assumes a level playing field on which women can state their
wishes and if necessary have recourse to rights to enforce these. There
are a number of problems with this assumption, which are exemplified by the issue of enforced caesarean section (Hewson 1994) and the
possibility of other enforced treatment (Dimond 1993).

The French philosopher Michel Foucault (1980) suggests that
knowledge and power are inseparable and that all relationships are
mediated through power. Thus, a dominant ideology such as the
medical model of birth not only claims exclusivity on knowledge, but
also attempts to suppress alternative views (Ehrenreich and English
1979, Arney 1982, Donnison 1988, Dalmiya and Alcoff 1993). This
conceptual framework is valuable in identifying power relations and
examining how these manifest themselves materially. The notion that
networks of power exist in complex, shifting patterns (Cowan 1996,
Eisenstein quoted in Shildrick 1997) shows women to be simultaneously powerless and powerful, while acknowledging the potential for
the dominant ideology to impose itself through power relations.

In concrete terms, this was through the practices of individual
midwives on the individual psyches and bodies of women. This could
be experienced as breaching boundaries in ways that would normally
be unacceptable.[11] In describing the birth of her baby, one woman in
the study expressed this powerfully:

> It sort of felt like she was just trying to rip me open.

If policies and practices are embedded in beliefs about birth that are
not focused on the individual woman and might be imposed when the
woman is most vulnerable, women cannot be in control. This could
set women and midwives apart from each other, in much the same
way that Paulo Freire describes oppressed groups oppressing each
other rather than challenging the oppressor (1972).

Furthermore, choice is largely defined by dominant ideologies
(Mander 1993). As I have already shown, women found that certain
choices, such as having a breech baby at home, were considered by the

medical model to be inappropriate. Recourse to rights involves adversarial engagement, which women wanted to avoid. Many women went to great lengths to maintain harmonious relationships with their midwives, even if this meant suppressing their own views and needs:

> I don't like to feel I make waves.

In terms of power, there appeared to be an underlying assumption that, in the final analysis, professionals know best. This has led to a greater emphasis on communication, and meaningful control is often displaced by informed consent. The onus is then on midwives to gain consent for their practices and keep women informed (see Ralston 1994). The following quotes seem to sum up this attenuated medical approach to birth, in which the emphasis is on 'steering' rather than empowering:

> There were the two midwives there, and they knew what they were doing, and they were quite happy to explain what they were doing because they had plenty of time to do whatever they were doing and it was... yeh, it was just great, much better [than hospital births].

> Every time there was something to be done, she did ask me if it was all right.

> [In hospital] I wasn't aware of getting that [Syntometrine] before, so they didn't even tell you, you got it, whereas this time [laughing] at least they're saying beforehand, you can have it if you want, and we're quite keen for you to have it [laughs].

To summarise, many women felt that their control was limited and was often more of a hope than a reality. Without adequate information and support to follow through on decisions, control remained, in Robin Gregg's (1995) words, more of an 'illusion' than a reality, and there was always the fear that decisions might be overridden:

> I don't want decisions to be made on my behalf, in the sense that I got this feeling about being given Syntometrine or vitamin K or something like that, you know, I got this worrying feeling that even if I said beforehand that I didn't want it, that at a vulnerable moment, they might try to persuade me; and I've heard that this actually happened to some people, you know, that even though they'd said something beforehand, people have tried to manipulate them with clever arguments at vulnerable times, and I didn't want to have to deal with that, I wanted my opinions to be respected, and just the control, yeh, just somebody not trying to dissuade me from what I want to do.

## Trust

Whether or not women felt supported and in control during their pregnancies related to how safe and confident, or how uncertain and fearful, they felt approaching the transition through birth to motherhood. It affected how trusting they felt towards both themselves and their midwives.

During the interviews, women addressed different levels of trust. They wanted to develop trust in the birth process and their bodies; they wanted to be able to rely on their midwives to trust and respect their decisions; and they wanted to be able to trust their midwives to support them staying at home, unless they both agreed that transferring to hospital was necessary.

The heart of the matter seemed to be whether or not women could trust their midwives in the face of vulnerability. From talking to women in this study, there appeared to be two main components to this. When the women and midwives held similar views on birth, and got to know each other, there was a core area of common ground on which to base trust:

> The difference of just knowing I'd have someone more in line with my thinking, I didn't feel that I needed a birth plan any more; I don't need all these things because I trust her opinion, and that way, I don't have any fears, so I don't need to swot up so much, and, you know, be so defensive.

Having the time to get to know each other further developed this trust and resulted in the relationship having reached a point of resolution for both woman and midwife:

> We'd done a lot of talking in the build up, so the talking was done, she knew where I was coming from and vice versa… so on the day it just felt very calm.

When they were able to form closer relationships, trust became part of that relationship. The woman trusted the midwife to do her best for her and knew rather than hoped that the midwife would support her.

Ironically, when the women felt they had different beliefs about birth, they felt that getting to know a midwife was more imperative in order to resolve some of the differences, rather than relying on the unsatisfactory 'wait and see' approach often mentioned:

Had it been somebody who I developed a rapport with, a lot of difficulties could have been a lot less.

Where there was little common ground, and little possibility of talking through these issues, the greatest fear was that the woman's knowledge about herself and her baby would be overridden:

I don't have any anxiety about things going seriously wrong and having to be rushed to hospital and having to have a caesarean, it's like, well, I don't want that to happen, but if it does, I'm really glad that that's something that's available to me... I think what I would find really difficult to cope with afterwards would be if I had been taken into hospital, or kind of pressured to have a birth different from the sort that I wanted, on the basis that there might be something wrong, and then to find out that there hadn't been anything wrong; that's the kind of scenario that I really feel would be very difficult to handle, the kind of aftermath of that, feeling very angry and cheated, especially if I'd been kind of resisting and saying, no, no, I think it's okay.

Women in the study also expressed the concern that they would not be able to make a responsible decision because they would be unsure of the grounds on which the midwife's advice was based. They were concerned that they and their midwife would come to legitimate but different decisions based on their different philosophies. They occasionally worried that the midwife's advice might be based on a preference not to attend homebirths at all:

If there was a good reason for me going into hospital, I wouldn't trust that it was for a good reason, because I wouldn't know that she wasn't just panicking or plotting to get me away.

Despite the fact that many women believed that their knowledge should contribute to these sorts of decision, most felt, because of the marginalisation of homebirth, and the associated blame and guilt, that they could not risk relying on this. In the event of a disagreement, they felt that they would have to override their own feelings and do as their midwives advised.

However the birth process unfolded, where trust was the foundation of the relationship between the woman and her midwife, the woman interpreted her experience in terms of growth and change. This was usually related to a general increase in confidence but could have wider implications:

If I have a crisis of confidence, I think back to the birth and it's a very good anchor for me; it makes me believe in my ability to make good decisions.

In a few instances, where a breakdown in trust occurred, women felt they were 'complying' with a system not designed to meet their needs:

I'm complying, I'm doing what I have to do.

They subsequently 'regretted' engaging with maternity care. These women sometimes felt disempowered because, although they could see that the maternity services were not meeting their needs, they often blamed themselves:

I think I let myself down, I should have been more forthright... but it's difficult to do that when you're relying on somebody.

## Conclusion

### *Summary*

The concept of different knowledges formed one of a number of possible axes with which to explore women's experiences of planning homebirths (class, race, educational status, age and personality being among others that women in the study identified). This framework illuminated the apparent discord/dedication dichotomy in a non-judgemental way and was best exemplified in the words of one of the women:

They [community midwives] do work for the hospital, they are connected, and their loyalties are on the medical side – that's the deal. I mean, they are wonderful people, they really are, but they are medical... at the end of the day they're going to rely more on their medical expertise than they are on their instincts, that's their job – it's to deliver a baby the way they've been trained. [The midwife] is truly amazing, I mean, she's just been extraordinary; she suggested the homebirth, she's been really encouraging throughout the whole thing, so this is not a criticism, but I think at the end of the day I would have been asking her to compromise her beliefs; I mean, she is a medical person, who has been trained in medical ways.

There was the potential for tension or similarity between women's and midwives' knowledges. This convergence or dichotomy could either undermine or increase information-giving, support for decision-making and control. For some women, homebirth was not far removed from hospital birth. The midwives' practices and artefacts were experienced by some as 'bringing the hospital into the home'. Thus, while many women had positive experiences of birth, the antenatal period could generate fear and uncertainty. Some of the interviews were emotionally painful as women attempted to reconcile feelings of vulnerability and distrust, and integrate their ideals with the reality that seemed to frustrate these. '*As much as they can* they'll go along with my wishes' (emphasis added) seemed to be a realistic assessment of NHS community care. In these circumstances, a common coping mechanism was for women to compare their experiences favourably with previous or imagined hospital births rather than with their own ideals.

While each meeting between a woman and a midwife was unique, in essence the relationships appeared to work best when the woman and midwife shared sufficient common values about birth for each to feel trusting of the other. This was further improved by a one-to-one relationship. The relationship seemed to work least well when fear and distrust were generated because the woman and midwife shared fewer common views on birth. This was further exacerbated when women saw different midwives at each antenatal visit.

The knowledge, structures and practices of the dominant model of birth limited midwives' abilities to develop supportive birth practices and prevented the development of partnerships with women based on mutual understanding, respect and trust. Lack of trust meant that women had to 'watch out' during labour despite knowing that the birth process needed them to be relaxed and focused.[12]

Within the NHS services, the importance of relationships between women and midwives was grafted onto a pre-existing hierarchy (echoing the way in which the rhetoric of choice has been grafted onto a model designed to steer women towards 'correct' choices). This hierarchical structure was experienced as divisive, and forming meaningful relationships depended on the efforts of individual women and midwives to resist its divisiveness.

This research has interesting parallels with Sheila Hunt's (Hunt and Symonds 1995) ethnographic study on how midwives interacted with women in a hospital setting, as well as with Helen Stapleton *et al.*'s (1998) study on the difficulties of midwifery supervision. What emerges is a more complete picture of women and midwives attempting to function in an unsupportive, hierarchical structure. In the same way that midwives felt unable to assert themselves for fear of reprisal, many women in this study felt unable to assert their needs for fear of causing further tensions in fragile relationships on which they would depend at a time of vulnerability. Disempowered midwives disempower women.

## Ways forward

Issues for exploration highlighted by this research include the socialisation of birth, the development of alternative knowledges of birth, the reconstruction of birth as a woman's issue and the reorganisation of maternity care around relationships.

One of the problems highlighted by this study was the dominance of a medical model of birth and the lack of robust alternatives. It goes without saying that technology and medical practices are invaluable when needed. None of the women in this study was against technology *per se*. Problems arise when the medical ethos permeates midwifery practice and imposes unnecessary or unwanted practices that reduce women's and midwives' abilities to construct their own birthing knowledge and practices.

Alternative philosophies do not exclude technical and medical assistance, but a medical model cannot easily extend itself to incorporate other knowledges and practices (Davis-Floyd 1992, Davis-Floyd and St John 1998). There is a need further to articulate a body of knowledge that is grounded in the respective experiences of women and midwives;[13] that can integrate a social approach drawing on technology appropriately; that can define its own education and practices rather than adopting those of another profession and attempting to humanise these;[14] that can align itself more closely with the physiological processes of birth; and that can find ways of supporting women through these processes (see Warmsley 1999 for a recent example of this).

Thus birth could be reconstrued as a woman's issue rather than a divisive issue between women and midwives, and different groups of women. This being the case, relationships between women and midwives may provide the key to the almost inconceivable move from a medical to a social model of birth. In this study, relationships between women and midwives were shown both to frustrate and enhance this process. It remains a relatively unexamined area, as one woman commented:

There's so much potential for the [relationship] and for whatever reason it's not being realised.

Jane Sandall's work (1995) and accounts from North America (Chester 1997) and New Zealand (Fleming 1994, 1996, 1998, Guilliland and Pairman 1994, Young 1996) provide ideas on the potentially radicalising effect on maternity care when these relationships become the organising principle around which care is structured (see also McCourt and Page 1996).

Finally, the midwife's role seemed to play a significant part in either extending the woman's role and knowledge or undermining it. Women could experience pregnancy and birth as part of a journey of self-discovery, personal growth and increased knowledge, or as more of a closing-down experience, undermining their knowledge, trust and confidence. That the midwife's potential role was indeed held in high esteem by many women can be seen from the following quote:

I realised that what I needed was... a midwife, I probably needed that more than I needed a homebirth.

## Notes

1.  The idea that suppressed groups have specific insights has been developed from the struggle between subordinated and dominant groups or individuals. It is usually attributed to Hegel's realisation that the viewpoints of slave and master are necessarily different (On 1993). This is not to say that oppressed peoples have the ability to stand outside their situation and see an objective 'reality', but that they have a different viewpoint (Holmwood 1995). Nor does this privilege experience or abandon theory or the researchers' critical faculties (Belenky *et al.* 1986, Roseneil 1996). Experience itself can also be said to be constructed (Scott 1992, Maynard and Purvis 1994). It does, however, allow the researcher to assume that women's accounts have their own validity (Stanley and Wise 1993) and are as valid as other accounts – although this is not necessarily widely accepted (Brown *et al.* 1994).
2.  In Britain, see for example journals published by the Association for Improvements in the Maternity Services, the Association of Radical Midwives and the National Childbirth Trust (NCT). There is also a small number of UK books on homebirth that include women's accounts of homebirths (Kitzinger 1991, O'Connor 1995, Wesson 1996).
3.  Research tends to show that women's views on the experiences of birth are subject to redefinition and change over the months following birth.
4.  Woman-centred researchers acknowledge that women may have difficulty in articulating their experiences in a largely male-constructed society (Smith

1987). The language available to women is often partial or missing, or reinforces dominant ideologies (Ehrlich 1995), and the area of childbirth is no
exception (Treichler 1990). Attentive listening to speech and silences is therefore essential (Burt and Code 1995). This enables both a critique of existing
definitions and a development of alternative theories (Braidotti 1997).

5.  The postmodern project has opened up challenging debates about the foundations of so-called scientific knowledge, with its basis in reason. Postmodernism undermines this cornerstone of modernity, questioning the nature of
rationality, objectivity and truth. The world is no longer to be discovered but
could be said to be under constant construction. Grand narratives are replaced
by Foucaldian 'fictions'. There are potential problems inherent in applying a
postmodern approach to woman-centred research, the full implications of
which are as yet unknown. The main concern is that, in destabilising previously stable categories and boundaries, the category 'woman' may be lost
altogether. There are complex debates on this matter (Flax 1990, Fraser and
Nicholson 1990, Hartsock 1990, Soper 1990, Phillips 1992, Code 1993, Nash
1994, Butler 1995, Fraser 1995, Holmwood 1995, McLennan 1995). I drew
extensively on Margrit Shildrick's (1997) ground-breaking work, which
suggests that postmodernism could be developed through feminism to incorporate 'woman' without stereotyping women. See also Cornell (1995).

6.  I use the terms 'model' and 'philosophy' purposefully in an attempt to draw
out the differences. 'Model' suggests a defined, less flexible system than
'philosophy'. In Davis-Floyd and St John's (1998) terms, the medical model
is a closed system that, by definition, cannot easily appeal to knowledge
outside itself unless a paradigm shift occurs (Kuhn 1970). Philosophies are
more open systems that can draw on other models and paradigms.

7.  Feminism and postmodernism have brought with them a growing awareness
that the Western worldview has been based on 'binaries'. These introduce
dichotomies, which include value judgements based on divisions between
male and female. Traditionally, the male has been associated with reason and
the female with nature. Nature is construed as unruly, unpredictable and in
need of governance (Williams 1993, Shildrick 1997).

8.  This is a crucial point. A valid criticism initially levelled at woman-centred
research was that it failed to recognise differences between women, and that
the category 'woman' referred to only white, heterosexual, academic women
(hooks 1990). This is particularly important in research on homebirth.
Women planning homebirths have typically been assumed to be a relatively
homogenous group, and stereotyping prevents us responding appropriately to
individual women. One of the interesting issues pointed up by this research is
that women held a wide range of views (Edwards 1996) and were different in
terms of age, class, race, educational status and income. Other research
confirms that it is not only white, middle-class, educated women who are
interested in homebirths (Ford *et al.* 1991, Martin 1995).

9.  Clarke (1995) describes the impossibility of midwives being able to fulfil
two opposing demands and clarifies one of the underlying problems in the
relationship between women and midwives. Their Code of Conduct requires
midwives to provide care focused on the woman, but their employers
demand that care be in line with Trust requirements. These potentially
opposing forces make a nonsense of the midwife's autonomy and threaten

her ability to provide woman-centred care. In the small number of cases in this study, when women moved from the NHS to being employers themselves (by engaging independent midwives), they interestingly reported that these problems were eliminated.

10. This mirrors some of the views seen in woman-centred debates that the systems developed thus far 'can only represent "otherness" as negativity' (Braidotti 1997:64). See also Irigaray (1985).

11. Sociology and medicine have been largely disembodied, that is, they have excluded the body as a site for consideration (Shildrick 1997). Research and awareness are developing in this area, but in woman-centred research this progress has been limited by fears that attunement to sexual difference may be used to reinforce gender stereotyping. (See, for example, Flax 1990, Soper 1990, Grosz 1993, Gatens 1996, and Marshall 1996 for an illuminating debate on this subject.) This is unfortunate as it has been suggested that power relations are played out most concretely in or on the body (McNay 1992).

12. We now know that the physiological processes of birth are more likely to progress smoothly when the woman is undisturbed and feels secure. Many women in this study felt the need to remain alert and watchful as they were uncertain about the midwives' practices and whether or not their stated wishes would be respected. Tess Cosslett (1994) criticises the 'natural' childbirth movement for failing to understand its own internal contradiction – that women need to focus solely on the birth process yet at the same time remain aware of and negotiate with the professionals providing their care.

13. Women in this study were able to expand their own knowledge of birth by drawing on experiential and other sources of information. They often found that the constraints on their NHS midwives did not allow the midwives to develop their knowledge in parallel. Thus, the women's knowledge could be threatening rather than complementary, and many women felt that there was little place for their own knowledge.

14. The humanising of the medical approach to birth has parallels with the attempts of early woman-centred empiricists (Harding 1987) to humanise research and include women. This was criticised for its failure to acknowledge or address inequalities and androcentricity (Eichler 1988). It seems unlikely that flawed systems can be greatly improved by superficial changes. Philosophical and structural issues require attention if real change is to be effected.

## Acknowledgements

The generosity of the women in this study, in sharing their knowledge with me, was overwhelming. It was a privilege to listen to their thoughts and feelings. There are many who assisted me in this particular social construction of knowledge. My thanks go to members of AIMS, especially Beverley Beech, Jean Robinson, Chris Rodgers, Pat Thomas and Sandar Warshal, for their continuing inspiration and support. The many conversations I have had with Miryam Bush, Peter Edwards, Mavis Kirkham, Andrea McLaughlin, Rosemary Mander, Helen Shallow, Cathleen Sullivan and Jan Webb have been invaluable. Without their insights and encouragement, this chapter would not have materialised.

# References

Ackermann-Liebrich U, Voegli T, Günter-Witt K, Kunz I, Züllig M, Schindler C and Maurer M (1996) Home versus hospital deliveries: follow up study of matched pairs for procedure and outcome. *British Medical Journal* **313**: 1313–18.

Alexander H (1987) *Home Birth in Lothian*. Edinburgh: Edinburgh Health Council.

Anderson K and Jack DC (1991) Learning to Listen: Interview Techniques and Analyses. In: Gluck SB and Patai D (eds) *Women's Words: The Feminist Practice of Oral History*. New York: Routledge.

Anderson R and Murphy PA (1995) Outcomes of 11,788 planned homebirths attended by certified nurse-midwives: a retrospective descriptive study. *Journal of Nurse-Midwifery* **40**: 483–92.

Arney WR (1982) *Power and the Profession of Obstetrics*. Chicago: University of Chicago Press.

Aspinall K, Nelson B, Patterson T and Sims A (1997) *An Extraordinary Ordinary Woman*. Sheffield: Ann's Trust Fund, School of Nursing and Midwifery, University of Sheffield.

Bastian H (1993) Personal beliefs and alternative childbirth choices: a survey of 552 women who planned to give birth at home. *Birth* **20**(4): 186–92.

Belenky MF, Clinchey BM, Goldberger NR and Tarule JM (1986) *Women's Ways of Knowing: The Development of Self, Voice and Mind*. New York: Basic Books.

Bortin S, Alzugaray M, Dowd J and Kalman (1994) A feminist perspective on the study of homebirth. Application of a midwifery care framework. *Journal of Nurse-Midwifery* **39**(3): 142–9.

Braidotti R (1997) Mothers, Monsters and Machines. In: Conboy K, Medina N and Stanbury S (eds) *Writing on the Body: Female Embodiment and Feminist Theory*. New York: Columbia University Press.

Brown S, Lumley J, Small R and Astbury J (1994) *Missing Voices: The Experience of Motherhood*. Oxford: Melbourne Open University Press.

Burt S and Code L (eds) (1995) *Changing Methods: Feminists Transforming Practice*. Peterborough, Ontario: Broadview Press.

Butler J (1995) Contingent Foundations. In: Benhabib S, Cornell D and Fraser N (eds) *Feminist Contentions: A Philosophical Exchange*. New York: Routledge.

Campbell R (1997) Place of Birth Reconsidered. In: Alexander J, Levy V and Roth C *Midwifery Practice: Core Topics 2*. Basingstoke: Macmillan.

Caplan M and Madeley RJ (1985) Home deliveries in Nottingham 1980–81. *Society of Community Medicine* **99**: 307–13.

Chamberlain G, Wraight A and Crowley P (1997) *Home Births: The Report of the 1994 confidential enquiry by the National Birthday Trust Fund*. Carnforth: Parthenon.

Charles N and Hughes-Freeland F (eds) (1996) *Practising Feminism: Identity, Difference, Power*. London: Routledge.

Chester P (1997) *Sisters on a Journey*. New Brunswick: Rutgers University Press.

Clarke RA (1995) Midwives, their employers and the UKCC: an eternally unethical triangle. *Nursing Ethics* **2**(3): 247–53.

Code L (1993) Taking Subjectivity into Account. In: Alcoff L and Potter E (eds) *Feminist Epistemologies*. New York: Routledge.

Comaroff J (1977) Conflicting Paradigms of Pregnancy: Managing Ambiguity in Antenatal Encounters. In: Davis A and Horobin G (eds) *Medical Encounters: The Experience of Illness*. London: Croom Helm.

Cornell D (1995) What is Ethical Feminism? In: Benhabib S, Butler J, Cornell D and Fraser N (eds) *Feminist Contentions: A Philosophical Exchange*. New York: Routledge.

Cosslett T (1994) *Women Writing Childbirth: Modern Discourses on Motherhood*. Manchester: Manchester University Press

Cowan JK (1996) Being a Feminist in Contemporary Greece: Similarity and Difference Reconsidered. In: Charles N and Hughes-Freeland F (eds) *Practising Feminism: Identity, Difference, Power*. London: Routledge.

Dalmiya V and Alcoff L (1993) Are 'Old Wives' Tales' Justified? In: Alcoff L and Potter E (eds) *Feminist Epistemologies*. New York: Routledge.

Damstra-Wijmenga SMI (1984) Home confinement: the positive results in Holland. *Journal of the Royal College of General Practitioners* August: 425–30.

Davies J, Hey E, Reid W and Young G (1996) Prospective regional study of planned homebirths. *British Medical Journal* **313**: 1302–6.

Davis-Floyd RE (1992) *Birth as an American Rite of Passage*. Berkeley, CA: University of California Press.

Davis-Floyd R and Arvidson P Sven (eds) (1997) *Intuition: The Inside Story: Interdisciplinary Perspectives*. New York: Routledge.

Davis-Floyd R and Davis E (1997) Intuition as Authoritative Knowledge in Midwifery and Home Birth. In: Davis-Floyd R and Sargent CF (eds) *Childbirth and Authoritative Knowledge: Cross-cultural Perspectives*. Berkeley: University of California Press.

Davis-Floyd RE and Dumit J (eds) (1997) *Cyborg Babies: From Techno-Sex to Techno-Tots*. New York: Routledge.

Davis-Floyd R and St John G (eds) (1998) *From Doctor to Healer: The Transformative Journey*. New Brunswick: Rutgers University Press.

Davis-Floyd R and Sargent CF (eds) (1997) *Childbirth and Authoritative Knowledge: Cross-cultural Perspectives*. Berkeley: University of California Press.

Devault ML (1990) Talking and listening from women's standpoint: feminist strategies for interviewing and analysis. *Social Problems* **37**(1): 96–116.

Dimond B (1993) Client autonomy and choice. *Modern Midwife* **3**: 1.

Donnison J (1988) *Midwives and Medical Men: A History of the Struggle for the Control of Childbirth*, 2nd edn. New Barnet: Historical Publications.

Durand AM (1992) The safety of homebirth: the farm study. *American Journal of Public Health* **82**: 450–3.

Edwards N (1996) Women's decision-making around homebirth. *AIMS* **8**(4): 8–10.

Ehrenreich B and English D (1979) *For Her Own Good: 150 Years of the Expert's Advice to Women*. London: Pluto.

Ehrlich S (1995) Critical Linguistics in Feminist Methodology. In: Burt S and Code L (eds) *Changing Methods: Feminists Transforming Practice*. Peterborough, Ontario: Broadview Press.

Eichler M (1988) *Nonsexist Research Methods: A Practical Guide*. London: Allen & Unwin.

Eskes M and van Alten D (1994) Review and assessment of maternity services in the Netherlands. In: Chamberlain G and Patel N (eds) *The Future of Maternity Services*. London: Royal College of Obstetrics and Gynaecology.

Expert Maternity Group (1993) *Changing Childbirth: Report of the Expert Maternity Group*. London: HMSO.

Finch J (1984) 'It's Great To Have Someone To Talk To': The Ethics and Politics of Interviewing Women. In: Bell C and Roberts H (eds) *Social Researching: Politics, Problems, Practice*. London: Routledge & Kegan.

Flax J (1990) Postmodernism and Gender Relations in Feminist Theory. In: Nicholson LJ (ed.) *Feminism/Postmodernism*. New York: Routledge.

Fleming VEM (1994) Partnership, Power and Politics: Feminist Perceptions of Midwifery Practice. Unpublished PhD thesis, Massey University, New Zealand.

Fleming VEM (1996) Midwifery in New Zealand: responding to changing times. *Health Care for Women International* **17**: 343–59.

Fleming VEM (1998) Women-with-midwives-with-women: a model of interdependence. *Midwifery* **14**:137–43.

Fleming VEM (1999) Seminar, Department of Nursing, University of Edinburgh, February.

Ford C, Iliffe S and Owen F (1991) Outcome of planned homebirths in an inner city practice. *British Medical Journal* **303**: 1517–19.

Foucault M (1980) *Power/Knowledge. Selected Interviews and Other Writings 1972–1977*, Gordon C (ed.) Brighton: Harvester Press.

Fraser N (1995) False Antitheses: A Response to Seyla Benhabib and Judith Butler. In: Benhabib S, Butler J, Cornell D and Fraser N (eds) *Feminist Contentions: A Philosophical Exchange*. New York: Routledge.

Fraser N and Nicholson LJ (1990) Social Criticism Without Philosophy: An Encounter Between Feminism and Postmodernism. In Nicholson LJ (ed.) *Feminism/ Postmodernism*. New York: Routledge.

Freire P (1972) *The Pedagogy of the Oppressed*. Harmondsworth: Penguin.

Furedi F (1997) *Culture of Fear: Risk-taking and the Morality of Low Expectations*. London: Cassell.

Garcia J, Kilpatrick R and Richards M (eds) (1990) *The Politics of Maternity Care: Services for Childbearing Women in Twentieth Century Britain*. Oxford: Clarendon Press.

Gatens M (1996) *Imaginary Bodies Ethics Power and Corporeality.* London: Routledge.

Giddens A (1991) *The Consequences of Modernity.* Cambridge: Polity Press.

Gregg R (1995) *Pregnancy in a High-Tech Age: Paradoxes of Choice.* New York: New York University Press.

Grosz E (1993) Bodies and Knowledge: Feminism and the Crisis of Reason. In: Alcoff L and Potter E (eds) *Feminist Epistemologies.* New York: Routledge.

Guilliland K and Pairman S (1994) The midwifery partnership: a model for practice. *New Zealand College of Midwives Journal* October: 5–9.

Harding S (1987) Is There Feminist Method? In: Harding S (ed.) *Feminism and Methodology.* Milton Keynes/Bloomington, IN: Open University Press/Indiana University Press.

Harding S (1993) Rethinking Standpoint Epistemology: 'What is Strong Objectivity?' In: Alcoff L and Potter E (eds) *Feminist Epistemologies.* New York: Routledge.

Hartsock N (1990) Foucault on Power: A Theory for Women? In: Nicholson LJ (ed.) *Feminism/Postmodernism.* New York: Routledge.

Heagarty BV (1997) Willing Handmaidens of Science? The Struggle Over the New Midwife in Early 20th Century England. In: Kirkham MJ and Perkins ER (eds) *Reflections on Midwifery.* London: Baillière Tindall.

Hewson B (1994) Court-ordered Caesarean: ethical triumph or surgical rape. *AIMS* **6**(2): 1–5.

Holmwood J (1995) Feminism and epistemology: what kind of successor science. *Sociology* **29**(3): 411–28.

hooks B (1990) *Yearning: Race, Gender and Cultural Politics.* Boston: South End.

House of Commons Health Committee (1992) *Maternity Services Second Report,* Volume 1. London: HMSO.

Howe KA (1988) Homebirths in south-west Australia. *Medical Journal of Australia* **149**: 296–302.

Hunt SC and Symonds A (1995) *The Social Meaning of Midwifery.* Basingstoke: Macmillan

Irigaray L (1985) *This Sex Which is Not One,* trans. C Porter. Ithaca: Cornell University Press.

Jordan B (1993) *Birth in Four Cultures: A Crosscultural Investigation of Childbirth in Yucatan, Holland, Sweden and the United States,* 4th edn. Prospect Heights, IL: Waveland Press.

Jordan B (1997) Authoritative Knowledge and its Contruction. In: Davis-Floyd RE and Sargent CF (eds) *Childbirth and Authoritative Knowledge: Cross-Cultural Perspectives.* Berkeley: University of California Press.

Kirkham MJ (1989) Midwives and Information-giving During Labour. In: Robinson S and Thompson AM (eds) *Midwives, Research and Childbirth,* Volume 4. London: Chapman & Hall.

Kitzinger S (1991) *Homebirth and Other Alternatives to Hospital.* London: Dorling Kindersley.

Kuhn TS (1970) *The Structure of Scientific Revolutions*, 2nd edn. Chicago: University of Chicago Press.

Levy VA (1998) Facilitating and Making Informed Choices During Pregnancy: A Study of Midwives and Pregnant Women. Unpublished PhD thesis, University of Sheffield.

McCourt C and Page L (eds) (1997) *One-to-One Midwifery Practice: Report on the Evaluation of One-to-One Midwifery*. London: Thames Valley University/Hammersmith Hospital NHS Trust.

Macfarlane A and Campbell R (1994) *Where to be Born? The Debate and the Evidence*, 2nd edn. Oxford: National Perinatal Epidemiology Unit.

Macfarlane A and Mugford M (1984) *Birth Counts: Statistics of Pregnancy and Childbirth*. London: HMSO.

McLennan G (1995) Feminism, epistemology and postmodernism: reflections on current ambivalence. *Sociology* **29**(2): 391–409.

McNay L (1992) *Foucault and Feminism: Power, Gender and the Self*. Cambridge: Polity Press.

Mander R (1993) Who chooses the choices? *Modern Midwife* **3**(1): 23–5.

Marland H (ed.) (1993) *The Art of Midwifery: Early Modern Midwives in Europe*. London: Routledge.

Marshall H (1996) Our bodies ourselves: why we should add old fashioned empirical phenomenology to the new theories of the body. *Women's Studies International Forum* **19**(3): 253–65.

Martin C (1995) Personal communication re unpublished data in Scottish Health Feedback Lothian Maternity Survey 1992, Report to Lothian Health Council.

Martin E (1989) *The Woman in the Body: A Cultural Analysis of Reproduction*. Milton Keynes: Open University Press.

Martin E (1990) Science and Women's Bodies: Forms of Anthropological Knowledge. In: Jacobus M, Fox-Keller E and Shuttleworth S (eds) *Body Politics: Women and the Discourse of Science*. New York: Routledge.

Maynard M and Purvis J (eds) (1994) *Researching Women's Lives from a Feminist Perspective*. London: Taylor & Francis.

Minister K (1991) A Feminist Frame for the Oral History Interview. In: Gluck SB and Patai D (eds) *Women's Words: The Feminist Practice of Oral History*. New York: Routledge.

Nash K (1994) The feminist production of knowledge: is deconstruction a practice for women? *Feminist Review* **47**: 65–77.

Nelson LH (1993) Epistemological Communities. In: Alcoff L and Potter E (eds) *Feminist Epistemologies*. New York: Routledge.

North West Surrey Community Health Council (1992) *Having Your Baby at Home: A Local Issue*. Available from NW Surrey CHC, St Peter's Hospital, Chertsey, Surrey.

Northern Regional Perinatal Mortality Survey Coordinating Group (1996) Collaborative survey of perinatal loss in planned and unplanned homebirths. *British Medical Journal* **313**: 1306–9.

O'Connor MT (1992) *Women and Birth: A National Study of Intentional Homebirths in Ireland*. Dublin: Coombe Lying-in Hospital.

O'Connor M (1995) *Birth Tides: Turning towards Homebirth*. London: Pandora.

Oakley A (1976) Wisewoman and Medical Man: Changes in the Management of Childbirth. In: Oakley A and Mitchell J (eds) *The Rights and Wrongs of Women*. Harmondsworth: Penguin.

Oakley A (1984) *The Captured Womb: A History of the Medical Care of Pregnant Women*. Oxford: Basil Blackwell.

Oakley A (1989) Who cares for women? Science versus love in midwifery today. *Midwives Chronicle and Nursing Notes* July: 214–21.

Oakley A (1993) Interviewing Women: A Contradiction in Terms. In: Oakley A, *Essays on Women, Medicine and Health*. Edinburgh: Edinburgh University Press.

Oakley A, Hickey D and Rajan L (1996) Social support in pregnancy: does it have long-term effects? *Journal of Reproductive and Infant Psychology* **14**(1): 7–22.

Ogden J (1998) Having a Homebirth: Decisions, Experiences and Longterm Consequences. In: Clement S (ed.) *Psychological Perspectives on Pregnancy and Childbirth*. Edinburgh: Churchill Livingstone.

Ogden J, Shaw A and Zander L (1997a) Part 1: Women's memories of homebirth 3–5 years on. *British Journal of Midwifery* **5**(4): 208–11.

Ogden J, Shaw A and Zander L (1997b) Part 2: Deciding on a homebirth: help and hindrances. *British Journal of Midwifery* **5**(4): 212–15.

Ogden J, Shaw A and Zander L (1997c) Part 3: A decision with a lasting affect. *British Journal of Midwifery* **5**(4): 216–18.

On, Bat-Ami Bar (1993) Marginality and Epistemic Privilege. In: Alcoff L and Potter E (eds) *Feminism/Postmodernism*. New York: Routledge.

Oswin J (1993) *Home Deliveries: How Mothers Who Planned to Have their Baby at Home Found the Experience*. Privately published, Bristol: J Oswin.

Phillips A (1992) Universal Pretensions in Political Thought. In: Barratt M and Phillips A (eds) *Destabilizing Theory: Contemporary Feminist Debates*. Cambridge: Polity Press.

Potter E (1993) Gender and Epistemic Negotiation. In: Alcoff L and Potter E (eds) *Feminist Epistemologies*. New York: Routledge.

Ralston R (1994) How much choice do women really have in relation to their care? *British Journal of Midwifery* **2**(9): 453–6.

Roberts H (1981) Women and their Doctors: Power and Powerlessness. In: Roberts H (ed.) *Doing Feminist Research*. London: Routledge.

Roncalli L (1997) Standing by Process: A Midwive's Notes on Story-Telling: Passage and Intuition. In: Davis-Floyd R and Sven-Arvidson P (eds) *Intuition: The Inside Story: Interdisciplinary Perspectives*. New York: Routledge.

Roseneil S (1996) Transgressions and Transformations: Experience, Consciousness and Identity at Greenham. In: Charles N and Hughes-Freeland F (eds) *Practising Feminism: Identity, Difference, Power*. London: Routledge.

Rothman BK (1982) *In Labour: Women and Power in the Birthplace*. New York: WW Norton.

Rothman BK (1993) Going Dutch: Lessons for Americans. In: Van der Mark A (ed.) *Successful Homebirth and Midwifery: The Dutch Model*. Westport, CT: Bergin & Garvey.

Sandall J (1995) Choice, continuity and control: changing midwifery towards a sociological perspective. *Midwifery* **11**: 201–9.

Scott JW (1992) Experience. In: Butler J and Scott JW (eds) *Feminists Theorize the Political*. New York: Routledge.

Shearer JML (1985) Five year survey of risk of booking for a homebirth in Essex. *British Medical Journal* **291**: 1478–80.

Shildrick M (1997) *Leaky Bodies and Boundaries: Feminism, Postmodernism and (Bio)Ethics*. London: Routledge.

Simpkin P (1991) Just another day in a woman's life?, Part 1: Women's long-term perceptions of their first birth experience. *Birth* **18**(4): 203–10.

Simpkin P (1992) Just another day in a woman's life?, Part 2: Nature and consistence of women's long-term memories of their first birth experiences. *Birth* **19**(1): 64–81.

Smith DE (1987) Women's Perspective as a Radical Critique of Sociology. In: Harding S (ed.) *Feminism and Methodology*. Milton Keynes/Bloomington, IN: Open University Press/Indiana University Press.

Soper K (1990) Feminism, humanism and postmodernism. *Radical Philosophy* **55**: 11–17.

Spurrett B (1988) Homebirths and the women's perspective in Australia. *Medical Journal of Australia* **149**: 289–90.

Stanley L and Wise S (1993) *Breaking out Again*. London: Routledge.

Stapleton H (1997) Choice in the Face of Uncertainty. In: Kirkham MJ and Perkins ER (eds) *Reflections on Midwifery*. London: Baillière Tindall.

Stapleton H, Duerden J and Kirkham M (1998) *Evaluation of the Impact of the Supervision of Midwives on Professional Practice and the Quality of Midwifery Care*. London: English National Board for Nursing, Midwifery and Health Visiting.

Tew M (1985) Place of birth and perinatal mortality. *Journal of the Royal College of General Practitioners* **35** (August): 390–4.

Tew M (1998) *Safer Childbirth? A Critical History of Maternity Care*, 3rd edn. London: Free Association Books.

Tew M and Damstra-Wijmenga SMI (1991) Safest birth attendants: recent Dutch evidence. *Midwifery* **7**: 55–63.

Towler J and Bramall J (1986) *Midwives in History and Society*. London: Croom Helm.

Treffers PE and Laan R (1986) Regional perinatal mortality and regional hospitalization at delivery in the Netherlands. *British Journal of Obstetrics and Gynaecology* **93**: 690–3.

Treichler PA (1990) Feminism, Medicine and the Meaning of Childbirth. In: Jacobus M, Fox-Keller E and Shuttleworth S (eds) *Body/Politics: Women and the Discourse of Science*. New York: Routledge.

Turner BS (1987) *Medical Power and Social Knowledge*. London: Sage.

Turner BS (1991) Recent Developments in the Theory of the Body. In: Featherstone M, Hepworth M and Turner BS (eds) *The Body: Social Process and Cultural Theory*. London: Sage.

Tyson H (1991) Outcomes of 1001 midwife attended homebirths in Toronto 1983–1988. *Birth* **18**(1): 14–19.

van Alten D, Eskes M and Treffers PE (1989) Midwifery in the Netherlands: the Wormeveer study; selection mode of delivery, perinatal mortality and infant morbidity. *British Journal of Obstetrics and Gynaecology* **96**: 656–62.

Wagner M (1995) A global witch-hunt. *Lancet* **346**: 1020–2.

Warmsley K (1999) Caring for women during the latent phase of labour. *Practising Midwife* **2**(2): 12–13.

Wayne FS, Barnes DE and Bakewell JM (1987) Neonatal mortality in Missouri homebirths 1978–84. *American Journal of Public Health* **77**(8): 930–5.

Wesson N (1996) *Home Birth*, 2nd edn. London: Vermilion.

Wiegers T, Kierse MJNC, Van der Zee J and Berghs GAH (1996) Outcome of planned home and planned hospital births in low risk pregnancies: prospective study in midwifery practices in the Netherlands. *British Medical Journal* **313**: 1309–13.

Williams A (1993) Diversity and agreement in feminist ethnography. *Sociology* **27**(4): 575–89.

Woodcock HC, Read AW, Bower C, Stanby FJ and Moore D (1994) A matched cohort study of planned home and hospital births in Western Australia 1981–1987. *Midwifery* **10**: 125–35.

Young D (1996) The midwifery revolution in New Zealand: what can we learn? *Birth* **23**(3): 125–7.

# Chapter 5

# Feeling Safe Enough To Let Go: The Relationship Between a Woman and her Midwife During the Second Stage of Labour

*Tricia Anderson*

## Introduction

Very little is known about women's experience of the second stage of labour and what aspects of midwifery care help or hinder them in the process of giving birth. As Kirkham and Perkins write, 'the voices of women are muted by the experts, although only women experience birth' (1997:185). The increasingly technological aspects and professionalisation of childbirth mean that women's experiences are too often neglected, yet unless we know what they are going through, how can we provide appropriate and sensitive care? This chapter is based on a study that tried to redress that balance by recording women's experiences of the second stage of labour and their perceptions of midwifery care during this crucial time (Anderson 1997). The impetus behind the study was this simple question: 'What can I do, as your midwife, to help you during the second stage of labour?'

Sixteen women, given pseudonyms in this chapter, who had given birth normally without epidural analgesia were interviewed in depth using the grounded theory approach. Full details of the methodology can be found in Anderson (1997). The women were asked about their experience of the second stage, which for them incorporated elements of the transitional phase of labour as well as the 'pushing' phase. Eight had given birth at home and eight in hospital; five were primiparous, eleven multiparous, and all gave birth normally with minimal intervention. These women are not representative of other women in their area, let alone all women giving birth in England. These findings cannot therefore be generalised to groups from other cultures or to women who experience, for example, augmentation, epidural analgesia or instrumental birth. These are, however, women who have achieved a normal birth with minimal intervention and analgesia within a Western cultural context; listening and analysing their stories may help midwives caring for women who want to give birth normally.

## The intense physical sensations of the second stage

The second stage of labour is associated with the onset of new and frightening physical sensations, which appear to follow a predictable pattern. Women describe sensations such as bulging, cracking, splitting, opening and breaking, as the uterine cavity is fully open and the baby begins its internal descent:

> I remember the sensation of my pelvis coming apart – unzipping. I suddenly thought 'Christ, my pelvis is cracking open'! I was really scared, because it was a bit like wild horses tied to either side of your pelvis, running in opposite directions... I didn't want to push, because I thought if my pelvis unzips any more, I'm going to come apart. (Anna)

On feeling these overwhelming sensations, women have to overcome a barrier of fear that initially prevents them pushing wholeheartedly. As Flint writes:

> I feel that when nature asks us women to push a baby out, it is probably the bravest thing we ever have to do. The feeling that trauma must ensue is so strong; in a way, a woman has to abandon her own comfort and safety in order for her child to emerge. (Flint 1997:186)

Women describe an initial sensation of holding back – for fear of opening their bowels, for fear of their backs cracking in half or their pelvis splitting open, for fear of nobody being there ready to catch the baby, for fear of losing control or for fear of simply more neverending and worsening pain:

You go through a sort of mental barrier, definitely. Before I stood up, it was like 'oh my god, this is so painful' and like just going with the pain. But when I stood up and started pushing, you suddenly just think 'well, I've got to do it. No matter how painful it is, I've got to get this baby out, and I've got to push and just forget about the pain.' You become a lot stronger all of a sudden. (Julie)

Price (1993) talks of the importance of body image and how this is constructed of, among other things, a concept of body boundaries – a perception of where one's body ends and the outside world begins. Any change in this body image can be profoundly traumatic, possibly no more so than during the process of giving birth, in which a woman's body literally opens up, the boundaries being breached and no longer clear and intact:

When I felt her first really descend, that was when I got a bit frightened... it was like a huge powerful thing that was happening to me... a fear that she was coming out beyond my control, there was a fear of the pain, and the fear that my body couldn't possibly open any more. (Anna)

In this process there is an inevitable loss of control. This is the 'regressive boundary-permeable phase'. One coping strategy is to seek external boundary control by grasping out for physical contact with something – with anything. If this need is not met, then, Price theorises, a woman will enter the third, aberrant phase, known as 'desperate-body boundary-diffuse phase', which may lead her to believe that her body is going to break up and she is going to die. Natalie, a primigravida, explains it thus:

I was convinced, absolutely convinced there was no way I could survive this kind of pain... I kept saying 'I can't survive another contraction.' I was desperate to die – I thought that would get rid of the pain. (Natalie)

### Fear of losing control

Perhaps surprisingly, however, the predominant fear seems to be that of losing control, which for many women is the main hurdle that needs to be overcome in order to give birth normally. Rhiannon talked of how women need to 'let go' in order to give birth, yet women report the greatest satisfaction in childbirth when they feel 'in control'

(Green 1993). Are these two states incompatible? As Bluff and Holloway (1994:161) point out, the issue of control is 'ambiguous, with women wanting to be in control of events even though they acknowledged that maybe they were not':

> It's quite nice to have the contractions stopping and a different thing happening, but it's scary at the time. It's almost like you're losing your control over the whole process and that's the scary bit. (Rhiannon)

Waldenstrom *et al.* (1996) explain how being in control seems to be associated with birth satisfaction, and, indeed, the women kept returning to this idea. The concept of control is complex and can mean different things for different women. Waldenstrom *et al.* suggest that it might be linked to a sense of being an active subject rather than the passive object of the event.

Brewin and Bradley (1982) also looked at women's perceived control and the experience of childbirth. Interestingly, they found that women who either perceived themselves to have control over labour or perceived the staff to have control over labour reported less pain. It would seem that the worst option of all is for no-one to have control over labour, that is, for the labour to be 'out of control'. Neither the midwife or the woman is in control, and, importantly, neither does the woman's body feel as if it knows what it is doing. This resonates with Daniella's experience: when the second stage of her labour seemed to be prolonged, she lost all sense of both internal and external control, and her saviour was a midwife, 'an angel', who came in and took charge of the situation:

> It was like at last somebody's here now who's in control and who's going to do something. (Daniella)

### Altered states of consciousness

The severity and intensity of physical sensations leads women to a instinctive primal survival technique, that of entering an altered state of consciousness. This equates with Rhiannon's suggested need to 'let go' or Isobel's 'just disconnect'. This was one of the strongest findings in this study; all but one of the women talked of a sense of separation of mind from body, which was not a frightening experience and paradoxically enabled them to retain control:

I was aware of having a kind of out of body experience... It was a
suddenly kind of floating feeling like I wasn't really there and then the
contraction would come again and wake me up. I was just floating away,
really comfortable, no pain, it was really quiet, really peaceful. There was
nothing around me. I could have been totally on my own, just not aware of
anybody. (Natalie)

The women did not equate entering an altered state of consciousness
with being out of control; on the contrary, it was a powerful coping
strategy that increased their sense of being *in* control. This corresponds
with Davis's (1989) paradoxical notion that, to gain control, one has
first to go through a process of losing it. She talks of how the key to
gaining control is often to lose it, to surrender ideas, desires and fears
in order to merge with and then master the experience:

I didn't feel in control. But I didn't feel like the midwife was in control,
either. I just felt like my body was in control. But not my mind at all.
(Emma)

## Letting go

The women talked a lot about their bodies being in control. It seems
that there is a sense of 'letting go' on a psychological level that allows
the physical body to take control. Thus, the woman still retains her
sense of control and physically embodies Waldenstrom's idea of being
the active subject. The woman is the body that is in control. In this
sense, there is no loss of control:

At that point you're not in control, society's not in control, no one's in
control apart from your body and what your body has learnt to do by itself
over generations and thousands of generations. (Rhiannon)

This psychological state is similar to that described by Cosmi
(1995) as a hypnotic trance. It is characterised by a perceptual shift
of awareness in an atmosphere of trust and security. Subjects
describe a 'distancing' that they later describe as a feeling of being
outside themselves, peripherally 'watching' what is happening to
them. Cosmi points out that severe pain and stress seem to enhance
the ability of an individual to enter this state. Machin and Scamell
(1997:82) described their participants as experiencing 'a trance-like

state of consciousness, indicative of the transitional state of a rite of passage'. Odent (1991) suggests that this might be similar to a 'near death' experience, in which there is a sudden, massive release of endorphins, which might explain the women's feelings of floating – a calm and peaceful euphoria.

Davis (1989) explores the concepts of different types of brain wave, the alpha, beta, theta and delta waves demonstrated on an electro-encephalogram. She suggests that women in labour are in the theta state, the same state that is induced by deep hypnosis or near death experiences, which would explain their euphoria, sense of oneness and lack of temporal or physical awareness. Isobel put this concept in her own words:

> What she [the midwife] said did get through to me though, even though I was on another level... it's like a different level of the brain picks it up, and that bit of the brain reassures the rest of the brain that's doing it that it's all right, even though it's not a big part of it. (Isobel)

The level of endorphins, the body's naturally produced powerful opiate-like substances, is at its highest during transition and the second stage, producing a sense of wellbeing and peace, altering the perception of place and time, yet curiously co-existing with the feelings of extreme pain (Odent 1994). To be able to 'just disconnect', as Isobel described, minimises the negative effect of the stress hormones (adrenaline and noradrenaline) on the strong oxytocic response needed to facilitate the contractions of the uterus and thus the birth.

Cathy was intrigued by this notion, and commented that 'it's not the kind of thing I've ever heard people talk about'. She pointed out that 'if you're talking to someone in labour, don't expect an answer straight away. Wait for something to happen, and then you'll get an answer.'

Entering this altered state appeared to be unconnected to use of analgesia (only three of the women being given pethidine) or the length or duress of the labour; even Rhiannon, whose entire labour was less than two hours in total, experienced a sense of separation. She gave birth at home without any intervention, any vaginal examination or any physical contact from the midwife, and was able to take this one step further:

> For me, it was not so much a separation but more a kind of 'oneness'. It was a separation from the intellectual side of life... when you're there and you're giving birth and your body is in total control. It's a trust and it's an

animal thing. It's a separation from thinking. You couldn't intellectualise
it. You have to separate your emotional thinking side of you to cope with it.
(Rhiannon)

## A sense of timelessness

All the women experienced temporal and locality distortion, and experienced a sense of timelessness. Beck (1994) studied this phenomenon
of temporal awareness and found that labouring women's sense of time
fluctuates throughout the process. This has implications for midwifery
practice: telling a woman that the anaesthetist will be here in 20
minutes or that the baby will born within half an hour may not be
helpful or relevant to her (although it may be of benefit to an anxious
partner!). The woman may be experiencing time at a completely
different pace, one in which half an hour may seem like a day or like a
few minutes. This is similar to the temporal distortion experienced by
those experiencing altered states of consciousness in other ways,
through meditation for example, or through hallucinogenic drugs
(*Scientific American* 1972). It may well be that, for the labouring
women, losing track of time is a very helpful coping strategy.

## Andrea's story: the exception to the rule

Not all women may feel that the sense of going into an altered
state applies to them, as seen, for example, with one woman in the
study. Rather than being an anomaly to be ignored, Andrea's experience is worthy of special mention as it throws up an important
point. She explains that, even while pushing, she was worrying
about her housework:

> I wasn't able to do that [go into another world]. I was worried about my
> husband. And you've got a lot of things going on in your head… Every-
> thing's got to be just right in this house. Housework, dusting and all the
> rest of it. Making sure my eldest was all right at school, making sure the
> other one was going to be in bed at the right time and just thinking 'oh
> dear, I haven't cleaned this and I haven't cleaned that and what are people
> going to think'. Thinking about the washing, thinking 'I hope this isn't
> going to make a mess cos I've got to wash more sheets!' I think it helped
> take my mind off things.

Rather than floating off into a private world, Andrea used her domestic worries as a distraction from the pain of the contractions. More than that, however, Andrea lived in an abusive relationship, her husband having a record of violent behaviour, towards both her and health professionals. Andrea's prime concern was to ensure the birth went smoothly so that her husband did not become violent. Thus, she had an overwhelming primacy of fear: in her rank of competing concerns, her fear of her husband and of her husband's abuse held sway over any fear of labour, pain or even death itself. This necessitated Andrea keeping herself very much 'together' and alert during the process of giving birth: any sense of separation or disconnection might have had disastrous consequences for her and her family. Had her husband's violence surfaced during the birth, Andrea knew that she risked having her children taken away.

Note how she quickly glosses over the fact that she is worried about her husband and moves onto a long description about housework. Women's lives are multifaceted and ongoing, and giving birth takes place in a complex context that has been long in its weaving. Midwives need to be aware of the whole picture, or at least be aware that the picture they see is not necessarily complete.

## Supporting or undermining: the power of the midwife

The women were unanimous in their belief that the contribution of the midwife was critical, having the power to make or break the woman's birth experience, and this centred on the issue of control. They agreed how vulnerable and susceptible to suggestion they were during the second stage of labour, which corresponds to the idea of an altered state of consciousness, and just how much power the midwife had to influence and direct them. Women in labour are in a vulnerable state of separation, a dangerous state in which the power of the surrounding people and their messages can be irresistible.

I felt completely in the midwife's hands, and would have obeyed anything she told me to do! (Tracy)

The midwife told me to stand up when I was laying down, and I did not want to stand up, but I just got up because she had told me to. I was told to get up, I got up. I was told not to push and pant, I panted. It's like being back at school... I remember looking at my husband and the GP, thinking 'she said pant, guys. Pant! The midwife says pant.' The midwife is more in control than you think. (Cathy)

## Midwife as safe anchor: feeling safe enough to let go

The women talked about having to trust the midwife: a failure to do what the midwife tells them could put their baby's life at risk (Kirke 1980, Beaton 1990, Bluff and Holloway 1994). Those women who gave birth at home had the opportunity to get to know their midwife, and without exception they rated this opportunity to build up a relationship of trust before the birth as being very important. Andrea talked about how the midwife was able to treat her as an individual as she had come to know the family and Andrea's own wishes regarding how she wanted to give birth, and then respected them. The trust was based on some foundation. Rhiannon agreed:

> The most important thing for me is to have somebody there who I trusted, who I knew beforehand, who was familiar with my family and was familiar with what I wanted, who I trusted and liked, and someone that I could feel completely at ease with and know that I could just get on with what I needed to do and give birth. (Rhiannon)

Isobel talked of how it was important that she knew and trusted her midwife 'not to laugh at me, or something'. Feeling safe enough to enter an altered state of consciousness was much easier in front of someone you knew, she thought. But even the women who gave birth in hospital and who had never met their midwife before labour talked of how they automatically trusted her and assumed that she knew what she was doing: 'You have to, don't you?' (Julie). Their trust was based on blind faith rather than any solid foundation. As they were in such a vulnerable state, they had no choice but to trust the unknown midwife. Tracy, a young woman having her first baby in hospital, goes one step further and talks of how the midwife takes on a mothering role to the mother-to-be, a firm-handed mother figure who has to be obeyed:

> You have to obey and listen to what the midwife's telling you. You know that she does it all day, every day. She's the expert. It's just automatic. There isn't time to rationalise it. You're in pain, the contractions are coming fast. You really want your mum, don't you? The midwife is the surrogate mum. (Tracy)

The midwife is in an extraordinarily powerful position. In her care, she has a woman who is vulnerable and in extreme pain, hyper-suggestible and experiencing perceptual distortions and loss of control:

> You're at the most vulnerable point, because you can't do anything. If someone starts telling you to do something, you just do it. When the midwife told me that I wasn't to push or to do something — like turn over – I felt like a little schoolgirl: 'Oh, all right then – if I have to.' So midwives are in a real position of power which they mustn't abuse. (Rhiannon)

This power on the part of the midwife can be used sensitively and wisely or, as Rhiannon points out, can be abused. Lukes (1986) explored how power affects behaviour. A has power over B to the extent to which A can get B to do something that B would not other-wise do. A (the midwife) may not exercise her power, but B's (the client's) knowledge of this power gains her willing compliance. Emma talked of how the midwife made her lie on her side, which Emma intuitively felt was wrong and subsequently proved to be so. On being asked whether she told the midwife this, Emma answered:

> No, I didn't say anything to her about not lying on my side. It was like 'OK, I'll lie here. Whatever you say.' The schoolgirl syndrome. If she'd said, can you just swing on this rafter, you'd go 'OK.' You haven't got time to think about it, have you? Everything is happening so quickly, you just don't have the time. You just do as you're told. (Emma)

## Trust sustained

When this power is appropriately channelled, a skilled midwife can provide a sense of security that enables women safely to enter the disconnected state and thus facilitate the birth process:

> It's the midwife's job to keep everything safe. She's the anchor that helps you go off into that altered state... I also felt really assured that they were competent. That was very reassuring, that they know what they were doing. It was all alright, it was all normal. They anchored me and allowed me to feel safe going through all that. (Isobel)

For this to happen, women need a midwife to be present yet unob-trusive. Berg *et al.* (1996) found that the midwife's 'presence' was key. If trust is lacking, if women feel undermined and unsupported, and do not feel that the midwife sees them as individuals, they perceive the midwife to be 'absently present':

> She [the midwife] didn't spend much time with me, coming in and out... she seemed quite distracted, like her mind wasn't really in the room. (Judith)

## Calm and quiet

Quietness and calm are attributes frequently mentioned by women, which they value in a midwife. Yet, paradoxically, when women are off in a disconnected state, the midwife's role is for many of them surprisingly peripheral, which may illustrate how well she can perform her task as guide, safe-keeper and anchor:

> I wasn't even aware of anything, even of which side she [the midwife] was standing. I don't remember much of what she was saying, I really don't. I'm sure it was all really good stuff... I'm sure probably if she hadn't been saying anything I would have noticed. (Natalie)

This idea of a midwife who sits, watches and is quiet is mentioned by Odent in his discussion of the role of the birth attendant (Odent 1987). He proposed that the fetus ejection reflex can only happen when the attendants are conscious that the process of parturition is an involuntary process and that one cannot help an involuntary process but simply not disturb it. If labour is going well, a woman needs little input from the midwife but her simple presence:

> The perfect midwife for me would be someone who would be able to understand when she was needed... But if everything's going well, just to be left by yourself, knowing that she's there, knowing that there's a woman there to deliver the baby, catch the baby, hold the baby. She's there if anything goes wrong. But it must be difficult – only experience can probably give a midwife that kind of knowing – when to step in and when not to step in. But I think that's the most important thing – not to spoil the whole flow of the birth process. That continuity of peace and tranquility and privacy. (Rhiannon)

> Just a guiding through, yes. Just to reassure you you're doing the right thing. But I would say that it's good for the midwife and everybody else just to stand back, really. You don't really want to listen to anybody. (Anna)

Yet for some women, the midwife, and in particular her voice, can be acutely important, the only thing that keeps them safe and holds them anchored in this world:

> I was very much tuned into her voice. If my husband had said anything, I probably wouldn't have heard it, but my ears were focusing back towards where the midwife was and very tuned in to what she was saying. It was very dark, and all I could hear was the midwife's voice, saying 'keep breathing'. (Joanna)

As well as quietness and calm, the women valued praise, positivity, simplicity, reassurance and gentle encouragement in their midwives to help them get through the second stage. They talked of how important it was that the midwife gave them confidence, confidence in both the midwife's skills and their own ability to give birth. The midwife needs to believe that the woman can do it and convey that belief to her.

Jones (1989) talks about the importance of care-givers having insight into the mind–body process of labour, which will result in them giving support that is far more appropriate to the mother's lived experience than if they only know the anatomical and physiological aspects of labour. 'As far as I'm concerned, teaching about the mother's altered state of mind is far more important than teaching about cervical dilatation', he writes (Jones 1989:19).

> The midwife said, 'you can do it…, you can do it'. She didn't tell me to push or anything. I didn't need telling to push this time. I felt really confident that I was in safe hands. (Isobel)

> No, what the midwife said, and the encouragement was just right. It wasn't too over the top. I think if she'd said more, I probably would have wanted her to shut up. You don't want to be bombarded with instructions. You just want it very simple, clear, consistent… You almost want to hear the same thing again and again… to reassure you that that's all you have to do. (Joanna)

## *Unobtrusive*

It is important that midwives know when to stand back and not intrude or distract women from focusing on the intense natural process of pushing. This important distinction was very well summarised by Berg *et al.* (1996), who described a woman's need to be supported and guided by the midwife *but on her own terms.* Supporting and encouraging women to listen to their own feelings and instincts is very different from imposing a pre-learnt arbitrary set of instructions. When guidance is given, women still need to be able to retain their sense of control. This idea was beautifully summed up by one of their respondents, who said: 'Even if I received expert help... it wasn't the intention of someone else that dominated, but my own desire' (Berg *et al.* 1996:13). The women themselves wanted to be the authorities at their own births, even though they all recognised and valued the need for professional assistance and guidance. Women – both multiparous and primiparous – acknowledged the expertise of the midwives but wanted to retain control and actively give birth:

> I was very much in control of the whole thing. And the midwife helped that. She could have easily cluttered the whole process. I liked the way that she was very, very easy, and didn't say 'right' and roll her sleeves up and say 'now, let's do this.. and let's examine you... and... I'll break your waters... and...' It just all happened and felt so natural. (Joanna)

Importantly, women value how the midwife does not take control of everything but facilitates their own ability and confidence to be in control. This leads to overwhelmingly positive feelings about the experience:

> After you've given birth, you can do anything. You could move a mountain... And the midwife helps you do that, doesn't she, as long as she doesn't interfere too much. (Cathy)

## Back to the school room: the naughty schoolgirl

Difficulties arise when midwives abuse their position, undermining the woman's sense of being in control rather than reinforcing it. Six women in the study talked unprompted of feeling like a naughty little schoolgirl, with the midwife that well-known authority figure, the harsh and unkind schoolmistress:

> You go back to being a schoolgirl and do as you're told. You feel vulnerable, and you think that somebody in authority, which the midwives are – they're the people that know about what's going on – you listen to them and do what you're told. (Julie)

Several women were called 'a good girl' when they did well. More often, though, they talked of a sense of 'not doing it right' or 'not doing it very well'. They were sure that there was a 'right' way to do it and that they were inadequate or deficient in some way:

> Everybody kept saying to me 'I've got to try and push harder' and I really felt inadequate that I wasn't doing it right at all. (Tracy)

Women were praised by the midwife if they got it 'right' – 'she kept saying I was doing it just right' and berated if they were not doing it 'right' – 'she shouted at me to stop shouting and start pushing'. All the women talked of times, either in this birth or from a previous birth experience, when the midwife had been at best intrusive, and at worst overbearing and rude. They cited examples of care by the midwives that had distressed them, and, in the case of the multiparous women who had chosen to give birth at home, it was their memories of poor treatment during previous births that had been one of the motivating factors in opting for a homebirth.

Two women mentioned how intrusive they found the midwife's constant note-taking during the second stage:

> I can remember the midwife was scribbling notes all the time. That's about all I can remember of what was going on around me. That's all she seemed to do. (Emma)

> Midwives should spend less time doing paperwork and give more attention to the women they're going to deliver! (Rhiannon)

The timing of a midwife's questions can sometimes be inappropriate and insensitive:

> Every time one of the midwives went to say something to me, I couldn't answer because it was at a time when a contraction was coming and you're trying to say something but you can't. It was irritating. (Sonia)

Sadly, some midwives can be rough, hard and insensitive:

> A lot of the midwives seemed very butch, very manly. Maybe that's the
> way they've got to be. They're all rough. (Judith)

Maybe 'doing things' helps the midwives to feel useful, rather than
being of help to the woman:

> It would just be an invasion of space if they leant in and said 'come on,
> dear…' Unless the woman is saying 'I can't do this', which I don't think
> happens at that stage. Maybe it would help the midwives, to think that they
> were helping, but I don't think you need to hear it. (Anna)

Some of the other women remembered being shouted at, which was
never appreciated:

> With my second daughter… by the end of it I was legs strapped up, big set
> of pliers and the midwife shouting 'you will fucking push this baby out!'
> like some headmistress! (Isobel)

Andrea recalled the second stage of her first birth, which she remembers as a terrible experience. While she was giving birth, a cleaner came
in and carried on cleaning the room as if nothing was happening:

> When I had my first baby, I had a cleaner walk in when I was pushing! She
> just walked in, had a dust round and off she went again. She picked me
> knickers up off the side to dust round them… I was pissed off about the
> whole thing. I had a husband who was sat there drunk asleep at the time.
> Great! And just people walking in and out all the time. It's not much fun.
> And then when you're in the stirrups, it's just… There is a lot of people
> there. I had forceps and so you end up with a paediatrician, doctors, junior
> doctor. It's like a side show. (Andrea)

### Feelings of anger

The imagery of the circus was used by several different women – they
described the medical staff as the circus and themselves as the freak or
side show. It was fairly clear from some of the women's accounts
exactly who was in control:

I was very angry because she'd taken him away. The midwife wanted to get him dressed instantly – instantly he came out! Quick, get his clothes on! Oh my god! They wanted to take him away and give me a cup of tea and it was like 'I don't want a cup of tea actually – go away! I want my baby in here with me and everyone else can go away... I was so angry. I was so angry. I was really angry. I felt that, after going through this whole empowering thing of giving birth where you've got so much strength, then all of a sudden in come the circus and you're totally disempowered. (Rhiannon)

So I screamed at L that I wanted to push, and she said 'No, don't push, don't push...' and then with every contraction then it seemed just more and more strongly that I wanted to push. And that's when she made me get out of the bath... I would have happily stayed in there – no problem at all, because it was really comforting actually being in the water., In the bath, she was saying 'we'll get you out of the bath and then I'll examine you to see how we're getting on'. (Natalie)

Note the use of the first person plural in the last sentence: exactly whose labour is this? Brook (1996) uses the term 'maternalism' to describe the way in which midwives may act towards a labouring woman more like the authoritarian mother of a small child rather than someone in a professional adult relationship:

The midwife [who] delivered my first baby was quite old fashioned. I didn't feel relaxed... I felt very stressed actually, because she was very kind of sergeant majorish – 'come on then, up you get, into the bath with you'... It was like 'what's this woman doing in my house!' She broke my waters and stuff. But now I think about it, she did want to control my pushing. I did listen to her. I did do what she said. I did, yes, I did. And at the time she said it, I found it incredibly irritating and I was quite angry because it was going against what my body was telling me to do. I didn't like it, and I just wanted to tell her to bugger off – just shut up! (Rhiannon)

Julie's comments are thought provoking:

It's not the midwife that forces you to be like that, is it? Like a schoolgirl? It's you. I suppose it's just going back to childhood really. The last time you felt so out of control, so helpless. I think it's just a natural thing. I don't think you can help it. (Julie)

As is obvious from some of the other women's stories, when a midwife uses her presence wisely, the adult labouring woman need not feel like a schoolgirl; it is not necessarily a 'natural' thing. Women do not equate entering the altered state with a return to childhood. Yet Julie believes that regression to childhood during labour is inevitable as a midwife has taken the schoolmistress role at both her births. Julie's belief in her ability to give birth as an adult woman is undermined by the midwife taking the power and exerting her influence as the adult, relegating Julie to the position of child. As Julie is on the brink of becoming a mother, this seems wholly inappropriate.

## Intrusive directions

> Giving birth is a completely free-willed thing and it doesn't listen. I think if it had to listen to something, that's when things start going wrong. (Rhiannon)

Interventions in the natural process of giving birth may be intended by the midwife to confirm normality, and she may believe it to be reassuring for the client. However, the very act carries with it the message that things might very possibly *not* being going well, for otherwise, why intervene at all? Professional surveillance brings doubt and anxiety into the process, and because of the supposed greater power, education and (assumed) gender status of health professionals, women are socialised into believing that the professionals' version of reality must be more accurate that their own.

That intervention in labour, such as monitoring the fetal heart, is of value is not in question, but, as an intervention, its proponents must be aware of its costs and benefits. If, by a simple procedure or examination, women are made to doubt their own bodies' ability to give birth ('I worried about it after that'), midwives must develop their communication skills of reassurance to try to root out the seeds of uncertainty that they have sown. This process also undermines a woman's sense of control and self-awareness: 'I feel X, but the midwife says Y; therefore I must be wrong':

> At one point I thought I felt a bit pushy and she was examining me at the time, and she said 'oh no, you don't feel like pushing yet'. And I thought 'Oh. No, OK then.' That made me feel a bit stupid, I suppose. Well no, not stupid, but just a bit like 'oh, I must be wrong. I'm not doing it right. I was

just a bit confused, really. I didn't feel angry – just confused, and like I was wrong and she was right, because she's the midwife and she must know. So I must have been mistaken in what I felt, which is stupid really. (Julie)

## Being undermined

Many women quoted instances when the midwife had completely undermined and disregarded what they were feeling, which made them feel angry and sapped their confidence in their own bodies. If the midwife's instructions were at odds with their physical sensations, this resulted in feelings of uncertainty and confusion. As already noted, women are so sure that the midwife must be right, and therefore their own body must be wrong:

> I thought I wanted to push, but she [the midwife] said I couldn't possibly. (Sonia)

Thomson, in her review of the management of the second stage of labour, writes:

> There appears to be an impression among the midwifery and obstetric profession that control has to be exerted over the labouring woman as soon as the second stage begins... the delivery room can resemble a rugby scrum with everyone present peering at the woman's vulva while urging her to exert greater effort. (Thomson 1988:77)

Midwives have traditionally exhorted women to 'take a deep breath in, hold it, and push.........sh' (McKay *et al.* 1990:192), responding more often than not to their own overwhelming urge to push (Sargady 1995). McKay *et al.* (1990) showed how the instructions that women received were more often than not completely at odds with their body's sensations, and Evans and Jeffrey (1995) found that pushing directions were the most frequently mentioned areas of conflict in information needs between midwives and clients.

## Trust betrayed

The women explained how important it is that the information given is accurate: 'white lies' are not appreciated, even when meant to encourage. For, if they are found out, the trust that the woman has placed in the midwife is instantly betrayed and any sense of control that the women has maintained is lost. None of the women appreciated being kept in the dark or being given inaccurate information or false hope. Dianne experienced this in her first birth: she had an epidural, the midwives were telling her how well she was pushing, yet in fact there was no progress whatsoever:

> You're not quite sure that when she says 'oh, you're doing really well' whether you really are doing really well, and you're thinking 'well, am I?' I obviously wasn't doing very well. Why didn't they tell me I wasn't doing very well? You're just lying there, thinking 'oh this is easy' with a big smile on your face, and then you find out that you're not doing it right at all. Nothing's happening. You just assume that everything's going all right, because they've just told me it is. (Dianne)

### Wrong assumptions

Many of the women incorrectly anticipated events, based on either past birth experiences or what they had learnt in antenatal classes. The multiparous women expected events to unfold in the same way in which they had previously, and kept waiting for the midwives to do or say certain things. Nowhere was this more evident than when to begin pushing:

> I was actually waiting for them to tell me what to do. That was a problem, in that I was waiting for them to tell me what to do, and of course they're letting you do what they want. I was waiting for permission to push, because that's what we'd been told in the classes... But then I didn't say anything to them anyway, so it was my fault as much as anything, because I assumed it would be the same thing as last time. (Julie)

Rose Driscoll has collected birth stories from 50 women of different generations and from differing cultures – England, Ireland and Italy:

> Something else many women agreed on was that once labour had begun there seemed to be great disagreement over the subject of when to push. When you're thrashing around in agony and wanting to push, it's not much fun to be told you can't. Unless you have the confidence of a gladiator you

do as you're told. You wait for them, you don't make a fuss, you submit to their demands. They know best. (Driscoll 1997:xvi).

But midwives are changing the way in which they practise towards more evidence-based care. One such significant change is the move away from the intervention of directed pushing to free women to follow their own body's instincts. This has a solid foundation in research evidence (Nikodem 1995). However, it is important to realise that this change has implications for women. First, all midwives do not change their practice at the same pace in the same way and at the same time. It is a piecemeal affair, with midwives even in one labour ward working the same shift using very different styles. Second, women clearly have a received knowledge of what they expect from the midwife, which is that she will tell them when to push. This is implied even in a very recent guide issued by the NCT (Nolan 1996), and Dianne mentioned how she learnt her birthing behaviour from what she had 'seen on the telly':

> I didn't go to any antenatal classes... so luckily, you've seen it all on the telly so you know more or less what you've got to do. (Dianne)

This illustrates nicely just how pervasive the notion of enforced pushing has become within Western society. It is possible that this received knowledge can be changed over a period of many years by consistency in childbirth classes, literature and other media, but in the meantime childbearing women are left in a very confusing situation. This was apparent from many of the discussions. The confusion over whether to push or not was widespread. All of the women had attended antenatal classes, for either this baby or a previous baby, and had clear expectations that the midwife would tell them when they could push. If this did not happen, they were left in limbo and not in control, not knowing whether or not to push:

> A lot of it, I was holding back for, because when I went to antenatal classes with the twins we were told 'don't push; if you want to push, then say so and we'll tell you when you can push'... because they check that there's no membrane across or something. So of course, I'm saying that I want to push, and I'm not being told 'no, don't' but I'm not being told 'yes, do!' And I'm thinking that they will tell me when I can. In the end I was saying 'if I want to push, can I push?' (Dianne)

For many women, there appears to be a conflict between their own and their care-giver's readiness to have them push. This can occur in one of two ways – the woman wanting to push and being told not to, or her not wanting to push yet being told she should. The most under-mining and confusing of all would be when both things happen, as it did with Daniella.

## Daniella's experience

'I was too exhausted to take her in. I was crying tears, but I wasn't even crying. I was crying from inside'.

Thus spoke Daniella about the birth of her baby. For her, the second stage was a repeating nightmare that was out of control: Daniella was the one woman in this study for whom the second stage of labour was a extremely negative experience. As we have seen with Andrea, the exception sometimes provides some interesting food for thought.

Daniella's first birth had ended in a long two-hour second stage and a bad perineal tear, which she remembers two doctors taking two hours or more to suture. She recalls not being able to walk for three weeks, and she could not resume sexual intercourse for a year and half. She felt brutalised, with her sexual identity in tatters. Daniella felt so traumatised by the memory of that second stage that she considered opting for an elective caesarean section for this birth, but decided in the end to have a vaginal delivery. The first stage went easily and quickly, and she needed no analgesia; then the second stage began, she panicked and it all started to go horribly wrong:

I thought I was pushing as much as I could. You can be pushing because you're told to push, or there's that point where I got these natural urges, they were real, and then I did really push for all I had. But the rest of the time I was having to force myself to push because they weren't sort of natural and the midwife was saying not to force it, so I thought well I won't push then, because I'll be forcing it. I was just so confused. Should I be waiting for the natural urges to push and then give it all I've got, all the welly, or should I just be pushing? The midwife was saying that I was using my breathing too much and I thought well, I've got to do something for this pain. (Daniella)

The midwife told Daniella to 'go with her body', which left Daniella confused over whether or not she should push. Yet when she did get an urge to push and tried, the midwife told her not to, which undermined what little confidence she had. Midwives were coming in and out of the room, and Daniella very quickly felt that everything was slipping out of control. The midwife was not taking charge, Daniella did not feel in control and, importantly, her body was obviously not to be trusted. Daniella did not know what to do, whether to push or to breathe, and then there was the continuing, excruciating pain. But then came her 'angel'. A second midwife came in after this had been going on for an hour and a half, 'took charge' and assisted Daniella to give birth vaginally by giving clear, precise directions:

> This midwife came in and took charge, almost with military precision, and you just felt confident with her. She said 'Right, Mrs X', and she just looked at me and she took my arm and she was an angel sent from heaven. I suddenly had a surge of energy. It brings tears to my eyes, because she really did. (Daniella)

There are two points to be made here. First, the lack of continuity of care is painfully obvious. The midwives did not know Daniella's history: she had asked for it to be documented, but when she arrived in labour they could not find her notes. So they were unaware of her fears of the second stage of labour and Daniella's trust in them was shaken. Second, the time for midwives to sit in the background is when all is going well, but all the women agreed that it was to the midwives that they expected to turn when things started to go awry. Daniella felt that the first midwife let her down for failing to initiate what Simkin (1989) has termed the 'take charge routine'. As previously mentioned, the worse scenario of all is if the woman feels things are 'out of control'; Daniella trusted the midwife to restore control, and felt betrayed when this did not happen.

Two key studies point to a significant discrepancy between a woman's perceptions of her own pain during labour and the midwives' perceptions of the pain that a woman is experiencing (Bradley *et al.* 1983), which point to a lack of connection. Rajan suggests that this phenomenon is self-perpetuating because it remains unspoken: neither women nor professionals fully understand the reality of each others' feelings and beliefs. They seldom truly listen to each other:

> They've got this way of saying to you 'that's not a very big one [contraction]!' I was in the hospital, and some woman was strapped up and she was having some quite nice peaks on there, and she was in a lot of pain, and

they were going 'you're not in labour, don't be so silly'. She was only 28 weeks, and she had the baby that afternoon. I mean, for goodness sake! It makes you feel like slapping them sometimes. (Andrea)

This echoes Kirkham's plea for the recognition of the value of story-telling (Kirkham and Perkins 1997) in the hope that women's voices may be heard, which will facilitate a sense of what Belenky *et al.* (1986) call 'connected knowing': through a process of collaboration, they can begin to measure personal knowledge against the authority of others and develop a constructed (or reconstructed) knowledge of childbirth based in lived experience. In an age when women-centred care is held up as the new ethos, this is surely essential.

## Anxiety-provoking interventions

The phenomenon of interventions bringing doubt and uncertainty was confirmed by many of the women. It prevented them from 'letting go'. They talked of how they were not at all worried about the baby's wellbeing until the moment when the midwife went to listen for the fetal heart or rupture the membranes. Then they worried:

She listened to it about every ten minutes or so, and every time she said it was fine. But it is a worry when she starts doing it because you think 'oh-oh is it going to be all right? Is there something wrong with the baby? (Julie)

I can remember the midwife wanting to break my waters. I said, 'why do you want to do that – is the baby OK?' 'Yes, yes, everything's fine – I just want to break your waters.' When she was talking about it I thought, 'oh my goodness, is something wrong? Maybe the baby's not OK.' (Rhiannon)

I always remember this nurse asking me continually if I wanted the gas. Me saying 'no, I'm fine. Why, am I not fine? Is there something I don't know? Is there something wrong with me?' (Cathy)

Anna highlighted how important it is for the midwife to give feedback quickly after every intervention. Having made the decision to intervene, silence is the worst possible outcome, implying that something is most definitely wrong:

I was worried for the baby's safety. Yes. When the midwife listened. I was really relieved when the midwife said 'that's fine'. So would it almost be better if the midwife didn't listen to the baby's heartbeat at all. And it would have been awful if the midwife hadn't said anything – if she hadn't said 'that's fine'. That's very important. Had she not said anything, I would have assumed that there would have been something wrong. (Anna)

Andrea took this concept one step further when she talked of how technology comes between the midwife and the women in labour and plays a disempowering role. At home, without access to cardiotocography, the midwife has to trust the woman far more:

I don't think you need to be strapped up the whole time, because then you spend the whole time staring at the monitor, watching the heart going up and down and thinking 'ohhhh'. And watching your contractions, and they say that they're a bit pathetic, not good enough – all this sort of stuff, whereas as home, the midwife couldn't tell me that my contractions were worth having or not. So without the monitors, the midwife has to trust us much more, and if I say I'm having a contraction, then I am! (Andrea)

Some of the women were pleased not to have any vaginal examinations whatsoever, which they felt allowed labour to progress very spontaneously:

She didn't do any. Even when she first arrived. That amazed me, because I thought she'd want to know how dilated I was. But because she didn't, it felt incredibly natural. (Joanna)

Andrea specifically did not want any vaginal examinations. She equated them with the midwife taking control away from her and asserting her professional power and authority over Andrea's labour. This is exactly the implicit function of vaginal examinations demonstrated in Bergstrom *et al.*'s study (1992) – a ritual to communicate the care-giver's control and the woman's corresponding passivity:

That was another thing. I didn't want any internals... I just felt that I would know. I know my body well enough now to know when it was all ready. I really wanted to trust myself. It would have been the midwife saying 'right, now it's time to push or no, you can't push'. I just wanted it to happen and be very natural. So I'm in control, I'm doing it. I mean, I know you can feel you want to start pushing before it's ready to push, but I just trusted my body to do it the right way. (Andrea)

Several multiparous women talked unbidden of how they were aware of a direct connection between them and the fetus they were carrying. They were very much conscious of how the baby was, and 'knew' that he or she was all right even though the professionals were thinking otherwise. They seemed surprised when asked to explain themselves more – to them it seemed self-evident:

> She did say that I'd been fully dilated for an hour and it's policy that we tell somebody, which I immediately thought sounded a bit suspicious! There's obviously something wrong. But I didn't *feel* that there was something wrong. In my body I didn't feel anything was wrong. (Julie)

> I wasn't worried about the baby at any point. I knew she was fine. When I had my second baby... I remember being on my knees and thinking, no, this is not right. The baby was not happy. It was wrong. It was just not right. At no time with this baby did I feel anything like that. When the waters broke, the midwife said 'they're lovely and clear' and I remember thinking 'that's all right, because I know she's all right'. I wasn't worried. I know if they're fine. (Cathy)

Several women quite disingenuously and intuitively suggested that there was a clear link between fear and distress – the mother being afraid and the baby becoming distressed:

> Not afraid. I don't think you're allowed to be afraid. I think if you're afraid, your baby is in distress. My sister was afraid, and her baby was in distress. Because she was afraid, because she did have distress. I think the afraid comes with it. I think if I was afraid, I wouldn't be so sure of myself that the baby was all right. I would say that you being afraid helps the baby get distressed. I think they definitely go together, fear and distress. (Cathy)

This intuitive idea is identical to the findings of Levinson and Shnider (1979), which looked at the role of maternal catecholamines, maternal fear and fetal distress. They found that the raised level of catecholamines in anxious labouring women resulted in a lowered uterine blood flow, thus reducing the amount of oxygen available to the fetus. A robust fetus will be able to compensate for this drop, but a previously compromised fetus is less able to do so and will show signs of distress. But how did Rhiannon, Cathy and the others know that?

Davis (1989:5) talks of women's intuition being the 'apprehension of reality exactly as it is'. The participants 'knew' something on an internal, subjective level that has only been recently confirmed by scientific method (and is not yet widely accepted). Belenky *et al.*'s (1986) work on women's ways of knowing shows how women pass through five stages of 'knowing'. The third stage (in which most of the women in their study were to be found) is a dualistic state of connecting with an inner voice that is contradicted by those on the 'outside'. The women 'knew' that maternal fear and fetal distress are connected, a notion that would be derided by many contemporary 'experts'.

The existence of intuition or 'gut feeling' is controversial. Baron (1988:26) defines it as an 'unanalyzed and unjustified belief', yet Orme and Maggs (1993:273) define it as 'a state of heightened perceptual awareness which emanates from subconscious thought'. By constant professional intervention and monitoring, a woman's own intimate knowledge of her own body and the fetus within is undermined and devalued. As Gilligan (1982:88) puts it, 'All knowledge is constructed, and the knower is an intimate part of the known.' In this instance, the 'knowers' – for example, Cathy and Rhiannon – are most certainly an intimate part of that which they know, for nowhere is there a greater, more tangible example of connectedness and intimacy than between a woman and her fetus. By not even recognising this knowledge, midwives undermine a woman's belief and confidence in her own body, which in turn makes her unable to feel in control of her labour.

## Conclusion

Midwives are called the experts of normal childbirth, yet so little work has been done exploring what normal childbirth is that it is hard to know how they can deserve this accolade. This study set out intentionally to study the normal second stage of labour. The women themselves described how, in order to cope with the enormity of the sensation that they experienced during a normal second stage of labour, they entered an altered state of consciousness, in which the mind 'let go' and allowed the body to be in control. The part played by the midwife is crucial to the success or failure of this strategy. A skilled and sensitive midwife can create a unobtrusive atmosphere of safety and calm, which allows a woman to feel secure enough to 'just disconnect' mind from body. An insensitive and intrusive midwife can just as easily block a woman's being able to do this, undermine her confidence in her own body and turn her experience of giving birth into a nightmare.

Midwives are extraordinarily powerful when a woman is in labour; these findings may help them to use that power wisely to the best advantage of the women in their care. By examining the components that go towards creating a normal second stage, listening to women's stories and establishing what they find helpful and what hinders them, midwives may create and use their own body of midwifery knowledge to help more women achieve the very thing that so many of them desire – to give birth normally.

## References

Anderson T (1997) Women's Experiences of the Second Stage of Labour. Unpublished MSc dissertation, University of Surrey.

Baron J (1988) *Thinking and Deciding*. Cambridge: Cambridge University Press.

Beaton JI (1990) Dimensions of nurse and patient roles in labour. *Health Care for Women International* **11**(4): 393–408.

Beck CT (1994) Women's temporal experiences during the delivery process: a phenomenological study. *International Journal of Nursing Studies* **31**(3): 245–52.

Belenky, MF, Clinchy BM, Goldberg NR and Tarule JM (1986) *Women's Ways of Knowing*. New York: Basic Books.

Berg M, Lundgren I, Hermansson E and Wahlberg V (1996) Women's experience of the encounter with the midwife during childbirth. *Midwifery* **12**: 11–15.

Bersgtrom L, Roberts J, Skillman L and Seidel J (1992) 'You'll feel me touching you, sweetie': vaginal examinations during the second stage of labour. *Birth* **19**(1): 10–18.

Bluff R and Holloway I (1994) They know best: women's perspective of midwifery care during labour and childbirth. *Midwifery* **10**: 157–64.

Bradley C, Brewin CR and Duncan SLB (1983) Perceptions of labour: discrepancies between midwives' and patients' ratings. *British Journal of Obstetrics and Gynaecology* **90**: 1176–9.

Brewin C and Bradley C (1982) Perceived control and the experience of childbirth. *British Journal of Clinical Psychology* **21**: 263–9.

Brook C (1996) Supportive interactions between midwives and childbearing women. *Birth Issues* **5**(2): 15–19.

Cosmi EV (1995) Hypnosis and birth. *Prenatal and Perinatal Psychology* **7**(4): 461–3.

Davis E (1989) *Women's Intuition*. Berkeley, CA: Celestial Arts.

Driscoll R (1997) *Plain Tales from the Labour Ward*. London: Minerva Press.

Evans S and Jeffrey J (1995) Maternal learning needs during labor and delivery. *Journal of Obstetric, Gynecologic and Neonatal Nursing* **24**(3): 235–40.

Flint C (1997) Using the stairs. *MIDIRS Midwifery Digest* **7**(2): 186.

Gilligan C (1982) *In a Different Voice: Psychological Theory and Women's Development*. Boston: Harvard University Press.

Green JM (1993) Expectations and experiences of pain in labour: findings from a large prospective study. *Birth* **20**(2): 65–72.

Jones C (1989) The laboring mind response. *Texas Midwifery* **VI**(2): 19–21.

Kirke J (1980) Mothers' views of obstetric care. *British Journal of Obstetrics and Gynaecology* **87**: 1029–33.

Kirkham MJ and Perkins ER (1997) *Reflections on Midwifery*. London: Baillière Tindall.

Levinson G and Shnider SM (1989) Catecholamines: the effects of maternal fear and its treatment on uterine function and circulation. *Birth and the Family Journal* **6**(3): 167–74.

Lukes S (ed.) (1986) *Power*. Oxford: Basil Blackwell.

Machin D and Scamell M (1997) The experience of labour: using ethnography to explore the irresistible nature of the bio-medical metaphor during labour. *Midwifery* **13**: 78–84.

McKay S, Barrows T and Roberts J (1990) Women's views of second stage labor as assessed by interviews and videotapes. *Birth* **17**(4): 192–8.

Nikodem VC (1995) Sustained (Valsalva) vs exhalatory bearing down in the second stage of labour. In: Enkin MW, Keirse MJNC, Renfrew MJ and Neilson JP (eds) *Pregnancy and Childbirth Module of the Cochrane Database of Systematic Reviews, 1995* (updated 24 Feb 1995). London: BMJ Publishing Group.

Nolan M (1996) *Being Pregnant, Giving Birth: A National Childbirth Trust Guide*. London: HMSO.

Odent M (1987) The fetus ejection reflex. *Birth* **14**(2): 104–5.

Odent MR (1991) Fear of death during labour. *Journal of Reproduction and Infant Psychology* **9**(1): 43–7.

Odent M (1994) The love hormones. *Primal Health Research* **2**(3): 3–7.

Orme L and Maggs C (1993) Decision-making in clinical practice: how do expert nurses, midwives and health visitors make decisions? *Nurse Education Today* **13**(4): 270–6.

Price B (1993) Women in labour: body image, loss of control and coping behaviour. *Professional Care of Mother and Child* November–December: 280–2.

Rajan L (1993) Perceptions of pain and pain relief in labour: the gulf between experience and observation. *Midwifery* **9**: 136–45.

Sargady M (1995) Renewing our faith in second stage. *Midwifery Today* **33**: 29–31, 41–3.

*Scientific American* (1972) *Altered States of Awareness. Readings from Scientific American*. San Francisco: WH Freeman.

Simkin P (1989) *The Birth Partner*. Boston: Harvard Common Press.

Thomson AM (1988) Management of the woman in normal second stage of labour: a review. *Midwifery* **4**: 77–85.

Waldenstrom U, Borg I, Olsson B, Skold M and Wall S (1996) The childbirth experience: a study of 295 new mothers. *Birth* **23**(3): 144–53.

# Chapter 6

# Being with Women who Are Economically Without

*Jean Davies*

## Introduction

This chapter draws on work carried out in an inner city area with a very high rate of long-term unemployment. It covers a period of 10 years from 1983, during which time two pieces of research were undertaken to examine enhanced midwifery care, and family networks and women's experience as mothers. Conscious efforts were made to bridge the gap between the experiences and expectations of the midwives as professionals and those of their economically deprived clients. In order to do this, attention was paid to how these women coped in their everyday lives and how midwifery care could be adapted to fit their coping mechanisms.

## Community Midwifery Care Project

The first piece of research used in this chapter was the Newcastle Community Midwifery Care (CMC) Project, which lasted for four years (Evans 1987). This looked at the impact of enhanced midwifery on pregnant women in two areas with particularly high indices of low income and poor health. One of the estates, Cowgate, had an above-average crime rate, more children taken into care per head of population than any other part of the city and the stigma of being considered the city's worst estate. Four midwives shared the work, working in pairs, and a sociologist undertook the evaluation.

The effect of enhanced care given to the women on two estates was compared with two control groups, one matched, the other a retrospective case note control. There was a combination of case note review and interviewing.

The enhanced care consisted of carrying out antenatal visits and one-to-one parentcraft sessions in the women's homes at least four times antenatally, visiting the women in hospital if there were any antenatal admissions, visiting the hospital when the mother was in labour and attending a few selected births, as well as postnatally providing extended visiting until the 28th day. The analysis showed that the average number of contacts between the women and their midwives was 10, but these were often meetings on the street as one aspect of the care was that it was geographically based and community centred.

The results showed that the women's experience of their birth was improved, as was their subsequent uptake of health visiting, immunisation services and family planning. The numbers were too small to be statistically significant, but there was a trend showing that the incidence of low birthweight babies was reduced with enhanced care, and in the group who had had a previous preterm birth, the subsequent pregnancy's incidence of this was reduced compared with that of the controls. There was also an effect on the smoking rate, and long-term improvement in nutrition was achieved (Evans 1987).

The sociologist involved in the CMC Project was struck by the fact that, when the questionnaires were being completed, during the interviews with the women, a number of the women said that the midwives were 'just like one of us'. Economically, this was certainly not the case as the women were practically all unemployed, and there was the professional divide between giver and receiver of care. The fact that this was said probably results from the mode of working: this was on the women's territory and done with a conscious effort to break down some of the barriers between 'them and us'. By working within a geographical area, it was possible to be identified with the community as 'their' midwife who worked 'with' the local women.

What also surprised the social scientist was that the findings were welcomed neither by the medical profession nor within midwifery. The comment was made by the doctors that if you give extra care, of course the women will be more satisfied; in addition, the clinical trends were discounted and not considered significant. There was little regard for the fact that the study illuminated the benefits of midwifery care for low-income women; it seemed to be taken as highlighting the deficiencies of the care given to the control women and, by inference, the midwives of the controls. The evidence was not used to promote the benefits that were clearly identified, probably because midwifery research was still in its infancy and there was still a resistance to it. There was an apparent reluctance to acknowledge the fact that it had occurred within the area of the local midwifery school, and was spoken about in their classrooms only years after its completion and publication.

## Networks

The second piece of research that forms the basis of this chapter was carried out in Cowgate (Davies 1989). Its aim was to construct a cultural profile through identifying kinship networks (Fox 1967), looking at day-to-day activity and asking what the women's perceptions of health were (Cornwell 1984). This research grew out of questions raised while working on the first project. It was clear that there were complicated family and social networks that deserved closer study. The data were collected through interviewing women with a questionnaire, mapping the kinship networks identified and participant observation. This research was built on much knowledge gleaned over the five years of working on the CMC Project.

The CMC Project had shown how closely families were connected, and the second piece of work built on the knowledge that had already accrued, as well as the interest in the networks that this had developed. It was an attempt to identify how the family connections worked on the estate. There was also an attempt to discover how health was perceived by the women.

One hundred and eighty women were identified who had had children over a five-year period, 80 of whom were interviewed. Seventy-six had moved away from the estate, a further 24 were not interviewed mainly because of time constraints, and one woman declined to be interviewed.

## Ethics

The ethics of doing research 'on the back' of a clinical relationship is not to be taken lightly (Murphy Black 1998). Midwives learn much about the parturient population, and to extend this into the research forum requires that all research should be undertaken with the full knowledge and agreement of those involved and within an ethos of service improvement, which is particularly important with such a deprived population (Reed and Procter 1995).

## The CMC Study

### *Background*

There seemed to be health sequelae to the cultural impact of living within this particular economic structure. The study of inequalities in health carried out on a ward-to-ward basis in the northern region (Townsend 1988 and the preceding Black Report – Department of Health 1980; see also Townsend and Davidson 1982) had identified that a poor health outcome is related to low income, social class and type of occupation. To address the link between poverty and poor health, it is necessary to examine the experience of living on a low income.

### *Community-based approach*

This midwifery initiative was funded by the Department of the Environment as a collaboration between the local and health authorities. A council house was converted, made into the Cowgate Neighbourhood Centre and given rent free by the housing department, who were working there at a very local level. After a time, a task group was established, all the professional groups working on the estates meeting on a regular basis to share concerns and plan the way forward: the police, probation, education, social and health services as well as the housing and recreation departments met regularly. From this locally based professional group was formed a working party that addressed the issues of the estate at local authority and eventually governmental level. This resulted in considerable extra funding being allocated to upgrade the estate. The houses, which had originally all been council houses, were modernised and privatised, many being sold.

### *Birth as a cultural event*

Before looking at the details of the research, there is a need to look at birth as a cultural event (Jordan 1995). Some of the findings showed that there were many variations from the broadly accepted cultural norms of the professionals. This not only highlights what is difficult to contend with, particularly with regard to economics and legality, but also approaches what is the essence of the cultural differences. If there is to be a real effort in addressing inequalities in health, these issues need to be addressed.

Birth is an important rite of passage; for parous women the transition is less dramatic, but the change is still marked. How this transition is organised and how women pass through it not only reflects the cultural beliefs within a society, but also affirms women as mothers within that society (Kitzinger 1978). To have a successful rite of passage, the attendants should confirm the person moving into the new position (Van Gennep 1908). To do this, they need to have some understanding of the cultural identity of the central person, in the case of birthing, the mother. Midwives attend during this transition. If there is no understanding of their cultural norm, of the world in which women are going to have to function, their affirmation as mothers will be discordant.

If a mother is attended through this transition by people who have no sympathy with her, or do not care who she is or where she is from, this will be a perilous passage, and she is likely to be confused as she emerges from it. To be a reinforced in the new role, there needs to be respect for the person and the role, and an understanding of the place where this role will played out.

Childbearing should not diminish but empower women (Yearley 1997). If the woman is not supported during childbirth, ways in which she may already feel undervalued could be exacerbated (Brown *et al.* 1994). Emotions are heightened around birth, and any experience of social and cultural division at this time could confirm individual low self-esteem (Littlewood and McHugh 1997) and reinforce prejudice. Pregnant women need to be comfortable whatever their cultural context if they are to be confident mothers. The word 'comfort' comes from the Latin 'with strength'. Midwives have a great responsibility to ensure that they are in fact 'with women' and give strength at this crucial time so that the difficult task of being a mother begins from a position of women feeling valued within their own cultural context, in effect, being comfortable.

Midwives know the extraordinary way in which it is possible to build up a rapport with very different women during labour, to support and care for them during the actual delivery, to help them give birth (Hunt 1995). The labour is extremely important and is the crucial transition that takes place in this rite of passage. Like many rites, it is conducted on a 'different' level and involves a removal into a special place for the actual ritual. Most mothers come into hospital, which is in itself is a reaffirmation of society as being highly medicalised. It is especially important in the strangeness of hospital for a woman to have a sense that there is an acceptance and understanding of who she is, where she came from and where she will return to. This is very difficult to achieve if the midwifery care is fragmented. It is important for a labouring mother to feel comfortable so that the physical pain is not made harder by social unease.

## The cultural impact of poverty

Low income and long-term unemployment, which lead to poverty, have a cultural impact and carry a stigma (Bradshaw and Holmes 1989). Midwives, in secure professional employment, need to be conscious of the cultural divide that needs to be bridged in providing appropriate care for poor women. Midwives have their share of social prejudice and views (see, for example, Bowler 1993), which can undermine childbearing women. It is not possible to be 'with' a woman if there is prejudice towards and a rejection of her. Instead, an openness is needed if different lifestyles are to be acknowledged. This may be hard, but discomfort that is not resolved can lead to rejection and could create dejection as in any social situation unless there is a willingness to acknowledge prejudices and work towards making them irrelevant, even getting rid of them

Behaviour develops in a variety of ways and for a variety of reasons, being a response to how and where people live; through becoming accepted, it becomes culturally specific (Wilmott and Young 1957). It develops to make sense of situations and also gives a way in which to live that is comprehensible. What was observed in the research was that ways of coping with living on a very low income appeared to have developed. For women with a low income, coping is central to their lives, and birth is also central to the lives of women.

## Findings

### Antenatal groups

Parentcraft classes were very difficult to establish: time was needed to set them up and remind women to come, and making classes welcoming was essential. The midwives puzzled over why they were so difficult to establish. They were held in the neighbourhood centre, which was accessible and which the women used quite freely at other times.

What was equally difficult was that, once the group was established and possessed a momentum, it became difficult to maintain it with any semblance of the intended structure of providing antenatal care. Postnatally, it became difficult to stop the women continuing to come. In the neighbourhood centre, it was difficult to establish a cut-off point, and new pregnant women sometimes found it hard to break into the established group. This was never properly resolved, except by women becoming pregnant again and therefore legitimising their presence in the 'antenatal' group. Another antenatal group, on an adjacent estate with women also on a low income, encountered exactly the same situation. Women really welcomed the opportunity to be together in an environment that was welcoming to them. What became clear was that establishing the group was more important than the intended reason of providing antenatal education.

The difficulties experienced probably arose from how the group was established in the first place. To get the women to attend, it had been necessary positively to encourage attendance and to have possible enticements. Nutrition was, and remained, a matter of concern, and it was consequently addressed at each session by having different foodstuffs prepared and brought to be talked about and of course eaten. There is no saying that the women came for this, but it was also done with the intention of breaking down the 'them' and 'us' barrier. A cup of tea was provided with the food, given by the midwives, even though the intention was always to go onto the antenatal session. However, the need to be welcoming had the effect of creating a social group, and this is what it became, possibly being a more important development.

It was hard work to run the sessions if the various planned topics of the day were to be addressed, and to keep the sessions from just being social. They often became boisterous, and on one occasion a fight concerning a man two-timing had to be prevented.

The greatest difficulty was accommodating what was, in effect, community development group work within midwifery. For example, it was considered at the time that taking the women swimming was outside the midwifery remit. Given colleagues' pressure of work, this was understandable. However, if inequality in health is to be addressed, care has to be a response to need. And the greatest health need was wellbeing, more likely to be developed in a swimming pool with a group of friends than in an antenatal clinic.

## With women

A different approach was adopted from that of the usual antenatal parentcraft class. This was not always easy as bringing barriers down can leave professionals, in particular, feeling vulnerable. It is easier to hide within a structure that is safe and can be closely defined and confined into a task-orientated approach. To adopt a more open way of working was a challenge, but it was seen as essential to acknowledge that health promotion is not possible without perceptions changing. For health promotion messages to be accepted, there has to be an openness between the people concerned and a belief in the individuals as well as the messages given. The upholding of women's self-esteem was of central importance, and antenatal education therefore had to enhance their feeling of self-worth. This demanded that what the women considered to be of worth was not discounted.

There were many discussions about food, which is as accurate a cultural definer as anything. At the time, there was a media debate on food, and an eminent politician had castigated people in the north for not eating better. The women's response to this was entirely related to the economics and impracticability of buying fresh and wholefood goods: not only were they not available locally, but they also cost too much. What money was available could be spent on food that was filling and cheaper.

## Smoking

Smoking was a big issue and a no-smoking period was imposed during the antenatal groups, not least for the midwives' lungs. The women would frequently either defy it or simply leave the building to 'have a tab' outside. This did raise smoking as an issue relating to health, and over the years there was some shift, a few women even giving up. As one woman put it, 'Before you lot came I just smoked; I think about it now.' This is one step nearer believing that it could be damaging, before hopefully moving on to knowing it is, and doing something about it (Marsh and MacKay 1994).

*Immediate issues*

Because of the way the group appeared to work, it was necessary to reflect and try to analyse what was going on. Trying to hang onto antenatal subjects was like being on a roller coaster. They kept on going off at different angles and up and down, as other usually more fascinating, but often completely extraneous, stories took precedence. What had happened the day before to so and so, who was in the fight in the pub, that someone was broken into, that the noise of joy riders racing around the estate at night had been the worst this year, and that the stolen car was eventually torched outside a house, and everyone knew who did it, but what could you do? You didn't want a brick through your window.

This local drama was a lot more gripping than the cervical dilatation that would be taking place in five months' time. In addition, there was the fact that a few of the mothers had already had children, five in one case, and consequently 'knew all about it'. This midwife has only three children, and, as for the midwife who had no children, the women 'could tell her a thing or two', and frequently did. Such maternal self-esteem could dint professional confidence.

The classes were difficult not because there was a lack of interest in the subject, but because there were more immediate issues. Once there was a regular attendance, it was very difficult to keep to the subject. What was also clear was that the women's male partners were not very happy about their attending. In the early days of establishing the group, there would be a whistle at the door and a man outside would summon 'his' woman home on some domestic pretext. And off the woman would go.

*A concrete achievement*

What emerged from the group was the realisation that the women were identifying different needs, and directly out of this, a children's centre was developed on the estate. The women stated that they wanted a place where they could go with their under-school-age children, so, together with the social services, this was forwarded and funding was made available – a prototype Healthy Living Centre as envisaged in the Green Paper *Our Healthier Nation* (Department of Health 1998). Proposals are emerging for different manifestations of Healthy Living Centres across the country in an attempt to promote healthy living.

They have already been in existence in a variety of ways in different places over the years – the neighbourhood centre was one, the children's centre another – but their success and continuance depends not just on secure funding, but also on local involvement in their use and development. Both these establishments eventually came under the aegis of the organisation Save the Children, but they had their beginning in the collaborative work between the health and social services, with a joint commitment to promoting health and wellbeing.

## The 'waterboatman theory' of coping

Throughout the project, an awareness grew of the particular way in which the women coped. Grounded theory (Glaser and Strauss 1967) was used when trying to understand some of the differences and difficulties experienced while working as a midwife, which were expressed in the interactions, in how the women were with each other and with the midwives giving midwifery care. It was an issue not of individual differences, as these are always there, but of the collective and hitherto unknown ways of coping that needed to be made sense of as they were possibly of cultural significance.

The women studied had just enough to live on through benefits. They lacked the resources for future planning; they were living very much for the here and now. Their awareness was not, therefore, that of the careful planner but they skittered about, checking the immediate situation and the various things that needed their attention. Some things might not be done, but others were picked up or left for something else. To stop and ponder would invite trouble; survival meant keeping on top, moving on the surface. To stop was to sink, so like waterboatmen on a pond, staying on top was not to stay anywhere for long. This image was later given diagrammatic form when mapping house moves.

## One-to-one health promotion

This aspect of the work was most effectively carried out in the antenatal discussions that took place on a one-to-one basis in the women's homes. A partner would occasionally join in, but usually either they were not there or they left as soon as the midwife came. The home, however, proved the most effective place in which to give the enhanced care that was established through the CMC Project. In the women's own setting and with increased midwifery time made available, it proved possible for midwives to develop their skills in acknowledging and educating women whose attention was of the waterboatman type. Information was provided as the women sought it, and further discussion could follow when they chose to return to a particular topic.

It was the first time that home bookings had been carried out in Newcastle. It was initiated, in the first instance, because of repeated non-attendance for hospital appointments.

## Targeting inequality: the networks study

The approach undertaken in the CMC Project, working very closely with social services, was effective. This approach has gained acceptance as in the Acheson Report (1998), which was designed to look at how inequality could be addressed. There is the recommendation that where there is inequality, care should be aimed at redressing it. The original work done for the CMC Project showed that enhanced care does have an impact on health improvement. The network research highlighted the way in which this care needed to be delivered – at a very local level and targeted towards addressing self-esteem and perceptions of health.

### *Questionnaires*

The questionnaires for the network research were designed to build up a picture of the women's social networks and activities. There were closed questions about kinship on the estate, as well as open-ended questions for comments. Looking at inequalities in health was a basic interest so there were questions about the women's perception of health, developed from what was already known. The question about diet and bowel function, for example, might not have been asked had this not been something that was part of an existing dialogue with midwives and in which there was interest because of its possible health implications having relevance to understanding some of the health sequelae of poverty. Nutrition does have a cultural basis, which is also affected by economics (Cole-Hamilton and Lang 1986).

One of the things that had been identified in the previous project was that frequent house moves were common, and this became a key issue in the research.

## *Mapping*

The actual mapping of the social network formalised the midwifery knowledge of the intricacies of family networks. The important aspect of this, from the point of view of mothers and midwives, is the practical impact of an extended matrilocal network on the provision of midwifery care. There were the informal contacts of knowing where to find a woman if she happened to be out, or of being stopped in the street by a woman who felt it important to tell the midwife of some concern about another woman, who might have been reluctant to instigate care on her own account.

The data were mapped to make them graphic, since 'Maps provide an efficient and unique method of demonstration of distributions of phenomena in space' (Howe 1986:127). The original plan had been to start with one family and map its kinship network on a map. This very soon became too complicated so a wider selection of women were included, which enabled information to be gathered systematically. From this, it was possible to follow not just one but several trails and to see where and to what extent they crossed.

Six different maps were drawn from the 80 women who were questioned.

1. Five groups of 16 randomly selected women had their networks mapped onto a stylised map of the estate.
2. Five maps from each group showed house moves on the estate.
3. The women and their proximity to their mothers were mapped.
4. The positions of the women and their sisters were similarly mapped.
5. Next, the 80 women and their brothers were considered similarly.
6. Finally, all the brothers and sisters of the 80 women were mapped.

Even though only 80 women were interviewed from a possible 180, all of them had received midwifery care over the preceding years and were consequently part of the research overall. When looking at the sister contact, for example, 42 per cent had no sisters on the estate. However, 54 per cent had sisters who were known to the researcher, showing that 12 per cent had sisters who had received midwifery care from the researcher and had subsequently moved off the estate. Of the 76 women who had moved away from the estate and were not interviewed, the whereabouts of the majority was known.

### *Findings*

The overwhelming observational evidence showed that this was a matrilocal society with very close family connections. Much movement occurred within the estate and some off it, but this was still fairly local.

There was a higher proportion of unmarried women, 37 per cent as against 35 per cent married, but 70 per cent lived with a partner. Three per cent of the partners were 'away' in prison. Of the 17 per cent living on their own, 8 per cent were divorced and one woman was widowed. In 1989, the national rate of birth outside marriage was 21 per cent so the women studied provided a figure well above the national rate. This rate continues to change annually. The majority of women had children by one partner, although 24 per cent of the women had children by two fathers, and 3 per cent by three.

### *What is normal?*

These findings showed some norms that could be obscured because of the colourful and therefore more memorable exceptions. This is a possible source of prejudice. A Lothario, with four children by four different women all within two streets, who appeared following each birth as the proud father, gave the impression of the presence of a rampant sexual code. Discovering the extent to which the majority did not live by this code redressed this impression, although apparent fidelity was no guarantee of a stable relationship. One woman with four children by the same man said that he always came to see her on his release from prison before going home to his wife: 'He's in for eighteen months, he comes once, and I'm away with the mixer again.'

Marriage and weddings are not very common; it is more the birth of a child that changes a girl into a woman. Being pregnant did not appear to be the reason for marriage that it might have been for women in a different social group, although this situation has changed radically in the past two decades. Some couples with children were open about not getting married as they could get more money as separate claimants. For others, marriage was calculated within apparently ephemeral financial considerations: 'I'd like to get married, have a big do, but right now I need a double buggy.' One woman got married the week before her second child was born. She was 'very large with child,' and 'hadn't meant to get married but me sister called hers off. There was the cake and all, seemed a shame to waste it.' Systematically collected data show these colourful examples to be exceptions, but they illustrate what is culturally encompassed.

The pattern of partnership was variable, as it is nationally, but there were some specific issues relating to low income that affected this pattern. Several women claimed state benefits as a single household and mentioned the fact that 'no-one knows he's here'. This had a marginalising effect on the man at the same time as giving him the appearance of 'having his cake and eating it', as the women usually financed the household and the man used his money as he pleased. The only authority that some men felt themselves to have was expressed through the control of violence and brutality.

With the heightened emotional atmosphere that surrounds a birth, any problems in the relationship often became very obvious. Fathers sometimes did not behave responsibly at this time; 'wetting the baby's head' was a good excuse or reason to go out and get drunk. Fathers turned up in hospital the worse for drink, and women who might be used to this in the privacy of their own home found it publicly very humiliating. Drinking was a problem that several women commented on. The midwife's observation reinforced the impression that the relationships between the sexes were often neither supportive nor mutually enhancing.

However, social situations do not remain static, and this was yet another example of 'waterboatman' skittering.

### Problems

The 80 women were asked whether they had any particular concerns, 60 (75 per cent) said that they had problems, most of which related to families, partners or health.

Three women spoke of child abuse. One had been abused by her father, from whom she had contracted syphilis, which was diagnosed on a routine antenatal blood test. Enhanced antenatal care had been given but without any knowledge of the abuse. Her results had been stored at the hospital and only came to light when there was a request for the baby to return to hospital for tests. Postnatally, this woman spoke of the horror of the birth, which brought flashbacks of the abuse. Several other women spoke of family traumas and bereavement, all relevant to their experience of childbearing and motherhood.

Fourteen out of the 80 women spoke of a problem with their partner. Three involved violence and threats, and four concerned excessive drinking. Two spoke of imprisoned partners: one was upset that this would deny her pregnancy, the other welcomed imprisonment as a contraceptive.

*Health*

Twenty of the women interviewed (a quarter of them) had been to the hospital or the GP in the week of interview. Ten women mentioned problems relating to reproduction. There were two stillbirths during the period of interviewing. Several spoke of their children's major health problems and others described the ill health of close relatives.

Nutrition and exercise are fundamental to health yet 52 per cent of the women questioned had had no fruit or vegetables the day before the interview, and 38 per cent had not eaten anything on the day they were interviewed. Ten per cent of the women opened their bowels only once a week and 3 per cent once a fortnight. Ninety per cent had had no exercise in the past week. The smoking rate was high, 76 per cent smoking, and 10 per cent of those smoking more than 40 cigarettes a day.

*Finance*

Only nine women mentioned that they had financial problems: four had debts, three needed to pay rates bills, one had had a loan refused and one spoke of low pay. Given that the majority of the women are on state benefit, the fact that this was not perceived as being a particular problem is of interest. A quarter of the women said that they had no problems, despite some of them having debts that would, taken as a proportion of income, have kept the middle class sleepless.

The three who mentioned the rates all lived on the same street and were interviewed at about the same time, which may have coincided with a 'blitz' on rates. Another 26 women, that is, 29 women altogether, admitted that they did not always pay their water rates, but this was not categorised as being a 'problem'. These rates had only recently been introduced, they were seen as 'unfair', no stigma was felt with regard to non-payment and no attempt was made to conceal it.

Finances were arranged through a complicated pattern of borrowing one day to repay on Giro day, often at exorbitant interest rates that were often charged within families and between neighbours. Using family allowance books as collateral was also common. It was a classic Catch 22 situation: money is borrowed because there is none; the DHSS would not give a loan because there was not enough to repay it, so goods were bought on the 'ticket' because people were too poor to pay with cash; but the interest rate nearly doubled the eventual cost. The poor become poorer simply because they are poor.

*Family contacts*

What the people of the estate did have in abundance, however, was family, which was matrilocal.

Eighty per cent of the women saw their mother at least once a week, 54 per cent daily. Only six per cent never saw their mother, and another 9 per cent of the mothers were dead. This contrasted with only 46 per cent who saw their father once a week. A quarter of the women's fathers had died, indicating a high death rate among a comparatively young group.

There was a lot of contact between sisters: 89 per cent of the women interviewed had sisters, 26 per cent of whom lived on the estate, and 47 per cent saw their sister every day. (Fifty-four per cent of the sisters were known to the researcher, indicating that they had only recently moved away from the estate.) Perhaps significantly, 36 per cent had no contact with their sister: having a family nearby does not always signify contact.

It is perhaps noteworthy that, while 89 per cent of the women had a sister, only 61 per cent of the women reported that they had a brother. Given that sex distribution at birth is almost equal, it is possible that some brothers were discounted. This oddity may be a reflection of some underlying tension. Of the 61 per cent who reported having a brother, 52 per cent of these lived on the estate, but only 36 per cent of the women saw their brothers on a daily basis.

This report of not having brothers may indicate that if these men do not remain in the area, they cease to be considered family. Whatever the reason, it is a curious finding.

*Activities*

A profile of the women's activities gave some impression of their lives. Eighty-four per cent had no employment; this was a lower rate than the estate rate of 92 per cent, which indicated that more women than men were actually employed. The women's work was, however, very spasmodic: part-time cleaning, bar and shop work. Only five women out of the 80 were employed five days a week.

Shopping and going to school to meet the children were the main activities outside the home. Most women (70 per cent) shopped once or twice a week. Only one woman bought in bulk and had a freezer, which she used in an efficient and economical way. She got a taxi home from the supermarket once a fortnight, saying 'if you shop daily you buy odds and ends'. She lived on her own and her husband was 'away' which, she said, made budgeting easier. Many others used the noisy mobile shops that toured the estate, which not only charged a high rate but, through giving credit, had a debt grip on the estate. (One of the mobile shop owners was murdered outside a local pub and the view was expressed by several people that, given the squeeze he put on people, he deserved it.)

Sixty-nine per cent of the women went to the school at least once a day. When asked about friends, a number of women commented that they met them 'at the gate', and seeing groups of women walking to and from school was common.

Going to the bingo and pub were both popular activities. Twenty-one per cent had been to the bingo during the week of interview and 26 to the pub. There were other activities away from the estate, but when asked about them, a lot of women commented on what boring lives they led, on how they did nothing. On the estate in the week they were interviewed, 13 women went to the neighbourhood centre, 9 of them daily, 14 women used the children's centre, and 10 used the leisure centre. These centres provide a kind of continuum: women having children tended to start at the neighbourhood centre, they then took their preschool children to the children's centre, and once the children were a bit independent they went on to the leisure centre, where there were various activities. Half of the women interviewed had used one of these facilities in the week of the interview, but this meant that half had not.

*House moves and tenancy*

In 1989, 99 per cent of the tenants of the estate were on housing benefit, and 95 per cent had been tenants for more than five years. This indicated a degree of stability of population within the estate, but it was not, however, a stability of tenancy of the same house. Forty-three per cent of the women questioned for the network research had visited the housing department, to pay rent and rates, to complain and to ask for a transfer. The number of times that the women actually moved house was evidence that these visits were fruitful. The frequency of house moving was one of the most extraordinary phenomena observed, even more so when mapped, as it showed 'waterboatman' movement in graphic form (see Table 6.1). Sixty-five per cent of the tenants on the estate had rent arrears, and there was a policy not to transfer these tenants off the estate; there were, however, frequent in-estate transfers.

**Table 6.1**     House moves within estate of women interviewed

| Moves | No. of women | % |
|---|---|---|
| 0 | 6 | 7.5 |
| 1 | 2 | 2.5 |
| 2 | 26 | 32.5 |
| 3 | 17 | 21.3 |
| 4 | 15 | 18.8 |
| 5 | 4 | 5.0 |
| 6 | 5 | 6.0 |
| 7 | 4 | 5.0 |
| 8 | 1 | 1.3 |

Only four women commented that housing was a problem. House moving is usually considered to be an extremely stressful event, not one to be undertaken lightly, but there was evidence that it was being undertaken with extraordinary frequency on the estate. Moving appeared to be a way of life. One of the largest families on the estate had been travellers within their lifetime, so frequent moving might be an extension of that.

These moves were undertaken by the women on their own account, independent of their parental home. They were central to the development of the 'waterboatman theory' as they exemplified constant shifting. There appeared to be a need to have something different, to achieve variety, and the only thing possible was a change of address. This gave some semblance of change, of something hopeful happening in the overriding sameness of everything and the unlikeliness of anything really changing.

Another example of the perpetual motion exemplified in the 'waterboatman theory' was identified through interviewing three sisters over the six-month period of the study. One brother appeared to live in a different house at each interview. The sisters told it as it was at the time, that the brother was spinning around from place to place.

Another apparently stable family had lived on the estate for 40 years and then suddenly moved away. Two women in this family had been interviewed, so during the time of writing up the work, their data had changed. Their individual questionnaires were used as they had been at the time of interviewing, but each told a different story of the family network. This highlighted the sometimes volatile nature of social datum, it does not remain static. It is in the duplication and repetitions that patterns begin to develop into trends. What became explicit from this work was that there was constant shifting but that it was contained within a very closed locality, where there was a similarity shared between the inhabitants of long-term unemployment and consequent low income.

## Deception

It sometimes benefited some families to present themselves as being something other than what they really were or others perceived them to be. Some depended on this, both for the sake of self-esteem and for financial reasons. Disconnection from the context of the wage- or salary-earning 'stable society' was inevitable. There was a pervasive tension of not staying still, of not being what you seemed, of where you seemed to be or of where you could be seen. To be safe, you skittered. This was exacerbated by a blitz on benefit fraud, people being encouraged to inform the authorities of neighbours' irregularities.

This resulted in several ugly neighbourhood 'squealings'. This kept some people on the move so that the external authorities could not prevail. Deceptions within families were also recorded.

## The midwife–mother relationship

Good communication between mother and midwife is essential if the relationship is going to be a fruitful one that results in wellbeing on the part of the mother and fulfilment on the part of the midwife. The interactions between woman and midwife in this study showed some evidence of cultural 'otherness', which prevented the full potential of the interaction being realised. It was usually the mother who was the loser because for her the action was so important. Where there is a lack of openness, communication is likely to come to grief.

Trying to be 'with' women who are economically without has the potential for misunderstanding and miscommunication. During the time of the studies, there was a change in the allowances, so that when a new tenancy was created, there was no longer any provision made for furniture and furnishings, and loans had to be taken out for these. This had an immediate and detrimental impact on internal housing standards. Midwives responded to this in various ways. One response was that expecting to get everything 'on tap' was not acceptable and that the change from grant-giving was good. This illustrates the social barriers, in this case, between the unemployed and the reluctant taxpayer.

Understanding the potential for stereotyping and stigmatising is important in an area where unemployment is long term, people have had no experience of work and state benefit is a fact of life. The unemployed are seen, and may see themselves, as being 'without', and in financial terms they are without the same security as the waged. They are without money in sufficient amount to ease living, without access to many of the things that only money can buy, and without escape from their low-income status as they are definitely excluded from the wage-earning sections of society. This becomes a defining factor, which is a divide.

There may be problems too with language and its understanding. A 15-year-old had decided to carry on with a pregnancy with gross abnormalities that ended with a stillbirth. The geneticist was gentle in his counselling and explained that it was unlikely to happen again – it was a one-off and 'it was in the genes'. The grandmother chirped up, 'I always said she wore them too tight.'

Limited literacy can also cause misunderstanding. A woman was distraught following her hospital booking and asked for a home visit. She had booked in very late and had missed appointments. She also smoked heavily. She said how difficult it was to organise getting five children up to the hospital, let alone coping with them once she was there. The woman had looked at her notes and was mortified to see that the consultant had written 'disgust'. After a referral to the notes, the context showed that the word was 'discussed'. The woman had taken a step in communication in saying how upset she was and in asking for reassurance and an explanation. Where women hold their own notes, midwives must routinely offer clear explanations in order to prevent such misunderstandings since many women do not seek out reassurance.

To be 'with' women who are living in an area of long-term unemployment poses a unique challenge for midwives because of the place that birth has in any society. Creating wellbeing for women who are going through the birthing experience could have, and does have, an impact on their psychology, which can make a difference to how they perceive themselves. The aim should be that women will be enabled to birth well and can then see themselves as 'women who can'. This is especially important for women whose experience of much around them is that they cannot.

Midwives can help women to feel, and be, more able. They have to make the effort, however, to be aware of the cultural and economic barriers to which they are subjected, and, for the duration of the interaction between them and the 'women without', midwives should strive to be fundamentally 'with' them. To this end, there needs to be an awareness and an acceptance of the individual woman's needs during this crucial transition.

The 'waterboatman theory' describes the geographical movement of the families studied and the skittering attention of the women in discourse. This can be used to highlight the very different cultural assumptions in the professional picture of the midwife–mother relationship. Professional assumptions, embedded in how care is organised and in antenatal education focused on topics, are clearly alien to the culture of these women. Where midwifery care adapts to their local culture, women gain immensely. Where their patterns of communication are accepted, women gain control of antenatal learning appropriate to their needs and learning style. Where the midwifery service is truly community based, complex links develop between midwives and families, which involve midwives in the lives of vulnerable women who would otherwise slip through the net of maternity care. Such cultural understanding and adaptation makes it possible for midwives to be with women and is educational for all concerned.

When starting to write this chapter, the researcher had the pleasure of bumping into two of the mothers cared for in the 1980s. Their children had left school, and they had been working at the neighbourhood centre over the years and been involved in its development. One of its activities is organising holidays and trips, which involves fundraising and enables families to have time together away from the estate. The two women were about to go to college to study sociology to be accredited for the knowledge that they have. They were keen to get more. It was good to see them.

# References

Acheson D (1998) *Independent Inquiry into Inequalities in Health*. London: Department of Health.

Black T Murphy (1998) Giving information, giving consent. *British Journal of Midwifery*, **6**(10): 618–19.

Bowler IMW (1993) Stereotypes of women of Asian descent in midwifery. *Midwifery* **9**: 7–16.

Bradshaw J and Holmes H (1989) *Living on the Edge*. London: Tyneside Child Poverty Action Group.

Brown S, Lumley J, Small R and Astbury J (1994) *Missing Voices: The Experience of Motherhood*. Melbourne, Oxford University Press.

Cole-Hamilton I and Lang T (1986) *Tightening Belts – a Report on the Impact of Poverty on Food*. London: London Food Commission.

Cornwell J (1984) *Hard Earned Lives*. London: Tavistock.

Davies J (1989) Tangled Webs. Family Networks and Activity Examined in One Inner City Area. MSc dissertation, Department of Behavioural Sciences, Northumbria University.

Department of Health (1980) *Report of the Working Group on Inequalities in Health* (Black Report). London: HMSO.

Department of Health (1998) *Our Healthier Nation – a Contract for Health*. London: Department of Health.

Evans F (1987) *The Newcastle Community Midwifery Care Project: An Evaluation Report*. Newcastle: Newcastle Health Authority.

Fox R (1967) *Kinship and Marriage*. Harmondsworth: Pelican.

Glaser B and Strauss B (1967) *The Discovery of Grounded Theory*. Chicago: Aldine.

Howe GM (1986) Disease Mapping. In: Pacione M (ed.) *Progress and Prospect*. London: Croom Helm.

Hunt S (1995) *Social Meaning of Midwifery*. London: Macmillan.

Jordan B (1995) *Birth in Four Cultures*. Prospect Heights, IL: Waveland Press.

Kitzinger S (1978) *Women as Mothers*. Glasgow: Fontana.

Littlewood J and McHugh N (1997) *Maternal Distress and Postnatal Depression*. London: Macmillan.

Marsh A and MacKay S (1994) *Poor Smokers*. London: Policy Studies Institute.

Reed J and Procter S (1995) *Practitioner Research in Health Care*. London: Chapman & Hall.

Townsend P (1988) *Health and Deprivation*. London: Croom Helm.

Townsend P and Davidson N (1982) *Inequalities in Health*. Harmondsworth: Penguin.

Van Gennep A (1908, reprinted 1965) *The Rites of Passage*. London: Routledge & Kegan Paul.

Wilmott P and Young M (1957) *Family and Kinship in East London*. London: Institute of Community Studies/Routledge & Kegan Paul.

Yearley C (1997) Motherhood as a Rite of Passage. In: Alexander J, Levy V and Roch S (eds) *Midwifery Practice*. London: Macmillan.

# Chapter 7

# A Three-way Relationship

*Margaret Chesney*

## Introduction

My work as a midwife with Pakistani women often required the presence of another, an interpreter. This chapter explores issues arising from this triad relationship that influenced my relationship with the women. The experiences described originated from my work as a community midwife in my home town of Rochdale and as a visiting midwife researcher to a maternity hospital in Sahiwal, Pakistan. This chapter will focus on four areas central to the relationship between the midwife, the interpreter and the woman. Pseudonyms have been used, and permission has been obtained from the people mentioned.

First, I will outline the context, background and experiences, and their effect on the relationship. Second, I raise issues from my findings in Rochdale. Following this, I will focus upon my dealings with individual interpreters during the field trips to Pakistan. Finally, following this very personal journey of learning from experience, I will examine some issues surrounding interpreter training so that a better relationship can be established when midwives and women are of a different culture and speak a different language.

## Context and cultural ignorance

I was brought up in a village in the Pennines where I knew of no ethnic minority families. During my midwifery training, I recall 'role-playing' a woman who had just arrived from Pakistan, attending a booking clinic. This was the sum total of my formal education on cultural awareness.

Culley (1997), in her critique of what she describes as the 'conventional culturalist approach', identified a lack of awareness of cultures other than our own. She states that while cultural awareness education is essential for all health professionals, it must go beyond conventional awareness-raising if it is to benefit professionals and clients. Balibar (1991) renames the culturalist approach the 'ethnic sensitivity model' and says that characteristics of the distinct cultures can be captured to explain health differences. This was confirmed by Stubbs (1993), who further identified a prevalence of the 'ethnic sensitivity models' within which a conceptual framework is developed, focusing on the differences between the ethnicity of minority groups and that of the majority 'white' culture.

I interpret the culturalist (sensitivity) approach to be the recognition of cultural differences yet acknowledge the potential to reduce the differences to problems, the consequence of which may be to ignore the power relations that exist between cultural groups. I wholeheartedly agree with Davies (1997:219) when she says that 'one cannot care for and be with women if there is a lack of understanding about their lives'. Essentially, the health professional must take this knowledge of both the distinguishing characteristics and the political power influences beyond the understanding the health beliefs and behaviour stage and into a critical evaluation of the complex ways in which ethnicity, socio-economic status, gender, age and geographical location may intersect.

When I began working with the Pakistani women in 1980, I was without doubt culturally ignorant: I did not even have the basic 'culturalist approach'. I was, however, without prejudice. I did not judge the Pakistani women's 'different ways' as being any less important than my own. Since then, I have kept that stance and, with eight visits to Pakistan and a significant study of the culture, I hope to be moving beyond the culturalist approach to what Gillborn (1995) calls 'plastic', fluid yet moulded, in which race and ethnicity continue to be of critical importance, their precise form and interaction with other variables, however, remaining amorphous. My aim in gaining knowledge and understanding is unambiguous: to provide what Leininger (1991) describes as 'culturally congruent' care.

## The clinic

As a relatively inexperienced midwife, I was promoted in 1980 to the level of Sister and given a community midwife post. My 'challenge' was to sort out a busy GP practice. Twenty per cent of the women giving birth in the hospital at that time originated from either Pakistan or Bangladesh. The clinic I was given was an all-Pakistani caseload with 15–20 women booking per month. The midwife who handed over the practice had held it for six months, having been the third that year, said, 'Every midwife should do a minimum of six months with this practice; then they would know what work was about.' I worked there for five very happy and satisfying years. The women would bring their sick children to the clinic; that was sometimes why they came. The doctor used to attend at the end of the clinic, and the women would wait hours for him (the clinic starting at 1 pm with as many as 30–40 on the list).

At first, 30 per cent of the women on the list chose not to attend, this figure being consistent with the available evidence (Hayes 1995). However, this was very simply addressed once I realised the confusion the women were labouring under. They were required to attend the GP clinic in one place, another hospital for the antenatal care, then a different hospital still to give birth. When I visited their homes and asked why they had not kept their appointments, they had no idea where to go: further to this, they did not understand why they needed to attend. If it were convenient for them, I would conduct the antenatal examination in the home. I remember a colleague saying that she had no intention of 'starting that, as all women would want it and purposely not attend the clinic'. This did not, however, happen. The norm was to attend clinic and the women wanted to be 'the same', so once they knew where to attend and felt that there was a purpose, they did. The confusion decreased as communication and attendance improved.

## Continuity

Continuity of care and carers for the women, both before and after birth, was the norm. Most women would see only between one and three midwives in the antenatal and postnatal period. Because I lived locally to the hospital and (initially for my own convenience) in order to reduce the initial loneliness of being the new community midwife, I called into the hospital every morning. I would visit each of the areas, talking to the staff and woman from *my* practice. Although I have to admit that it was not initiated for this purpose, I soon realised that this daily contact with the women served as the cement of trust

for the relationship with the women. It was as if we 'connected'. Halldorsdóttir (1996) relates to this concept, using the metaphor of a
bridge, symbolising the openness in communication that takes the
relationship onto a 'professional intimacy'. This is developed in the
presence of mutual trust, respect and compassion.

The women's eyes would light up at my familiar face. This would
reflect on me and it felt good. If necessary, I would call the interpreter
(who worked on the wards in the morning) from our clinic and ask her
to check whether the women needed anything. This visit also enabled
me to provide extra information to the hospital staff on the women,
usually of a personal, social or psychological nature, the type that is
difficult to commit to paper, for example, 'This woman is having a
hard time with her mother-in-law.' I could see that such information
brought the woman 'alive' to the hospital midwife. So they saw not
only the 'outer' physical woman, but also the inner, hidden, silent,
often neglected one. Through 'seeing' the whole, the hospital
midwives could then offer an 'extra' smile and gentle warmth, which
crosses all cultural communication barriers.


## 'Bad care days'

During my visits to the women's homes, I developed a 'patter' of
pidgin Punjabi and learned to *talk* with my hands, face and body,
developing a virtual, designer sign language. Although this was developed on a trial and error basis, if it served *my* purpose it was reinforced, and if not I sought alternative means. The effectiveness was
judged by my getting the answers I wanted. It is only in retrospect and
with embarrassment I recognise this and other strategies that I used to
employ on Tuesdays, when the antenatal clinic began at 1 pm and
finished at 6 pm. I sometimes had to assist with another clinic from
9 am for an hour or so, and in between there were often eight or more
antenatal and postnatal visits. There was no concept of necessary or
unnecessary (selective) visits. I carried out the ritual visits twice daily
for the first three days, then daily for ten; only thereafter could visits
be as needed until the 28-day watershed.

The quality of the visits on Tuesday must have been different. Now
I recognise them as 'bad care days'. My strategy was to pray on the
doorstep that there were no problems. If it was a visit for my
colleague's practice and non-Pakistani women, I would pray for the
woman not to be in, but the Pakistani women would always be home.

I would breeze in chirpy and cheerful, with the pidgin 'OK Tak-hai', 'no problems', an effective 'blocker' for any problem. The obligatory top-to-toe examination of mother and baby was conducted, using my agenda, at a speed that I judged the woman would not detect as being rushed. If I had a student, this was wonderful, as both 'top-to-toes' could be conducted simultaneously. If there was a problem that I had initially 'looked through' on arrival or that arose during my swift record-keeping, I would move into superefficient mode and deal with it quickly, with little thought.

I look back and recognise that I was using what Foucault (1980) describes as the 'professional gaze'. According to the time I had, that is, how much 'work' I had on, I would use this gaze to enable or disable the women. As the women were always pleased to see me, I used to kid myself that I did not need an interpreter, and, when my conscience told me otherwise, I would rationalise that it was the way the women wanted it. The women, however, knew no different; they did not have an expectation of me being able to understand or help them. Speed certainly does not allow time for really listening or for the provision of essential psychosocial care. On reflection, I had nothing to listen to because I could not understand. On non-clinic days, I tried to make up for the care shortfall. This must have been very confusing for the women as I probed and actively listened one day and was professionally distant the next.

While we had the good fortune to have an interpreter at the antenatal clinic one half-day a week, there was throughout the rest of my working week no-one, other than family members, to assist with communication. An on-call rota for volunteer interpreters (paid when called) was briefly set up, but the service was poorly funded and, not surprisingly, unreliable. If ever there was a dire need for an interpreter, such as the times I wanted to admit a mother or her baby to hospital and she did not understand, I would ring the GP's surgery and ask the Pakistani receptionist or the doctor to explain to the woman. On rare occasions, I arranged with the interpreter from the antenatal clinic to meet me at a woman's home. I am ashamed to admit that this situation lasted for the five years I worked there and to my knowledge continues today.

Those five years were the happiest and most satisfying times of my midwifery career. I spent many long interesting visits asking anyone who could speak English about the Muslim culture and learnt as many Punjabi phrases as I could. I admired the strong family ties and values; I saw unconditional love, and children given priority. This was very refreshing compared with my own life, which involved full-time work with others caring for my (at the time) young children. The latter provoked feelings of guilt and inner conflict. For the first year in the community, I was lonely and missed the support of my hospital colleagues. I remember being thrilled to be allocated a student so we could chat between the visits, share our feelings and views on practice and the women, and learn from each other.

Parveen was the very first interpreter whom I worked with; she was attached to the GP clinic referred to above. Parveen was based at the hospital on the postnatal ward, as an auxiliary, and then came to the clinic for one half-day a week. In the hospital I had not noticed her attitude towards the women but in the clinic I was shocked by her authoritarian manner. I listened horrified as she berated the women, chastising them if they had forgotten their sample of urine, ordering them to the chair or the couch to lie down. The final straw came when I asked her what she had said to one women and she blandly informed me that she had told her to 'speak when she was spoken to'.

I learned that Parveen lived in and was part of the community of women attending this antenatal clinic. When I informed Parveen that I would like her to speak to the women kindly, she became surly, withdrawn and unhelpful. Her power in the triad relationship revealed itself clearly as she failed to facilitate the communication between myself and the women. The worst scenario I suspected her of was distorting the message. It was evident that the cultural conflict and the power relationship lay not between the women and me but between Parveen and me. It became an issue of great concern as I was aware that my reputation in the community would rest with Parveen. Her power as the gate-keeper to the community neutralised in one stroke any control I had of the situation.

An opportunity for change arose when Parveen's pregnant sister attended the clinic. The difference in Parveen's attitude was palpable. I took hold of this and informed Parveen afterwards that that was how I wanted her to be with all the women. Her reply was, 'the women did not want or expect this' and 'I would not be accorded the respect I was due, by virtue of my professional role, if I continued this way.' She made the comparison with the doctor, who, like their husbands, must be looked up to and obeyed (Rafiqul-Haqq and Newton 1996). As such, she considered her authoritative behaviour to be entirely appropriate.

Our differences were initially and superficially resolved in an authoritative way. As I was 'in charge', she would do my bidding, yet she made it abundantly clear that I was 'going about it the wrong way'. This solution to our cultural conflict only served to fuel her existing cultural and socially inculcated reaction to power and authority. Her belief system upheld the view that the only way to gain respect was to command it. My belief system was based upon the principle that one cannot command respect, it has to be earned. Earning respect, however, takes more time.

Following the birth of her sister's baby and my visits to their home, there was a distinct change in Parveen's attitude and behaviour. Parveen's acceptance of my methods became evident as she used her links and extensive knowledge of the community in the care of the women. My role as a detective, tracing families that had been re-housed, or women who had gone home to their mothers, became much simpler as Parveen shared with me information about the community. Her insider knowledge of important issues such as family feuds, second wives or abusive husbands became crucial to my under-standing and subsequent care of the women. I knew I had passed the acceptance test because she trusted me with this information. I was, however, very 'careful', despite some very clever questioning from some women, never to divulge any information. I had earned Parveen's trust and respect, and she saw and experienced an alternative belief model in operation.

The relationships blossomed from then on; Parveen began to address the women as *Baji* (sister); she was able to be 'kind' to the women when she made them honorary members of her family. Consequently, through the process of my using my position in the hierarchy and wielding power and authority, including ingredients such as persistence and kindness, a change in Parveen's attitude to the women was achieved. Parveen and I became a team working for the benefit of the women in her community. On reflection, I was aware that I had imposed my values and was in no doubt that the motive behind Parveen's action was to protect and guide me.

## Ethnocentricity, power and authority

Contrary to the role of the interpreter in most codes of ethics (Kaufert and Putsch 1997), Parveen did not show 'neutrality or objectivity'. Whether neutrality is a realistic expectation for interpreters has been debated by Solomon (1997). She found that principles easily slip over to dogma when they are applied ethnocentrically (in believing in the superiority of the cultural group from which one comes); this can create sterility in the triad relationship, which itself becomes a barrier.

It could be argued that both Parveen and I were applying ethnocentric principles dogmatically. The situation was initially resolved, albeit not satisfactorily, by the use of power and authority. My 'do it to prove it' approach possessed an ethnocentricity, but the clinical damage and potential sabotage might have continued without the key learning opportunity brought about by Parveen's sister attending the clinic. Friedson (1985) focuses upon issues of power and dominance in clinical communication, but he refers specifically to health care providers and clients rather than interpreters and health care workers. There is much value to be gained from morally sensitive persons in a particular situation bridging the cultural gap, in this case initially via the interpreter. It should be remembered, however, that the right to the moral high ground must always remain in question, especially cross-culturally.

Policies that restrict the role of the interpreter, and emphasise cultural neutrality and invisibility, may ignore the important other dimension that Parveen and others bring to their role of interpreter, that of broker or mediator. There are many important issues that surface when the interpreter takes on this role, not least the ethical dimension. It would not be possible to gain the consent of the community prior to Parveen's divulging information, but it should have been a consideration for the individual. In the early 1980s, a utilitarian approach was instituted, but almost two decades later it would be important to consider the rights of the individual more carefully.

Parveen's story provides an example of problems that occur outside the woman when the interpreter and midwife do not share the same culture. It does not, however, highlight another fundamental issue surrounding the interpreter–midwife–woman triad, that of demonstrating how interpreters make sense of the uncertainty surrounding the direct translation.

## Interpreting: more than just words

In my naïveté and ignorance, I believed and trusted that Parveen had interpreted my words verbatim. Neither Parveen nor I had received any training for this part of our role, and I often asked why it took so many sentences to effect the translation of a single sentence. Kaufert and Putsch (1997) found that some interpreters introduced a bias into the messages they gave. It was only after I had worked with different interpreters and had myself studied Punjabi and the Islamic culture that I realised how a straight verbatim interpretation might not get the message across.

In the provision of a straightforward interpretation, Kaufert and Putsch (1997) confirm that interpreters often need to extend upon or adapt the message so that it is understandable in a different language or culture. This is often conducted in a mediating way to prevent conflict or to protect both parties. Managing the information to the benefit of both parties involves what Schott and Henley (1996) identify as cultural brokerage. However, there is the potential for suspicion (from either the giver or receiver) around this cultural adaptation. The interpreter as the carrier of the message may suspect direct translation is inappropriate, or the owner of the message may suspect the interpreter of altering the meaning of the message.

Trust is needed on all sides: the interpreter, who has worked and lived in both cultures, who has a knowledge of the topic and culture, and who also possesses the skills of a good communicator, may be the best person to make a judgement on how the information is best managed. There are also other factors that need to be considered – the interpreter's standing in the community, personality, gender, religion, dress and attitude – which all have the potential to make or break the vital link to effective communication.

## The status of interpreter

The literature about communication has emphasised language and culture as 'barriers'. Kaufert and Koolage (1984) found that interpreters or bilingual health workers were usually represented by ancillary members of the health care team. Thus, despite the importance of the interpreter's role, the power structure, the culture of the health service and the low status of the women can easily lead to interpreters being marginalised. There is the ever-present potential for misunderstanding, leading to a breakdown in communication. Schott and Henley (1996: 94) quote a community midwife who said, 'I am never sure what she [the interpreter] tells them, she seems to make their decisions for them... I feel she looks down on the women as uneducated and stupid and feels she knows better.'

It is understandable that the interpreter identifies with the 'higher-class' health professional, which further emphasises the disparate elements of class. Parveen considered herself 'a cut above' the women who came to the clinic, even though they were of her community;

until she elevated them to being a member of her family, she did not treat them as equal. The major issue that set her apart was her education, which ultimately accorded her access to the health system, a freedom denied to most Asian women generally (Hayes 1995). As discussed, Parveen worked as an auxiliary in the local hospital so some of the terminology would be familiar, but the concepts, importance and relevance might not have been understood. There is also the ever-present possibility that there may not be a linguistically equivalent term for the interpreter, which presents her with a dilemma. This is especially important if it is superimposed upon a total lack of understanding of the true meaning in one language. Tests for screening fall into this category.

## *Bad news*

This is a direct translation of an untrained interpreter's interaction with a woman following the confirmation by scanning that her baby was abnormal (Rizwana, personal communication, 1998):

> Your baby is handicapped and ill; how are you going to cope in looking after it? It will be a burden to you and your family, and you must think of them; you can always have another baby. The doctor wants you to have an abortion.

This approach is incredible to believe, yet it took place in an antenatal clinic in 1998. The woman had conceived this, her much-wanted, eighth child, while visiting Mecca to pray for one last chance at motherhood. This conception was a 'blessing from Allah'. The psychological effect upon this woman following this interaction was devastating, 'her world fell apart' and she was left feeling that the health service and all its personnel had failed her.

Giving bad news through an interpreter is a cultural double-edged sword. Truth as a concept may not be upheld or valued, especially if it has the potential to do harm or hurt someone's feelings. This generates a culture that supports an 'emperor's new clothes' value system and is reminiscent of my own upbringing with regard to the maxim 'If you cannot say anything good, do not say anything at all.' However, a problem denied cannot be one solved. This has been evident to me many times during my work with Pakistani women and their families.

One example of this occurred when a child born with a severe heart defect was transferred to a distant regional unit. The mother did not want to visit or learn of the child's problem; all she asked was whether a child with this condition had ever lived.

There seems no doubt that one's use of language affects one's perception of reality. Carrese (1995), working with Navajo Indians, found that their core values prohibited the discussion of bad news. Protecting a relative from bad news is a common value in many cultures (Felema and Teklemarian 1992). It is interesting to note that other groups hold a parallel belief that telling the truth may be considered disrespectful and has the potential to attract harm by tempting fate.

This belief underpins the true story of a woman attending a GP in Pakistan with severe anaemia. When the GP asked how many children she had had, she replied that she did not know: 'five or six maybe...'. The GP subsequently learned that she had given birth to nine children in eight years. He rationalised her reluctance to tell the truth by saying that it was her belief that if she spoke about her success and luck in having nine live children, she would be tempting fate and some harm might come to them. A parallel to this is the Western woman who is afraid of discussing cot death just in case she 'makes it happen'.

There is also the unfamiliar (to English) polite and impolite/ respectful and non-respectful terminology in Urdu and Punjabi. A small parallel can be made with the English language. I have heard other midwives use (and indeed have myself used before I knew) the term *pishab* when asking a Pakistani mother for her specimen of urine. When I learnt that this word translates into a rough common term likened to 'piss', I realised the potential to offend.

## Interpreters in Pakistan

Following on from the examination of the cultural context, the stark realisation of the effect that interpreters and interpretation have upon the relationship between the women and the midwife, I propose to explore experiences that I have had with different interpreters in Pakistan. It is not my intention to 'dramatise' and thus increase the potential to stigmatise the interpreters, the women or their culture. Some of the information has been collected systematically through ethnographic study while the rest has come through practising as a midwife. Davies (1997) might refer to this as 'practitioner observation'. I would like to make it very clear the findings can in no way be generalised as each relationship was unique.

The interpreters allocated to us during the early field trips to Pakistan came from a multitude of backgrounds: a lady health visitor, a civil defence worker and a GP's wife. We had no choice in the selection as it was made by officials from the town, the Chairman of the Town and Municipal Councils and the Chief Engineer. This occurred because the twinning was between town councils. The relationship with each of the interpreters had its own uniqueness. The success (from my perspective), or otherwise, of the triad relationship with the women–staff was dependent upon trust, and whose agenda was being served.

There was no doubt that the Pakistani council officials required feedback from the interpreters on our behaviour and the questions we were asking, and it was inevitable that the loyalty of the interpreters lay with these bureaucrats. We were treated with reserved suspicion. I was even asked whether I was an evangelist trying to convert women to Christianity. Discussions with the elder men of the community at social events left us in no doubt that Western women are considered to be decadent and of loose morals. They took the statistics on teenage pregnancy and divorce as a proof of this. As a consequence, we were aware of the 'fear' felt by some of the men that we might lead their women astray into decadent Western feminist ways.

They could not, however, have been further from the truth. My strict Methodist background gave me a grounding similar to theirs. In addition, I have a high regard and respect for all cultures. Communication through an interpreter, however good, is never likely to be as effective as direct communication between a midwife and woman who share the same language and culture (Schott and Henley 1996). This is undoubtedly true, but in research on birth in Pakistan, the women agreed to be interviewed only because I was a Western women and midwife (Chesney 1998a). The reason given was that they trusted me not to gossip. Whether this is trust or subservience from the colonial past is a matter for further analysis. Mumtaz and Rauf (1997), in their study of the silence surrounding reproductive health in Pakistan, found a reluctance to talk to other women from their own community or background, especially about private matters such as childbirth. This further extended to a division between married and unmarried women. The latter would never be included in any discussion that involved reproduction.

Although each of the indigenous Pakistani interpreters proved fluent in written and received spoken English, their ability to understand our northern accent, cope with the speed of our spoken English and follow our terminology caused both them and us great difficulty. This lay outside the sensitivity of the topic, that of birth. After a particularly frustrating third visit, I informed the twinning group that we would return if we could take an interpreter from Rochdale.

### Razia

The first of the interpreters to accompany us from Rochdale was Razia. She was 'allocated' to us by the town hall in Rochdale, her name having been proposed by one of the members of the twinning group. Razia was a single girl who was doing voluntary work with a youth group in the town.

Our first mistake was to meet her for the very first time at the airport, although I had requested a meeting many times before. On reflection, this should have raised my suspicions. During the flight we discussed her role. I tried desperately to overcome her passive, subservient demeanour, but it seemed that I did not have the key to free her to be my equal, so I changed role to that of 'maternal protector'. I did not know whether this was natural shyness or a fear of me or of the situation. It is almost impossible to build a relationship of trust during a 10-hour flight to a 'mission of fear', which was how I perceived Razia to feel.

Unfortunately, Razia's premonitions were realised. To summarise the key elements of a particularly frustrating field trip, we were first met at the airport by her relative (a male cousin slightly older than Razia), who had been instructed by the family to chaperone her throughout the trip. I explained that he would not be allowed to be present in the maternity hospital, but he was not happy to let Razia out of his sight. He even insisted that Razia stay with the family rather than with us in the rest house. Naturally, I did not want to offend any cultural norm and gave Razia the choice of where she wished to stay, understanding her wish to please the family.

Razia (along with her chaperone) accompanied us on our first 'official' function. A politician called her over and asked her who her father was and what was he doing allowing her, a single girl, to be in the mixed company of women and men. I spoke to the politician but the damage had been done and Razia was frightened. The only time we saw her on the trip thereafter (until the return journey) was when we went to visit her at her aunt's house to check that she was not being kept there against her will.

Not being able to communicate freely with the women and the staff at the hospital was the most frustrating part of our work together. I had studied Punjabi, and although this helped a little when combined with pidgin, signing and body language, no-one was able to understand me fully. In sheer frustration, we would end up smiling, nodding, shrugging our shoulders and moving on to the next equally frustrating experience. This formed a web of communication that was frequently devoid of common words, but over the seven visits we built an abundance of common experience. This served as an umbilical link containing veins and arteries of mutual respect and admiration. We cared for and looked out for each other, as women would do in a war situation. For example, one time when I was upset over a stillborn baby, the staff, despite being surprised at my reaction, comforted me. Another time, one of the staff had been transferred, and we pulled out all the stops to get her back.

In a bid to span the language gap and prevent a recurrence of Razia's unfortunate experience, I informed the co-ordinator at the town hall that I would select the next interpreter to accompany me. As it happened, we self-funded the next trip in order to conduct the evaluative research for my MSc. This was primarily to free us of the social commitments that the town-twinning arrangement required of us. Such civic duties, for example prize-giving at the local schools, took priority, in the official's eyes, over our work in the maternity hospital.

### Nadia

When I was a teacher in the West Pennine College, Nadia was a student midwife. Before I seriously considered her offer to act as interpreter, I asked her to confirm her parents' permission. They asked to meet me and the others in the team who were to accompany Nadia to Pakistan, and after only a brief introduction we were served a delicious meal by Nadia, ate alone and left. We had been vetted, and Nadia was given permission to travel with us and act as our interpreter. Her own student group raised money for Nadia's fare. We had frequent meetings about the trip; Nadia was involved in the piloting and development of the interview schedule, and we role-played the interview situation. The relationship built into one of mutual respect, with a clear focus and direction.

In total contrast to the previous visit, our pre-existing relationship made the trip a resounding success. Nadia had a warm, non-judgemental, humanistic approach and she bowled everyone over with her serene 'mother Theresa' presence. Even the socially sensitive GP and his wife who provided our accommodation were impressed with her, when she asked the GP whether she could possibly move the Koran in her bedroom to another place as she was not happy to sleep with her feet pointing towards it. She was, in everyone's opinion, the epitome of a good Muslim girl, yet she was breaking the social norm by being in our company. To overcome this, we took on a parental role. We totally avoided the political and social scene, and as a consequence Nadia did not suffer the male prejudice that Razia had encountered.

Nadia was undoubtedly the ideal interpreter, whispering in my ear, filling me in with conversations that she felt were appropriate to the research, yet managing to maintain everyone's trust. When I asked a question that could not be directly translated, she would check any adaptations made with me and explain the relevance to me. Her thinking was woman centred, and she knew the aims of the study by heart; in addition, because she was halfway through a 78-week midwifery programme, she had a firm grounding of the terminology and practice. We spent some time working on the wards, and together we experienced emergencies such as shoulder dystocia and a fresh stillbirth. These experiences, although extremely traumatic, built the relationship between us and the staff in the hospital. On reflection, the relationship with the women was transient, almost secondary.

By then (our fourth trip), the staff had come to accept our different 'sisterly' care of the women. It was ironic that the staff were insatiably hungry for our knowledge, yet the one thing that they could give within their own resources was 'care' – which did not appear to be valued. However, Nadia and I agreed that the tender loving care we saw given by a mother to her daughter, first day post-caesarean section, could not be matched by that of any nurse or midwife.

Nadia and I reflected upon the need for the staff to protect themselves psychologically from the tragedy that went with their daily work. I thought of the women who asked me to remove my (as I saw it) comforting hand from their arm in labour: they had built a wall of protection and did not want it breaking down by my touch; or perhaps, because I was a white person, they were suspicious of my presence and 'odd' behaviour. Further reflection took Nadia and I into an analysis of the camaraderie and relationship with the staff following major incidents: no angry black cloud of litigation hanging over us, making us defend our individual practice, just an honest, genuine desire to do it better, try something different next time.

Although this fourth field trip was the most traumatic and challenging in a midwifery practice sense, it was, paradoxically, without doubt the most satisfying. The reasons were multifaceted:

1. our relationship with the staff, made possible by a more effective communication system
2. the oneness (philosophy) of the interpreter (Nadia) and myself
3. trust built through working together
4. separation from the male bureaucracy.

I consider attaining these goals to be essential before effective care can be given. What is considered 'effective' is, however, culturally determined. Saving lives is clearly cross-culturally valued, but dealing with the psychological as well as the physical trauma is not yet on the agenda for the poor women or the staff in this hospital. On a Maslow (1969) type hierarchy, the basic level of survival has to be achieved before considering morbidity, either physical or psychological. As a consequence, in this hospital and in Pakistan, we are at the opposite ends of a cultural continuum. The relationship with the women remains in limbo: they neither wanted nor understood our tender loving care. The relationship with the staff, however, has moved onto a different plane. They observed holistic care, saw the women's reaction, so did not value or emulate it for the women, but did admit that they would like to receive it.

### Amrith

Nadia was unfortunately not available for the sixth field trip as she had by then qualified as a midwife, was married and was pregnant. I thus considered myself very fortunate to have Amrith offer to accompany me as my interpreter. We held a similar position in higher education and had studied together at undergraduate level.

My lasting memory of this field trip is of a huge, painful learning curve; being in a minority group, I realised just how uncomfortable a situation that is. My relationship with the women and the staff took a downward spiral as my confidence was sapped. I was no longer the one with the knowledge – someone else had that and possibly more understanding of the culture – but most importantly, she had the means of communicating it, in a warm, friendly, empathetic way. I felt helpless, and the very same useless invisibility that engulfed me as student midwife returned with a vengeance. The women looked through me to the person who could help the midwife, or in this case the interpreter, who was also a midwife.

A multitude of feelings and thoughts sprung from the uncomfortable position in which I found myself. I felt marginalised as the women grouped around Amrith. I felt a failure when I had to ask her to explain what the women were trying to say, and I knew that I was not needed for the answer as Amrith could give it. I experienced grave reservations about my role within the project. I had been happy with the communication through a non-informed interpreter or a student, who did not know as much as me – how inflated my ego must have been. This field trip made me think for the first time that it was not good enough. I had been selling the women and the staff short when what the women and the staff needed was what Amrith could give them and I could not. A mother must feel this way when her child is on a special care unit. I recognised my feelings as being those of jealousy: I wanted to help the women whom I had come to care for but I could not. I had compromised the women, given them second best, and they deserved more.

I recognised, however, that the culture would not allow Amrith to address the men (the bureaucrats) in the town as I did. I was able to challenge them and at times shame them into taking on their responsibilities, such as clearing the hospital drains and decorating the hospital. I had built a long-standing, trusting relationship with the staff at the hospital, and they often asked me why I did not stay longer or come more frequently. Perhaps my cultural difference could complement a partnership, if I could overcome my jealousy.

The partnership was not to be, however. I had detected reluctance from the twinning group when I proposed Amrith as my interpreter, their reluctance being based upon the issue of her coming from the Indian Punjab and on her religion as a Sikh. I told the group that they were bigots. However, I lost the bid to return with her, not because of Amrith's religion but on the issue of her not originating from Rochdale!

## Nasreen

Nasreen's father was a founder member of the twinning group and he proposed his second eldest daughter, Nasreen, to be the interpreter for the eighth field trip to Pakistan. My personal aim for this trip was to interview women on their birth experiences in Pakistan. I really did

need a reliable interpreter, and I knew that Nasreen was also a Registered Sick Children's Nurse (RSCN), which I initially saw as being
beneficial to the project. I had known Nasreen's mother and father for
many years as I had been their midwife for the last four of their 15
children. I was, however, suspicious of Nasreen's father's offer as I
knew that Nasreen had never visited Pakistan before. As such, I made
it very clear that she would not be able to spend time with her relatives
in Pakistan. I insisted that Nasreen come to visit us at home before I
agreed. Nasreen visited us a number of times. She was 25 years old,
both her RGN and RSCN had been completed in the north west of
England, and she had recently graduated with the Open University.

It was a shock when we met Nasreen, as she was articulate, very
forceful and politically opinionated. Her nervous, high-pitched laugh
belied her maturity, and she had a somewhat naïve perspective on life.
She jumped into a defensive paternalism with a protective stance
towards the Pakistani population of Rochdale without apparent provo-
cation. It was almost as if she did not believe us when we talked of
caring for the women in Pakistan. The source of this might have been
the strong 'caring' extended family network. Nasreen had a likeable
openness about her; she would joke with my husband but then sulk
like a teenager. We never knew what she was really thinking. I had
never come across a more complex young woman and wondered
whether this was a result of living in one culture and being educated
in another, yet Nadia had had an almost identical background but was
quite different. I came to the conclusion that this must have arisen
from personality and social differences. On reflection, I was disgusted
with myself for expecting them to be similar as it showed that I was
thinking in absolute categories, demonstrating what Rattansi (1992)
called a 'culturalist approach', which has the potential to collapse
diversity and complexity into a destructive stereotype.

It was Nasreen's expressed wish that we were not to let her out of
our sight in Pakistan as she herself was suspicious of her father's and
other relatives' intentions in Pakistan. We had discussed Nasreen's
role as interpreter, stating clearly my requirements during the trip. I
did not have to wait long before I saw the effect that Nasreen had
upon the relationship with the women. We hit a problem that had not
been anticipated during the very first interview. This was with an
older woman who did not speak any English. Following the introduc-
tions and purpose of the interview, as a part of the woman's 'life
story', I asked Nasreen to enquire how old the woman was when she
started menstruating. Nasreen turned to me indignantly and stated, 'I

can't ask her that, it would be disrespectful; she is my elder.' I was taken aback. We had discussed the interview questions and they contained more personal information on life and the birthing experience in general. How on earth was I going to conduct the interviews if the interpreter could not ask the questions? I explained to Nasreen that it was not she asking the questions but me; reluctantly, and with some embarrassment, the question was asked.

I had never experienced difficulty with the non-acceptance of young students caring for Pakistani women before. Thus, I had never considered the age of the interpreter or midwife relevant before this incident. However, I have since then read Gatrad's (1994) study on the attitudes and beliefs of Muslim mothers towards pregnancy, which confirms that Muslim labouring women prefer to have older female attendants. (This may contribute in part to the difficulty experienced in recruiting Pakistani student midwives.) The incident also made me realise the difference between asking a mother about her child (a familiar occurrence for Nasreen as a children's nurse) and asking a woman across a generation gap about personal matters. This also accentuates the bad practice of using a younger member of the family as interpreter.

Schott and Henley (1996:101) say that using children to translate matters that are distressing or highly personal can cause long-term damage to both the children and the family relationships. Yet I am ashamed to admit that, when there has been no other possible alternative, I have had to resort to seeking the help of relatives who have accompanied the women. Most parents wish to shield their child from distressing or sensitive information, as with the woman who was advised to abort her 'blessed child' (Rizwana, personal communication, 1998), whose eldest daughter, aged 15 years, accompanied her for the antenatal booking interview. When the question of consanguinity arose, the woman was embarrassed: she did not want her daughter to be influenced against her extended family wish and the norm of marrying her cousin.

### 'Get it over with'

A further difficulty with Nasreen's lack of understanding of midwifery and with her background was exposed when she stated that she could not see a problem with 'getting the labour over with as quickly as possible' and thought that induction and the use of oxytocin was 'modern midwifery practice'. All her brothers and sisters had been born during the 1970s and 80s, and she had under-taken her maternity placement during her RGN training in a regional high-technology maternity unit. Nasreen had grown up in a world steeped in the medicalised model of midwifery, with induction and intervention as the norm. I learned later that she considered me 'way out' and 'radical', much like the doctor at the maternity hospital in Pakistan, who judged my non-interventionist approach to be on a par with that of the untrained, uneducated *dai*.

One interview that stands out as being the most successful, in terms of really communicating with the woman and feeling the relationship between us build exponentially, was with a women whose husband was the gardener at our accommodation. On reflection, and with an analysis of the chemistry that gelled the relationship, a multitude of factors emerged. The key one over which I lingered was the accep-tance of the woman by Nasreen and vice versa. I feel that this came from the initial exchange of information prior to the interview when we explained the purpose of our being there, our personal interests and professional backgrounds, and, very importantly for this partic-ular interview, our personal backgrounds.

I had noticed in previous interactions, not just with interviewees, that Nasreen avoided answering the inevitable question 'What does your father do?, as well as the next most asked question of how many siblings she had. Whenever it could not be avoided, I always added to her almost whispered reply that I would have loved such a large family, sensing Nasreen's diffidence. There was undoubtedly a prickly defence reaction in Nasreen when she felt she had been cornered into replying. When we asked the gardener's wife how many siblings she had, her reply matched Nasreen's in both number and gender. There was an immediate snap of acceptance, a common empathic experiential bond. I had sensed and experienced this so clearly only once before, when observing a student midwife book a woman who had had a previous stillbirth, and the student saying, 'This also happened to me.' Thus, it was apparent to me, but too sensitive to discuss with Nasreen, that she had become ashamed of the size of her family, much as I am reluctant to 'tell the truth' about my daughter cohabiting with her boyfriend when I am questioned in Pakistan. It is almost as if I am confirming their belief that Western norms and values are decadent.

## Interpreter training

My experiences working with different interpreters, in both Rochdale and Pakistan, directed my thinking towards getting it right more often. To achieve this, specific training must be the key. I have been involved in the training of link workers who have a primary interpreter role. What information could or should not be given was a major theme in the training. Because of their link worker status, basic health care information on hygiene and child care, plus information on whom to contact and where, was included in the content of the training. The screening tests and the different pathways that women would tread through the childbearing continuum were covered in some depth, but the other very important elements of what to do with bad news and problems in translating medical terms were not addressed. The training also involved trying to get the interpreter to accompany the women through the antenatal clinic to act as their advocate. Despite clear directions, this has never been achieved. The reason given was that the interpreters wanted to be separate from the women and sit in the staff room until summoned by the midwife or doctor; this was a recognition of their status. Indeed, this training was superficial compared with that outlined by Solomon (1997), Zimmerman (1996) and Woloshin (1995) currently offered in some states in America. Although they identify the lack of nationwide standards for language interpreters, some states have training programmes and certification. Similarly, they further maintain that the goal of the medical interpretation should not be maintaining a distant neutrality but building a shared meaning.

Following training, Kaufert and Putsch (1997) suggest that interpreters should be given the freedom to interpret, to provide the additional context, to say more than the professional has said, or to ask questions of the health professional that *patients* may not have asked. These authors recognise the potential for harm, that is, crossing the line into inappropriate persuasion or how interpreters may avoid conveying critically important information, particularly if the message is considered rude or improper.

Wasongarz (1994), cited by Solomon (1997), recommends a 'transparency' rule. Such a rule requires the interpreters to explain to the health care professional whenever it is difficult to make the required translation, revealing what they have omitted, changed or added. On reflection, the relationship that developed with Nadia and myself embodied such transparency, and it is apparent that we had developed a practice standard that is validated by research. The responsibility now is to create an educational programme to disseminate this through education.

## Professional interpreter

It is possible, but may not be practical, to overcome some of the language and interpreter dilemmas by employing midwives (professionals) from the cultural group being served. However, to achieve this we would need successfully to recruit many more ethnic minority nurses and midwives. This would seem to be an oversimplistic solution to the problem as conflict may arise between the roles of midwife and interpreter.

French *et al.* (1994) examined factors that are influential in the choice of 'nursing' (as a lead-in to short midwifery programmes) as a career choice. They identified the importance of the family in any career decision-making. The primary reason identified within my own ongoing work (Chesney 1998a) points to the status of midwifery, not in Britain but in Pakistan, as an influencing factor. The bond between the branches of families in Britain and Pakistan is very strong. Thus, when a Pakistani family in Britain write to their relatives in Pakistan about their child's career aspirations, wanting to become a midwife is taken by the extended family as entering a lowly 'dirty' profession that no 'decent' family would condone. Another obstacle is the issue of unmarried Pakistani women being forbidden to discuss sexual activity or reproduction. Mumtaz and Rauf (1997), in their study of intergenerational knowledge transfer, found an imposed silence on issues of sexuality between generations.

Murphy and Macleod Clarke (1993) reported that health service staff consider cultural barriers to be largely of language origin only. They argue that staff are less likely to be aware of the structural constraints within which the communication operates. Such structural constraints include a uniculturally designed health service. Bowes and Domokos (1995) found other barriers, including gender, class and racialisation. Similarly, the King's Fund study (1990) of racial equality and the nursing profession found an overemphasis on culture and language, rather than equal opportunities and antiracism.

In the first instance, I considered the major issue inhibiting understanding to be the absence of a common language. I naïvely felt that if we communicated, women's needs could be met. However, following my experiences working with interpreters at home and in Pakistan, I now see that the issue is much more complex and needs to be addressed holistically. This could be demonstrated in a model using the onion skin analogy, with the core of culture or language being encircled by gender, age, class, personality, attitude and racialisation as the outer layers of the onion. To put this in context, each person has these (and more) layers as the organisation and environment will have their own; the complex whole is dynamic and may never be describable.

## Conclusion

Such was my ignorance that I practised hypocrisy and self-deception. Reviewing my past experiences caring for Pakistani women in Rochdale has enabled me to address my previous complacency, cultural blindness and imperialist approach to care. The spark that ignited the fire of change came from being deposited in the minority position myself. Unable to articulate my needs, being the lone *different* served as a shock to open my eyes and increase my awareness of how Pakistani women may feel receiving care from a British midwife imposing a British system of care. For the women in Rochdale, living in a strange country, passing through a major life event and being processed in a service not designed for them is surely bad enough, but to superimpose on this the inability to understand, or be understood, is persecution.

Moreover, there is a definite complacency surrounding the provision of care of ethnic groups in the NHS. This is evidenced by the lack of priority and resources to train link workers or interpreters. I have recognised that providing care through a third person, an (untrained) interpreter and/or a relative, increases exponentially the potential for problems. Caring for women across a language and cultural difference is beset with problems at the outset. Even if there is no language difference, the cultural values and norms related to childbirth are the strongest in any society. Some of the problems encountered have been uncovered in the text: conflict, power, control and ethnocentricity provide some evidence for the complexity of this area.

Care provided through a third person requires specialist knowledge and at least some training and preparation. In the UK, there is a void where this training should be. As a consequence, professionals and interpreters muddle through, much as I have done, and are lucky, as I have been, to get it somewhere near right the odd time. This is, however, not good enough; the women are casualties of this, and their lives and those of their families are affected by it. Good maternity care requires intimate and sensitive communication between women and those who care for them (Hayes 1995). To work effectively, however, the midwife may not be required to become an expert in the ethnocultural group, or the interpreter need not necessarily be a midwife. It is essential, however, to have cultural flexibility, acceptance and understanding, and to perceive the woman as an individual, as well as to develop a self-awareness and openness to cultural diversity in relation to our own beliefs, values and culture.

Interpretation needs may not be immediately evident, but communication is the key to the success or failure of the therapeutic relationship between midwife and woman. A woman's needs are, as stated, individual and unique to her. Thus communication needs will be broad and complex, but solutions must be found to provide the care that all women deserve. *The Patient's Charter* states 'there should be respect for privacy, dignity, religious and cultural beliefs' (Department of Health 1995:6). This care should undoubtedly encompass information so that choices can be made; the very best form of information is 'people attached' and context framed. Paper information should supplement this. It is, however, apparent that many sections of the community are denied both.

These are the key learning experiences that arose while working with professional, but untrained, interpreters. They demonstrate the uniqueness of and effect that each person has on the relationship with the other. When there is an interpreter, this will increases the potential for disharmony by a third, but, as I have suggested, one simple but unrealistic answer would be to have midwives who can communicate through a common language. Until such time, trained interpreters are an essential component of health care. Zimmerman (1996) identified an agenda for action, which involved three simple steps:

1. There is a need for a rigorous review of education with the development of a core component on ethnicity and health, race- and culture-specific health problems.

2. Models and frameworks of care need to be adaptable, and the assessment of need should include the use of a cultural assessment tool (Tripp-Reimer *et al.* 1964, Giger and Davidhizer 1990).

3. A rigorous programme of research is required to establish the needs of ethnocultural groups.

It is every policy-maker's and professional's responsibility to take Zimmerman's steps beyond the 'words' stage and into action.

## References

Balibar E (1991) Is There a 'Neo-racism'? In: Balibar E and Wallerstein I (eds) *Race, Nation, Class, Ambiguous Identities*. London: Verso.

Bowes AM and Domokos TM (1995) South Asian women and the GP: some issues of communication. *Social Sciences in Health* 1: 22–3.

Brooks G (1996) *Nine Parts of Desire: The Hidden World of Islamic Women*. Harmondsworth: Penguin.

Carrese JA (1995) Western bioethics on the Navajo Reservation, benefit or harm. *Journal of the American Medical Association* 274(10): 826–9.

Chesney M (1998a) *Birth Experiences in Pakistan*. MPhil/PhD dissertation, University of Sheffield.

Chesney M (1998b) Dilemmas of interviewing women from Pakistan. *Nursing Research* 5(4): 57–70.

Culley L (1997) Ethnicity, health and sociology in the nursing curriculum. *Social Science and Health* 3(1): 28–39.

Davies J (1997) The midwife in the northern regions homebirth survey. *British Journal of Midwifery* 5(4): 219–24.

Department of Health (1995) *The Patient's Charter*. London: HMSO.

Felema E and Teklemarian M (1992) Telling Bad News: An East African Perspective. Cited in Kaufert JM and Putsch RW (1997) Communication through interpreters in healthcare: ethical dilemmas arising from differences in class, culture, language and power. *Journal of Clinical Ethics* 8(1): 71–87.

Foucault M (1980) In Gordon (ed.) *Power/Knowledge: Selected Interviews and Other Writings, 1972–1977*. New York: Pantheon.

Freidson SET (1985) Approaches to the measurement of explanation and information giving in medical consultations: a review of empirical studies. *Social Science and Medicine* 18: 571–80.

French S, Watters D and Mathews RD (1994) Nursing as a career choice for women in Pakistan. *Journal of Advanced Nursing* 19: 140–51.

Gatrad AR (1994) Attitudes and beliefs of Muslim mothers towards pregnancy and infancy. *Archives of Disease in Childhood* 71: 170–4.

Giger JN and Davidhizer R (1990) Transcultural nursing assessment. A method for advanced nursing practice. *International Nursing Review* 37(1): 199–202.

Gillborn D (1995) *Racism and Anti-racism in Real Schools*. Oxford: Oxford University Press.

Halldorsdóttir S (1996) Caring and Uncaring Encounters in Nursing and Health Care – Developing a Theory. Linkoping University Medical Dissertations No. 493.

Hayes L (1995) Unequal access to midwifery care: a continuing problem. *Journal of Advanced Nursing* **21**: 702–9.

Kaufert JM and Koolage WW (1984) Role conflict among culture brokers. The experience of native Canadian medical interpreters. *Social Science and Medicine* **18**: 3283–6.

Kaufert JM and Putsch RW (1997) Communication through interpreters in healthcare: ethical dilemmas arising from differences in class, culture, language and power. *Journal of Clinical Ethics* **8**(1): 71–87.

King's Fund (1990) *King Edward's Hospital Fund for London. The Work of the Equal Opportunities Task Force 1986–1990. A Final Report.* London: King's Fund.

Leininger MM (1991) *Culture Care, Diversity and Universality: A Theory of Nursing.* New York: National League for Nursing Press.

Maslow A (1969) *The Psychology of Science.* New York: Harper & Row.

Mumtaz K and Rauf F (1997) Inter and Intra-generational Knowledge Transfer and Zones of Silence around Reproductive Health in Sunnakhi. In: Harcourt W (ed.) *Power, Reproduction and Gender.* . London: Zed.

Murphy K and Macleod Clarke J (1993) Nurses experiences of caring for ethnic minority clients. *Journal of Advanced Nursing* **18**: 442–550.

Rafiqul-Haqq M and Newton P (1996) *The Place of Women in Pure Islam.* http:debate.domini.org/newton/womeneng.html

Rattansi A (1992) *Racism, Modernity and Identity.* Cambridge: Polity Press.

Schott J and Henley A (1996) *Culture, Religion and Childbearing in a Multiracial Society. A Handbook for Health Professional.* Oxford: Butterworth Heinemann.

Solomon MZ (1997) From what's neutral to what's meaningful: reflections on a study of medical interpreters. *Journal of Clinical Ethics* **8**(1): 88–93.

Stubbs P (1993) 'Ethnically Sensitive' or 'Anti-racist'? Models for Health Research and Service Delivery. In: Ahmed W (ed.) *Race and Health in Contemporary Britain.* Buckingham: Open University Press.

Tripp-Reimer T, Brink T and Saunders JM (1984) Cultural assessment: content and process. *Nursing Outlook* **32**(2): 78–82.

Wasongarz D (1994) Bioethics and the Intermediary Role of Interpreter; Negotiating Language, Culture and Emotion. Presented at the Annual Meeting of the American Anthropological Association, Atlanta GA. Cited in Solomon MZ From what's neutral to what's meaningful: reflections on a study of medical interpreters. *Journal of Clinical Ethics* **8**(1): 88–93.

Woloshin S (1995) Language barriers in medicine in the United States. *Journal of the American Medical Association* **273**(9): 724–8.

Zimmerman PG (1996) Use of interpreters in the emergency department. *Journal of Emergency Nursing* **22**(3): 225–7.

# Chapter 8

# Midwives' Personal Experiences and their Relationships with Women: Midwives without Children

*Chris Bewley*

## Introduction

At some point in a midwife's professional relationship with a pregnant woman, the question 'Have you got children?' is almost inevitably asked. As a midwife who does not have children, I found myself thinking about how best I could answer the question without losing credibility and without feeling that I had to justify my childless state. When I was younger, people's responses were generally that I had plenty of time, or they speculated on whether seeing many women in labour had put me off. As I got older, and it became obvious that I was of an age when pregnancy was unlikely, I noticed that women responded in a different way when I answered 'no' to their question. I could almost see them wondering why, and it was sometimes difficult for me not to feel I had to tell them why. I also noticed that the nature of the question changed as I got older, and was more likely to be 'How many children have you got?', the assumption obviously being that I was a mother.

Once the question had raised itself and I noticed the effects it had on my relationships with women, even if on only a temporary basis, I began to observe how other midwives reacted in response to the question. I was particularly interested since many of my midwife colleagues had quite sad obstetric and reproductive histories. One had a long history of infertility and desperately wanted a family. Another, after many years of infertility, conceived only to find that she had a ectopic pregnancy. Yet another had a termination of pregnancy for gross fetal abnormality, and another had a baby with a chromosomal abnormality who only lived a few hours. On one occasion, I was with a community midwife whose preterm baby had died at only a few hours old and we were visiting a woman who had given birth to twins, one of whom had died. The midwife was extremely supportive, and at one point in the conversation the woman asked her 'Have you got children?' The midwife replied 'No', but I wondered how she felt and I realised what a loaded question 'Have you got children?' is. How do midwives respond when they have had a baby and something has happened to it? Do they spend their days being constantly reminded of their loss? Do they feel they have to tell women that they have shared the birth experience but that their baby died? How do they relate to women, and what happens to that relationship when such intense emotions are involved?

Flint (1989) suggests that some midwives treat women insensitively and that much of this thoughtless treatment arises from the unresolved grief of childless midwives. She also offers this as a reason for the unkind treatment of young midwives by their older, childless colleagues. Walton (1994:113) comments that 'women on the whole, prefer the midwife to be a mother'. These sweeping statements are made confidently by Flint and Walton, women who have children, operating from an apparent power base of knowledge and privilege. They may be sincere and compassionate in their call for midwives to be supportive of one another, but they imply that midwives who do not have children are somehow lacking.

Gaskin (1994) suggests that midwifery training does not place sufficient emphasis on the midwife's personal life experiences and their potential effects on the midwife–mother relationship. Thomas (1994:2) asks 'What do midwives bring to the birth arena?', observing that life issues that affect a proportion of women, such as eating disorders, sexual abuse, depression, domestic abuse, stillbirth and homosexuality, must, by their widespread existence, impact on the personal lives of some midwives. She comments that very little work has been done on the psychodynamic nature of the midwife–mother relationship, speculating that a failure to explore oneself conceals good or bad influences that midwives may bring to their practice.

With the above in mind, this chapter considers how midwives' personal obstetric and reproductive experiences impact on the midwife–mother relationship, using information gained from an in-depth study of six midwives who do not have children. As will be seen, the respondents and their backgrounds were very different from what was anticipated. The study revealed, among other things, that the issue of being a midwife without children is important, not only to those who have had adverse reproductive experiences, but also to those midwives who have not yet tested their fertility. What follows is a brief description of the study design and methodology, a presentation of the findings, and a discussion of issues raised in conjunction with the available literature.

The study was formulated to determine how midwives without children deal with the everyday experience of being with mothers, babies and families, and how their childlessness affects their relationships with women. The term 'childless' is used throughout the chapter, although I am aware that for some midwives without children, 'childfree' is more appropriate. That term does not, however, apply to the midwives in the study, and using 'childless' is less clumsy than repeating the phrase 'midwives who do not have children'.

## Study design

The chosen research method was phenomenology. Phenomenology concentrates on the lived experience of individuals, recognising the reality of the situation to the person who has undergone it and valuing it as that individual's truth. It does not seek to generalise findings but to describe and interpret them. In this study, midwives without children are not considered a homogenous social group for whom an explicated social structure is sought. Phenomenology is congruent with the heterogeneity of these midwives, allowing a recognition of the uniqueness of each midwife's perception while acknowledging the spatial, temporal and sensate limitations of experience. It is, therefore, concerned with ontology – the study of being. In this case, it is used to study the experience of being a midwife without children.

### Credibility

The use of phenomenology as a research method in nursing and midwifery has increased over the past 10 years, but some researchers feel that credibility is being damaged as researchers adopt a 'mishmash' of qualitative methods under the umbrella of phenomenology

(Omery 1983, Morse 1991, Baker *et al.* 1992, Taylor 1993). All the writers mentioned call for a strict differentiation between phenomenology and other qualitative methodologies. While the debates and critiques are valid, the justification for the use of phenomenology becomes a complex philosophical defence.

In view of these criticisms, I turned to the original philosophical work of Heidegger, a student of Edmund Husserl, the so-called father of phenomenology. Heidegger's work is a vast, philosophical treatise spanning many years, which examines the nature of being and time. Heidegger's work is creative, visionary and imaginative; his thoughts are boundless, yet explained with academic rigour. When language becomes insufficient to express his thoughts, however, he makes up his own expressions and gives words new meanings, which he then has to explain. His work forms much of the thinking behind existentialism and should be considered a way of philosophising rather than a philosophy with fixed, unmoveable boundaries (MacQuarrie 1977). The Heideggerian approach involves description and interpretation to cast new light on taken-for-granted situations and meanings.

Phenomenology does not seek to generalise its findings and places importance on credibility rather than validity and reliability. In phenomenology, only the participants can validate their statements (Baker *et al.* 1992). Further validation may, however, occur when others reading the study recognise their own experiences and say 'Oh, yes! That's exactly what happened to me' (Brink 1991). This may or may not lead to generalisability.

### Framework for data collection and analysis

Hycner (1985) suggests that the emergence of highly structured frameworks for data analysis in phenomenology represents attempts to legitimise its use in areas such as psychology, nursing and midwifery, which traditionally revere a rationalistic approach to research. There is debate over whether such a restricting approach is congruent with the philosophy of phenomenology, in which the experience of the informants should dictate the direction that the study takes (Oiler 1982, Omery 1983, Hycner 1985). To fulfil the need for some form of academic rigour, however, a simple guiding framework devised by Collaizzi with input from Hycner (1985), and modified by Beck (1992), was used. Thus the study design was formulated to reconcile the philosophical underpinnings of phenomenology with the need for an academically rigorous framework.

## Selection of participants

Participants were recruited from a team of 18 qualified midwives working in a hospital but rotating on a daily basis to all practice areas. A maximum of six midwives was sought as this was felt to be manageable by one researcher within the timeframe available. Inclusion criteria were that participants should be practising midwives who did not have children and were available for interview during the months of December 1994 and January 1995. Thus, the sample was purposive and self-selected. There was no way I could know in advance what the reproductive experiences of team members was, so an invitation letter was sent to every midwife in the team. Ethical approval was gained and specialist counsellors were available for debriefing and follow-up counselling if required.

Data collection occurred by tape-recorded interview in a location of the participant's choice and was conducted using non-directive, active listening techniques (Rogers 1967). Interviews were transcribed as soon as possible after the interview.

From the transcripts, the essence of the individual's experience had to be elicited by 'reduction'. The issue of reduction is interesting – it is not reductionist, as in rationalistic research, but is rather like the process by which thousands of tons of flower petals are reduced to essential oils (Bewley 1995). Reduction involved reading each transcript through in its entirety. Significant statements and phrases relating to midwives' reproductive status and its perceived effect on practice and relationships were extracted. These significant statements were re-read and meanings formulated from them. Transcripts and formulated meanings were shown to the participants and discussed to ensure that the reduction of their lived experience to an essence had been faithfully carried out.

## The participants

The six participants were Hannah, Jenny, Catherine, Sarah, Mary and Rosie. They were all in their mid-twenties to early thirties and, with the exception of Rosie, were unaware whether their childlessness was temporary or permanent as they had not yet 'tested' their fertility. Rosie had been diagnosed as being infertile and knew that she could not have children.

## Findings

Following an analysis of the data, the formulated meanings were grouped together in theme clusters, from which three main headings with subheadings were noted:

● 'Have you got children?'
● Expertise versus experience
● Prospective motherhood.

The findings are presented here under their respective headings.

### *'Have you got children?'*

All the midwives confirmed that they were frequently asked whether they had children and thought that they were asked for a number of reasons, the question operating at a number of levels. Some saw it as a social question, developing the mother–midwife relationship by seeking common ground. Mary recognised that women look for kindness and sympathy, and wondered whether women think that having had a child makes midwives more sympathetic. Others felt that their credibility as a midwife was being challenged and wondered whether the question was asked to determine that the midwife was 'suitably qualified' in the woman's eyes if she had not experienced childbirth herself.

Rosie, who knew that she could not have children, cited instances of aggressive attacks on her credibility as a midwife because she did not have any. One concerned the mother of a labouring woman:

> She was very forceful and direct… she says 'How can you look after women in labour without any children?'… she went on and on for twenty minutes, half an hour… really personal, really digging.

On another occasion when a partner asked whether she had children and she said no:

Then she [the labouring woman] pipes up, 'Then how the **** can she look after me?'

Sarah felt that women need reassurance that, even though the midwife has not experienced labour, she will believe what women tell her, particularly in relation to the pain they experience. She further suggested that women who do not have children are viewed by society as being odd, and she sought to distance herself from them by assuring women that she wanted children in the future.

Despite some midwives' comments that the question 'Have you got children?' is a chatty, social, getting to know you question, some also saw it as being of a personal nature. Rosie, who could not have children, said:

When they ask me about children they're asking my person, not my profession, my Being.

Although all the midwives answered no to the question, the nature of their response varied. Where she thought that there was perceived doubt about her credibility as a midwife, Catherine had developed answers designed to assure women that she was an experienced and competent midwife:

I always say I have been a midwife for a long time... I tell them which areas I've worked in... I tell them I'm doing a further course... and they think oh, she must know.

Despite feeling that her credibility was challenged, Rosie made the point that her professional knowledge was, to her, the most important element and no amount of challenging could take that away.

Some were clearly unhappy at issuing a direct and unqualified no and felt they had to justify their childlessness. Jenny said:

I usually say, no, not yet, I feel too young.

Mary was unhappy at just saying no but was unsure what else to say:

I feel sometimes I should make a bit of a joke, but I think, no, that's not the right answer.

For some of the midwives, however, making a joke or giving a light-hearted answer was exactly how they dealt with the need to say more than just no. Hannah said:

> I say no, I've got enough babies here, I don't need any more, and they take that as a funny gesture and laugh.

Rosie also joked, but her joking had evolved after much thought and some difficult conversations with couples. Rosie found out quite suddenly at the age of 26 that she could not have children. The underlying condition that rendered her infertile did not require her to have time off work, so she returned to work on the labour ward in a state of grieving and sensitivity. She was initially unsure how to respond when asked whether she had children but found that if she told the truth about her condition, she was overwhelmed by the sympathetic reaction of the people she was supposed to be caring for, and the caring roles were reversed. Like some of the other midwives, she felt that she could not say no without justifying her answer, and she became defensive in her responses. She felt that her infertility created a barrier between her and the people she looked after, and she gradually evolved a joking response with replies such as:

> 'Do you think I'm mad' or 'Do you think I'm crazy!' I want to sleep every night for the rest of my life.

and

> I just laugh [when they ask], I haven't got children, don't be silly, try to keep it light, have a laugh.

The joking fulfilled the need to maintain herself as the carer rather than the cared-for:

> It [the joking] protects me. It's very strong this need to be protected from their sympathy.

Rosie acknowledged the barrier created by her infertility, but she also acknowledged that joking created its own barrier:

> They laugh, just in response, but there's this unspoken thing that says...
> don't ask me any more about this because that subject's closed and it's a
> defence thing.

Hannah also realised that making a joke had a definite effect on the
conversation:

> When I say no, I have enough here to look after, they sort of laugh, they
> don't talk about it any more, it's just dead – that's it.

Thus responding to the question with the answer no seemed to
require some sort of justification, involving a personal statement,
whereas joking prevented further discussion without the need for self-
disclosure on the part of the midwife.

### Expertise versus experience

Some of the midwives differentiated between the midwifery expertise
gained from attending many births and the personal experiences of
women who had given birth. They recognised that the personal
experience could enhance practice, but they also recognised that
midwives who had given birth could be capable of making assumptions that their own experience was universal.

Rosie felt that midwives who had children were less committed to
the profession than those who did not, and she put this down to the
intense emotional commitment of motherhood.

Some of the midwives tried to learn from the birth experiences of
their friends, the women they attended at work and their midwifery
colleagues. Sarah, however, felt threatened when midwives discussed
their personal experiences and the effects that their own pregnancies
and childbirth had had on their practice:

> I feel a bit envious and it makes me feel threatened, as though I don't know
> what I'm doing or I can't understand.

The issue of not having children was powerful; some midwives
cited instances of their colleagues lying to women when asked
whether they had children, by saying yes when they actually did not
have children.

Although Rosie could not have children, her jokes gave a misleading picture to the couples she cared for, implying that she was childless by choice:

> I can look them straight in the eye and lie... the choice is mine and as far as they are concerned I have made the decision not to have children.

Rosie wondered whether her responses ensured her control of the relationship:

> Although it's always taken as a joke... there's a hidden agenda... by responding the way I do, I'm trying to gain some superiority over them. It's almost as if I've done a 180 degree turn, 'I wouldn't have children if you could give them to me.' It's as though 'I'm better than you because I've chosen not to have children.' I haven't, but they don't know that.

This bending of the truth has the effect of giving the midwife the upper hand. As with Rosie's misleading responses, the midwife's withholding of information, or her selective disclosure, maintains her control of the relationship.

### Prospective motherhood

The midwives in the study felt that it was important to assure women that they fully intended to have children in the future. Sarah felt strongly that women who choose not to have children are somehow viewed as deviant and abnormal by society, and she wanted to distance herself from that.

When midwives told women and their partners that they did not have children, they were often met with the response, 'I suppose this has put you off', and they went to great lengths to emphasise that the reason they did not have children had nothing to do with witnessing women in labour.

All the midwives except Rosie discussed prospective pregnancies. Being too young was the reason that most of the midwives gave for putting off their decision to have children. They had a 'magic age' for themselves that they considered the optimum time for them to have a baby, and most of them made comments to the effect that they were 'not ready' to have children. It also seemed that, for some, as they approached the magic age, it became higher:

Maybe I'll decide that I want to have a family but I'll wait until I'm 35...
it was 32 but now I'm getting nearer to it it's gone up.

In spite of their responses, all the midwives were of an age when
they could well have had children and were certainly midwives with
considerable experience and expertise, often caring for women much
younger than themselves.What was clear was that although some felt
that there was a right time to have children, it was not now!

The issue of age also arose in other circumstances. Hannah was
particularly conscious of her youth although she was, in fact, 25.
These are some of the significant statements she made:

A lot of people say 'you're very young – midwives are old'.

My dentist said I was too young to be a midwife.

My boyfriend says to me, do people say you're too young to be a midwife?

Jenny, aged 28, told of one 18-year-old she looked after in labour who
asked if she was 'old enough to be doing this'.

Catherine (in her early thirties) also perceived herself to be too
young looking to be a midwife or a mother. She told me about an
older colleague saying that she had children when she did not. I asked
Catherine if she would ever do that, and she said:

If I said that they'd look at me and think I look too young.

Some spoke of the expectations and pressures of society and their
families on them to have children. They differentiated, however,
between pregnancy and childbirth as experiences, and the long-term
commitment of parenting. Most felt that they would like to experience
childbirth, and they expressed wonder at the reproductive process.
Some had actually imagined their labours, often in terms of pain, but
they viewed the long-term responsibilities of parenthood differently.

Rosie's thoughts about herself and children had undergone a
change as she came to terms with her infertility. She felt powerful
emotions towards babies and expressed empathy for women who
actually abduct babies because of such emotion. She did not feel bitter
about being childless but occasionally found herself thinking about
the injustice of babies born to women who did not want them or who
abused them.

At this stage in her life, Rosie felt able to admire babies and then give them back to their parents without any sadness. Her loss of prospective motherhood had obviously had a profound influence on her as a person, and as a midwife, but she concludes that:

> There are other things in life, this [having children] isn't the be all and end all.

The midwives' observations seem to relate to the formation of caring relationships, power bases within these relationships and the use of humour, truth and self-disclosure in caring relationships. It is also important to consider the pressures on women to conform to society's views on motherhood, and on women's own views of themselves as prospective mothers. Additionally, the issue of credibility as a midwife arises in connection with age and with having borne children, which may arise from the lay perception of midwives.

## Discussion

In phenomenology, the emphasis is on description and interpretation. The findings from the study form the descriptive component, and, from there, literature was searched in order to shed light on and interpret what the midwives had revealed. Literature was searched under the following headings:

- Motherhood and status of women as mothers in society
- Formation of caring relationships
- Age, motherhood and midwifery.

### *Motherhood and status of women as mothers in society*

Much is written about motherhood as women's natural function and biological destiny (Ong 1986). In many societies, women are defined by their biological ability to give birth. Thus, for some, the inability to reproduce renders them nameless and pariahs within their cultural group. In the Western world, Woollett (1991) suggests that today's climate is pronatalist. Despite recommendations on family spacing and the avoidance of 'unwanted' pregnancy, the emphasis is on having a child, or children, but not too many.

The dominant cultural view of motherhood as life fulfilment for women is reinforced by its idealisation. Bartlett (1994) discussed the idolatry of the Virgin Mary and the Christ Child in the Christian religion, suggesting that all new mothers are subsumed into a hagiography. Pictures of new mothers are sentimentalised and shot in soft focus lighting, no real credence being given to the underlying emotional and physical upheaval that childbirth and childrearing bring. Despite the fact that some mothers beat their children, starve them physically and emotionally, and neglect them, their status as women is valued and their existence as women confirmed (Ong 1986). In contrast, society views women without children in very different ways.

Pfeffer (1993) observes that assumptions are made about childless women: either that they are in control of their fertility or that, if they are married, they are infertile and to be pitied. She suggests that involuntary childlessness within a heterosexual relationship brings forth images of the 'dark and irrational side of nature', which she equates with the biblical concept of the barren woman and the barren land. As Bartlett (1994) observes, the word 'barren', with its meanings of aridity, emptiness and uselessness, is only ever used when describing infertile women or land on which crops will not grow; it is never used when describing impotent or sterile men. This emphasises the view that the sole expression of women's entity is denied them if they are infertile.

It is not only involuntarily childless women who are viewed with pity and suspicion. Bartlett (1994) studied groups of childless women in the UK and suggested that, in popular terms, voluntarily childless women fall into two categories: the 'sad spinster' and the neurotic 'career bitch'.

The selfishness of voluntarily childless women is echoed in other work. Childless women are selfish because they refuse to babysit for their friends (Dowrick and Grundberg 1980), because they have a higher disposable income and spend it (Webb 1986), or because they diet and exercise to fit into skin tight clothes whereas mothers diet and exercise in order to live long enough to see their children grow up (Morell 1994).

Morell (1994) studied 40 women in the USA who were voluntarily childless, ranging in age from 40 to 70 years. Many of them spoke of their difficulties and the constant need they felt to justify their childlessness. They had evolved strategies for responding to the question

'Have you got children?' in which they sought to refute popularly held assumptions that they were selfish, thoughtless child-haters.

The literature suggests, then, that motherhood is seen as a desirable state for women and that childlessness, for whatever reason, leads to bitterness, self-recrimination and selfishness. How does this relate to the midwives in the study?

Sarah talked about women who do not want children as being deviant or abnormal, and, as the above shows, this view is widely endorsed. The midwives in this study also spoke of their desire to be seen as 'normal' in the eyes of the women they cared for, part of this normality being that, apart from Rosie, they fully intended to become mothers themselves.

Bartlett (1994) analysed the decision process that women follow in their reproductive careers and documented the transitional period in a woman's life during which she has the capacity to chose whether or not to have children. During this transition, her fertility is untested; as far as she knows, the choice is hers. The removal of that choice led to responses from women indicating that they grieved, not only for the loss of the children they could not have, but also for the loss of choice. As one pointed out, when so much of the female identity is invested in motherhood, at least those who are childless by choice can boost their femininity by making the point that they could have had children had they wanted.

Woollett (1991), however, observed that for some women who were voluntarily childless, self-disclosure involved running the risk of disapproval, accusations of selfishness and a criticism of affluence consequent on not having children. Rosie, in her infertile condition, sought to protect herself by implying that she was childless by choice. This was, to her, preferable to the pity, also documented by Woollett (1991), that she experienced when she disclosed that she was infertile.

The responses that the midwives in the study gave to women when discussing their reproductive futures were not the same as they gave to me and, in Rosie's case, not the same as she would give to a colleague if asked. Argyle (1990) and Goffman (1976) studied relationships in which deception is used to avoid censure from other parties for behaviour or views that are not approved of. Given the above discussion on the status of childless women, it is hardly surprising that midwives sought to confirm their normality and estab-lish common ground with the women for whom they cared.

In Britain, where the majority of midwives are female, there is a potential for a shared, lived experience between woman and midwife, but evidence of this shared experience must be elicited by questioning on the part of the woman and disclosure on the part of the midwife. There is nothing immediately evident that marks out mothers from non-mothers.

## Formation of caring relationships

Argyle (1990) suggests that self-disclosure is important in the formation of relationships and that people who self-disclose are well liked, as long as what they disclose is acceptable. As previous discussion has suggested, childlessness is not necessarily accepted in society, and, on the whole, the midwives were questioned about their childlessness rather than disclosing it. A parallel may be drawn with women who conceal from midwives behaviours that may be considered unacceptable, such as smoking, drinking, substance abuse or being abused by a partner.

This accords with Goffman's (1976) assertion that self-presentation may include deception in order to maintain face and status. The midwives thought their childlessness less important than their midwifery skills. Their joking responses prevented a further discussion of childlessness, yet they employed self-disclosure to confirm their professional competence. In this way, the midwives maintained control over the agenda of topics that could be discussed and, in Rosie's case, protected her from the sympathy that she found inappropriate in her professional relationships with women.

Kirkham (1986) has written widely on the subject of communication in labour, showing how midwives use one-line *non sequiturs* to halt conversations and maintain control of the situation, Similarly, the childless midwives in this study prevented further enquiry on the subject of their childlessness by joking. Kirkham suggests that, by responding to women with phrases that cause them to be silent, we are effectively telling them to 'shut up'. However, as the next section of the discussion shows, some sources consider that humour is an acceptable means of avoiding self-disclosure and maintaining control.

Writers on humour (Mulkay 1988, Fox 1990, Sumners 1990) agree that humour may be used in a positive way to convey kindness and affection, and to relieve tension. Conversely, it may be used aggressively to ridicule, belittle or embarrass. Humour used in social interactions, as opposed to being created simply for fun and entertainment, is termed 'applied humour', and this is the nature of the humour used by the midwives in the study.

A byproduct of humour is laughter; Argyle (1990) discusses the functions of smiling and laughter in social interactions, suggesting that the human smile has evolved from the 'bared teeth scream' of lower primates. This gesture is one of submission, and Argyle suggests that in humans, smiling and laughter convey a message of non-aggression.

Similarly, perhaps, the midwives in this study joked to illustrate that they did not have children, but that they were caring and not representative of popular views on childless women. They were also able to send out the message 'Don't ask me about this any more' in a way that did not embarrass the couple. Whatever the reason, the result was the same, that the midwives retained control of the conversation and thereby the relationship.

Hugman (1991) suggests that power and control are linked to knowledge, documenting a hierarchy of knowledge in which specific forms of knowledge are systematically discredited by the dominant professional group. He cites the subordination of midwifery knowledge to that of obstetricians, a view further endorsed by Dalmiya and Alcoff (1993), who suggest that midwifery knowledge has been relegated to a series of 'old wives' tales'. Within this hierarchy of knowledge, pregnant and labouring women's knowledge, although first hand and experiential, has traditionally occupied an even lower position.

Kirkham (1986) suggests that pregnancy (other than that deemed deviant, for example teenage pregnancy) constitutes a state of absolute approval in society because it embodies all that is natural for womanhood. Pregnant women may draw on a personal knowledge of motherhood that is approved and endorsed by society as woman's biological destiny. The midwives in the study confirmed their admiration and fascination with the state of pregnancy and speculated on the increased knowledge that their own pregnancy would bring to their midwifery practice. For women, however, the power that ensues from a first-hand knowledge of pregnancy and an enhanced status in society must be balanced against systems and attitudes that have historically devalued and disempowered them.

Hunt and Symond's (1995) ethnographic study of midwives documents many instances of midwives belittling women by expressing disbelief at their statements and suggesting that women's observations about their own bodies were to be doubted and had to be checked against professional expertise. It seems that midwives and others who care for labouring women assert their professional knowledge over the 'natural' knowledge of women, establishing their knowledge as being superior in the hierarchy to which women must concede power. For the midwife without children, professional knowledge and expertise occupy a higher status in the knowledge–power hierarchy, but the childless midwife has an experiential knowledge deficit.

This may place her at a disadvantage, by calling into question her authority, but it also places her at a disadvantage as a women who has not (yet?) fulfilled her biological destiny. The asking of a personal question in what is essentially a professional relationship throws the midwife into a complex situation of protecting her person, her Being, and re-establishing her professionalism. In that momentary interchange, it would seem that, in a hierarchy of power, the woman who has children occupies a higher status than the childless midwife, with all her professional knowledge.

When Walton (1994:113) states that having children makes the midwife an 'equal' to the women for whom she cares, she is, albeit unconsciously, implying that there is an imbalance in the relationship consequent on the midwife's childlessness. In order to be equal, both parties must be on the same level so, in Walton's terms, who is superior? Is the midwife brought down to the woman's level or raised up to it? According to Walton, childless midwives would say that this makes no difference to the way in which they care for women; Walton implies that she knows better!

Morell's (1994) study draws on feminism and post-structuralism to construct an argument against the dominant discourses of childlessness. The women in Morell's study did not confine themselves to one-line responses that blocked further discussion; instead they formulated complex statements that affirmed their belief in themselves and their choices. Rather than being defensive and overcompensatory, Morell suggests that these responses reverse the dominant discourses and lead to the production of alternative forms of knowledge. She calls for childless women, by their affirmation that childlessness is not to be pitied as the 'vacant opposite of motherhood', to seize power rather than wait for it to be conferred (Morell 1994:59).

While the midwives in the study identified that their childlessness could place them at an experiential disadvantage, they recognised another factor that some of them felt was a disadvantage – their age.

## Age, motherhood and midwifery

The issue of age arose a number of times. There were conflicting and ambiguous meanings associated with the midwives' use of terms such as 'young' and 'old', which suggest that they meant something other than, or in addition to, biological age. The midwives made links between age, motherhood and midwifery competence. With these three areas in mind, the literature was searched to determine what, if any, these links were.

Qualifications for midwifery vary world wide. Priya (1992) speculated on whether suitability for midwifery practice should relate to the candidates' personal experience of birth or to their academic ability. Donnison (1988), however, pointed out that, even until the end of the seventeenth century in Europe, the major requirements for a midwife were maturity and maternity. She suggested that, nowadays, 'direct entry' midwives are generally older and usually married with children, so that their experience of childbearing equips them to give women 'better understanding and care' (Donnison, 1988:206). Once again, the inference is that women who are older and who have children will be better midwives.

Kirkham (1986) suggests that the skill of 'grounding' a labour in the minute-by-minute observation of a woman is more likely to be evident in 'older, experienced midwives' (Kirkham 1986:42). She also suggests (1989) that midwives tend to infantilise the women for whom they care, particularly in labour, and she describes how midwives may be seen as mother figures in the immediate postpartum period when new mothers have much to learn. What, then, is the difference between a mother and a mother figure? Does a mother figure always have to be a biological mother? Can the attributes of a mother exist in a woman who is childless? How do these attributes relate to midwives, and do they relate to the age of the midwife?

Of all the midwives in the study, Rosie in particular talked about how, as she grew older, she would respond to questions about her childlessness in a different way and how people would view her differently as she aged. She felt that people would see her as a mother figure. This is an irony in that she cannot be a mother, yet it suggests that there is a difference between being a biological mother and a mother figure.

Morell (1994:125) suggested that there are forms of mothering other than biological motherhood. She cited the African–American women who use the term 'blood mothers, other mothers and community other mothers'. Rich (1976) called for motherhood to be viewed as a continuum based on women's emotional and physical relationships with children and babies. Midwives would thus fall into the category of 'other mothers'. They have close relationships with childbearing women and with babies, and in the mother–midwife relationships they may be cast in a mothering role.

The links between age, mothering and midwifery are complex yet indeterminate, perhaps hinging on the expectations of society of mothers and others who adopt a nurturing role. Unger and Crawford (1992) distinguish between the ideal of the mother, which is socially constructed, and the reality of motherhood. Perhaps the view of midwives as mother figures represents a continuing search for the socially constructed ideal.

### Strengths and limitations of the study

This study is undoubtedly limited, and any recommendations for practice or education should not rely solely on the findings from this small group. One of the study's strengths, however, lies in the interest that it has generated on the part of the participants and all those who have heard about it. From the point of view of midwives without children, it seems to be an unexplored area about which they are keen to talk. One of the strengths, therefore, is the identification of a new and perhaps important topic.

Given that the intention was to study a selection of midwives, the final range of experiences was limited and, other than Rosie, who was infertile, did not include midwives whose pregnancy and childbirth experiences had left them childless, or those who had opted to be child free. This is not to devalue the input of the participants since it is clearly an important topic for those who fully anticipate having children at a later date. Whatever research approach is used, a wider range of age and experience in the respondents is, however, needed, and a larger, national study is currently in progress.

Above all, in the study, the approach of the midwives to the women for whom they cared was based on the desire to understand and accept in the absence of their own experiences. Apart from Rosie, their responses indicate that their childlessness was expected to be temporary, and, the literature suggests, they were not alone among the female population of the Western world in their anticipation of pregnancy. However, slightly fewer than 10 per cent of couples in the UK are affected by infertility (Condy 1995), and 1 in 5 women in Britain do not want children (Condy 1995). These statistics begin to challenge the view that motherhood is woman's biological destiny. How, then, does this impact on midwives and midwifery practice?

The Second Report of the Expert Maternity Group (Department of Health 1993) lays great emphasis on the formation of good relationships with women. The midwives in this study had not, apart from Rosie, given much thought to their status as women without children caring for childbearing women, or to how that would impinge on the relationships they formed. If, as the literature suggests, women would prefer to be cared for by midwives who have had children, what are the implications for midwifery recruitment and education? If we purport to be consumer led, and want to give choice to women, should we explore their views on the subject? Perhaps an important area for research is women's perceptions of midwives and the expectations they have of them in terms of professional and personal experience. As an area for further research, this would be interesting yet fraught with methodological problems.

A recent questionnaire from the Royal College of Midwives (1995) formed part of a study aimed at changing midwifery to achieve woman-centred care. One of the questions invited midwives to strongly agree or strongly disagree with the statement 'Motherhood has made me a better midwife.' The phrasing is interesting; if a midwife had begun her career when she already had children, how could she know what sort of midwife she would have been without them? Furthermore, there is no question suggesting that midwives may think that not having children has made them better midwives.

Childbirth, for the women who experience and for those who witness it, is a time of great emotion, when some of the most elemental human feelings are evoked: pain, fear, loss of control, help-lessness, as well as joy and a sense of fulfilment. An unpublished study by Williams (cited in Simms *et al.* 1994) suggests that childless student midwives early in their training were distressed by seeing women in labour. Work by Kitzinger (1992) suggests that the birth experience triggers memories of sexual abuse and rape, and brings carers of women in labour into direct confrontation with their sexuality. It is difficult and purely speculative to wonder how students deal with their emotions in a way that enables them to function. The routinised care described by Menzies (1981) as a defence against anxiety is disappearing from the maternity services, but there is no supporting mechanism to replace it.

The progress and successful outcome of labour are not governed solely by physiology. The input of the midwife and other carers can directly influence the labouring woman, suggesting that midwives must be free of emotional baggage. In programmes of education for midwives, it would seem appropriate to consider preparing students to cope with the question 'Have you got children?' Perhaps they can be helped to avoid the joking responses that serve to halt conversation. They should be helped to formulate responses with which they are comfortable and which do not alienate women.

A strong call for emotional support for midwives comes from Thomas (1994), a psychotherapist specialising in pregnancy and childbirth. Thomas suggests a scheme of co-counselling for midwives. This would provide a supportive strategy, but would need input from suitably trained counsellors in the first place; as Thomas points out, poor counselling can do more harm than no counselling at all.

All midwives should take care, in conversation and in writing, to avoid sweeping statements suggesting that midwives without children are less well equipped to provide understanding care. Perhaps they are, but what should they do if their childlessness is voluntarily or involuntarily permanent? Are they expected to leave the profession? Midwives with and without children need to explore the nature of the client–midwife relationship and to realise how the personal and professional aspects overlap.

Gaskin (1994) makes a plea for openness and acceptance among all midwives, mothers or otherwise so that extremes of views can be accommodated in a cherishing atmosphere. In this way, she maintains that polarisation of opinion will be avoided and all midwives will be valued for their varying knowledge and experience.

## Conclusion

There is some indication that being a midwife without children raises issues that are unconnected with an adverse outcome of pregnancy but are clearly important for the midwives concerned. I have heard subsequently that the midwives in the study group derived benefit from their interviews and chose to reveal to their colleagues that they took part, despite my assurance that I would maintain confidentiality. I certainly valued their open discussion of sensitive and personal issues.

From the initial study, a further study has now been completed (Bewley, 2000) recruiting from a much wider group and using a questionnaire format. Once again, the response has been rapid, suggesting that there is a need for an exploration of the midwife's personal experience and its effects on the midwife–mother relationship. Greater recognition is needed of how the midwife's experiences as a woman can influence the relationships she forms with pregnant and labouring women, and how those life experiences can act in negative and positive ways. The emphasis should be on helping midwives come to terms with their feelings about themselves and their reproductive lives in ways that leave both feeling emotionally whole.

# References

Argyle M (1990) *The Psychology of Interpersonal Behaviour*. Harmondsworth: Penguin.

Baker C, Wuest J, and Stern PN (1992) Method slurring: the grounded theory/phenomenology example. *Journal of Advanced Nursing* **17**: 1355–60.

Bartlett J (1994) *Will You Be Mother: Women Who Choose to Say No*. London: Virago.

Beck CT (1992) The lived experience of post partum depression: a phenomenological study. *Nursing Research* **41**(3): 166–70.

Bewley C (1995) Clinical teaching in midwifery; an exploration of meanings, attitudes and perceptions. *Nurse Education Today* **15**: 129–35.

Bewley C (2000) Feelings and Experiences of Midwives who do not have Children Caring for Childbearing Women. *Midwifery* **16**.

Brink PJ (1991) Issues of Reliability and Validity. In: Morse J (ed.). *Qualitative Nursing Research*. London: Sage.

Condy A (1995) *Family Policy Bulletin*. April 3. London: Family Policy Studies Centre.

Dalmiya VA and Alcoff L (1993) Are Old Wives' Tales Justified? In: Alcoff L and Potter E (eds) *Feminist Epistemologies*. New York: Routledge.

Department of Health (1993) *Changing Childbirth: Second Report of the Expert Maternity Group*. London: HMSO.

Donnison J (1988) *Midwives and Medical Men: A History of the Struggle for Control of Childbirth*. London: Historical Books.

Dowrick SA and Grundberg S (1980) *Why Children?* London: Women's Press.

Flint C (1989) *Sensitive Midwifery*. London: Heinemann.

Fox S (1990) The ethnography of humour and the problem of social reality. *Sociology* **24**(3:) 431– 46.

Gaskin I (1994) Beyond Spiritual Midwifery. *AIMS Journal* **6**(3): 6–9.

Goffman E (1976) *Presentation of Self in Everyday Life*. London: Pelican.

Hugman R (1991) *Power in Caring Professions*. London: Macmillan.

Hunt S and Symonds AS (1995) *The Social Meaning of Midwifery*. London: Macmillan.

Hycner RH (1985) Some guidelines for the phenomenological analysis of interview data. *Human Studies* **8**: 279–303.

Kirkham M (1986) A Feminist Perspective in Midwifery. In: Webb C (ed.) *Feminist Practice in Women's Healthcare*. Chichester: John Wiley & Sons.

Kirkham M (1989) Midwives and Information Giving During Labour. In: Robinson S and Thompson A (eds) *Midwives, Research and Childbirth, Volume 1*. London: Chapman & Hall.

Kitzinger S (1992) Birth and Violence Against Women: Generating Hypotheses from Women's Accounts of Unhappiness after Childbirth. In: Roberts H (ed.) *Women's Health Matters*. London: Routledge.

MacQuarrie J (1977) *Existentialism*. London: Pelican.

Menzies I (1981) *Function of Social Systems as a Defence Against Anxiety*. London: Tavistock.

Morell CM (1994) *Unwomanly Conduct: The Challenges of Intentional Childlessness*. London: Routledge.

Morse J (1991) *Qualitative Nursing Research*. London: Sage.

Mulkay M (1988) *On Humour*. Cambridge: Polity Press.

Oiler C (1982) The phenomenological approach in nursing research. *Nursing Research* **31**(3): 178–81.

Omery A (1983) Phenomenology: a method for nursing research. *Advances in Nursing Science* **5**(2): 49–63.

Ong Bie Nio (1986) Child Abuse: Are Abusing Women Abused Women? In: Webb C (ed.) *Feminist Practice in Women's Healthcare*. Chichester: John Wiley & Sons.

Pfeffer N (1993) *The Stork and the Syringe*. Cambridge: Polity Press.

Phoenix A, Wollett A and Lloyd E (eds) (1991) *Motherhood: Meanings, Practices and Ideologies*. London: Sage.

Priya, JV (1992) *Birth Traditions and Modern Pregnancy Care*. Shaftsebury: Element.

Rich A (1976) *Of Woman Born: Motherhood as Experience and Institution*. New York: WW Norton.

Rogers C (1967) *On Becoming a Person*. London: Constable.

Royal College of Midwives (1995) *Changing Midwifery: Survey of Royal College of Midwives Members*. Surrey: Department of Sociology, University of Guildford.

Simms C, McHaffie H, Renfrew MJ and Ashurst H (eds) (1994) *The Midwifery Research Database – MIRIAD – a Sourcebook for Information about Research in Midwifery*. Hale, Cheshire: Books for Midwives Press.

Sumners AD (1990) The professional nurses' attitude towards humour. *Journal of Advanced Nursing* **15**(2): 196–200.

Taylor B (1993) Phenomenology: one way to understand nursing practice. *International Journal of Nursing Studies* **30**(2): 171–9.

Thomas P (1994) Accountable for what? New thoughts on the midwife–mother relationship. *AIMS Journal* **6**(3): 1–5.

Unger R and Crawford M (1992) *Women and Gender: A Feminist Psychology*. New York: McGraw-Hill.

Walton I (1994) *Sexuality and Motherhood*. Hale, Cheshire: Books for Midwives Press.

Webb C (ed.) (1986) *Feminist Practice in Women's Healthcare*. Chichester: John Wiley & Sons.

Woollett A (1991) Accounts of Childless Women and Women with Reproductive Problems. In: Phoenix A, Woollett A and Lloyd E (eds) *Motherhood, Meanings, Practices and Ideologies*. London: Sage.

# Chapter 9

# The Midwifery Partnership in New Zealand: Past History or a New Way Forward?

*Valerie Fleming*

## Introduction

In August 1990, section 54 of the 1977 New Zealand Nurses Act was amended by the government to allow midwives in New Zealand to take responsibility for the care of a woman throughout her pregnancy and labour as well as in the postnatal period. This was an area that, since 1971, had been legally restricted to medical practitioners, although for many years prior to this the practice setting of midwives in New Zealand had mainly been within hospitals. Here they worked alongside nurses, from whom there was little differentiation in terms of their expected duties. Midwives had therefore, like nurses, become entrenched in rigidly defined structures, which were controlled by the medical profession and bureaucratic regimes.

The enactment of the 1990 legislation was hailed by the then Minister of Health, Helen Clark, as offering 'greater choice in childbirth services to pregnant women and their families' (Department of Health 1990:3). However, the legislation was simply the vehicle through which change could occur; it was the challenge for midwives to foster creative ways of practising.

This chapter critically analyses the notion of partnership, which has been adopted as a slogan by midwives in New Zealand. Consideration is first given to some of the key factors that led to the change in the legislation. Midwifery practice generally since 1990 is examined and critiqued. The chapter concludes with an analysis of the author's own practice as a midwife in rural New Zealand.

## The consumer movement

New Zealand in the 1960s, as elsewhere in the world, experienced a surge of 'alternative lifestylers' seeking to remove themselves from the increasing technological developments of the Western world. Although these groups sought to distance themselves from such developments rather than directly challenge them, they laid the foundation for the wave of feminism that developed during the following decade and *did* challenge the *status quo*. The feminist movement in New Zealand encouraged women from varied backgrounds to join together and seek alternatives to the patriarchal social structures that had dominated New Zealand throughout the twentieth century.

Nowhere was this challenge more visible than in the area of childbirth, which feminists challenged as rightfully belonging to women, a right that had been eroded with the rise to power of the profession of obstetrics. As Mein-Smith (1986) notes, the power of the obstetric profession was visible in New Zealand very early in the twentieth century, earlier than was apparent in many other Western countries. The registration of midwives based upon 1904 legislation did not prevent the medicalisation of childbirth in New Zealand. Instead, it was the beginning of the medical control of both midwives and clients.

## Homebirth Association

One of the first tasks of feminist activists in New Zealand was therefore to challenge the medicalisation of childbirth. The group that is mainly credited for doing this is the Homebirth Association, which was founded in Auckland in 1978. While birth at home had always been legal in New Zealand, it was not a common option. This was mainly the result of successful campaigns in the 1920s and 30s by medical practitioners who publicised the perils of homebirth (Gordon 1957, Mein-Smith 1986).

The 1937 Social Security Act, which was passed only after much negotiation with the medical profession, provided 14 days free hospital care for all women following childbirth. This must have seemed an attractive option for many New Zealand women, particularly those in rural areas. Small cottage hospitals sprang up throughout the country, providing relatively home-like environments for birthing women and thereby reducing the perceived need for homebirth. However, with the growth of the Post Graduate School of

Obstetrics and Gynaecology in the 1950s and 60s, Donley believed that there was a need by the obstetricians for more 'clinical material' (Donley 1992:9).

Thus began the centralisation of obstetric services throughout New Zealand. In response, however, there arose a growing interest in homebirth as an alternative to the impersonal and increasingly technological hospital experience. Donley (1992) details the history of the homebirth movement, which fought to preserve women's rights to choose their place of birth. The early group consisted mostly of women who were consumers of maternity services, but also of one or two midwives who supported their goals and were willing to provide a homebirth service. The aim of the movement was to raise awareness of the option of birthing at home in both potential consumers and their attendants.

A major success of the Homebirth Association in New Zealand was, unlike its counterpart in Australia, its bringing together of midwives and consumers to work together for a common goal. Although Donley's history does not specifically acknowledge it as such, this joining together of midwives and consumers was the first tacit acknowledgement of a partnership between women and midwives, that moved from the level of the individual to a more political level. While the impetus had come from the consumer, there was the realisation that 'women need midwives need women,' a slogan that was to become popularised later in the 1980s. Together, consumers and midwives publicised the positive aspects of homebirth and lobbied for medical practitioners to supervise the midwives' practice, as was required by law.

Such radical movements as the Homebirth Association naturally did not go unchallenged by obstetricians from the Post Graduate School of Obstetrics and Gynaecology. The Maternity Services Committee (1979) published a document condemning homebirth as endangering the safety and the intellect of the baby. This was widely circulated and gained general acceptance among midwives and medical practitioners who practised in hospitals. This publication, however, only served to fuel the debate, and in the years since then the Homebirth Association has continued its struggle to establish homebirth as mainstream rather than as a radical alternative. The Association has been extremely successful and plans in the future to continue its campaign.

## Save the Midwives Association

Just as the Homebirth Association had its beginnings in Auckland, so too did the Save the Midwives Association, founded in 1983 to emancipate midwifery from the domination of the medical and nursing professions through the development of direct entry midwifery education programmes. The Save the Midwives Association, consisting mainly of consumers, rapidly gained national support and served to unite hospital and domiciliary midwives, both of whom were threatened by the proposed legislative changes. The Homebirth and Save the Midwives Associations worked together and raised awareness among the general public of the abilities of midwives to practise according to the World Health Organization's (1966) definition of a midwife.

The Save the Midwives Association communicated with its growing number of members through regular newsletters that exhorted its members to lobby women's groups in particular, as it was these which the Association's executive believed would have the most influence on women in childbirth. The tactics of this group were also successful as women's groups took up the cause of midwifery and, in turn, lobbied Members of Parliament to recognise the potential contribution that midwives could offer women. The Homebirth and Save the Midwives Associations were two of the most politically active groups in raising the profile of midwives, but other groups, such as Parent Centre and the Domiciliary Midwives' Society, also assisted in helping midwives to achieve their independence. Midwives themselves were also active and, through their own structures, were trying to overcome the obstacles that had previously prevented independent practice.

## The New Zealand College of Midwives

The New Zealand College of Midwives had its beginnings at the second National Midwives' Conference in 1988. Following this conference, a working party was established to develop a constitution for the new organisation, and by early 1989 the New Zealand College of Midwives was officially launched. It offered a unique opportunity for a partnership between midwives and consumers as membership, including voting rights, was open to both groups. The major task of the new organisation was to continue the drive towards the independence of midwifery practice through amendments to legislation.

The college members, many of whom had not previously been politically active, achieved this in a remarkably short period of time. Each region worked hard to promote midwifery as a viable alternative for childbearing women and the only birth option that was women centred. Members used every opportunity to meet with women's organisations and Members of Parliament to educate them in the potential of midwifery.

Finally, the Nurses Amendment Bill was introduced to Parliament in 1989. Following its first reading, it was referred to a Select Committee that advertised for submissions, setting a closing date of 9 February 1990. The amendments to the 1977 Nurses Act were eventually passed in August 1990, and midwives were once more permitted to practise independently of doctors. The first National College of Midwives' Conference was held three weeks prior to the passing of the Act. The keynote speaker, Helen Clark, then Minister of Health, who was an acknowledged supporter of midwives, suggested that the next challenge for the College was 'to make autonomy work' (Clark 1990:10). The mood was celebratory.

## Changes in midwifery practice since 1990

When the 1990 Nurses Amendment Act was passed on August 15, there were a few practitioners throughout the country who were immediately ready to take up the challenge of independent practice. The reality of the 1990 Amendment was, however, that it was a beginning rather than an end, and the majority of midwives had to become confident with new and innovative ways of practice. In addition, since its enactment, the government-funded health services have faced several major structural changes presenting other challenges for midwives.

The concept of partnership between midwives and clients, which was stated by the New Zealand College of Midwives (1990) to be pivotal for midwifery practice, had to contend with stiff resistance from within the profession at the International Council of Midwives at its triennial meeting in 1990. Member organisations felt that midwifery was a profession and that it was therefore inappropriate to include consumer representation on its Board of Management. The New Zealand College of Midwives was nearly expelled from the international body, and its representatives had to lobby members from other countries to ensure its continued membership. Since then, however, the notion of partnership has continued to gain in strength and added to the impetus for change both in New Zealand and overseas. In 1993, the International Council of Midwives unanimously accepted New Zealand's constitution.

Changes in New Zealand have affected both midwifery education and practice. In the education sector, direct entry programmes were quickly introduced in Dunedin and Auckland, registered nurses and others being able to apply the principles of prior learning to gain entry at an appropriate level.

Current midwifery practice is comprehensively documented in the text by Calvert (Calvert I 1998) so will only be alluded to here.

## Independent midwifery practice

Prior to 1990, the majority of practising midwives were employed in hospitals. Of the few who were community based, most carried out postnatal care for women who had opted for early discharge from hospital, while only a few practised as domiciliary midwives providing a full range of services for their clients. With the amended legislation, however, the requirement for a doctor to supervise the pregnancy and birth was removed. The financial remuneration for midwives was also much greater as midwives were able to claim a standard fee for attendance at labour and birth, which was the same as that paid to GPs. For either or both of these reasons, a number of midwives moved from being employees in hospitals to being self-employed and community based and to practising continuity of care.

Approximately 800 midwives currently practise as independent practitioners. With approximately 57,000 births throughout New Zealand in 1997, this implies that many more women are opting for maternity care that provides for continuity of midwifery care throughout pregnancy, labour and birth, and the postnatal period up to six weeks postpartum. By accessing midwives early in the pregnancy, women and their chosen midwives are able to form a relationship and establish a trust in each other before labour. In this way, the woman can know and have confidence in her birth attendant (Flint 1986). It is now generally acknowledged, however, that to provide midwifery care on a caseload basis needs total commitment on the part of the midwife, and many midwives have been unable to offer such a commitment as they often have other commitments of their own.

At this level of individual midwife–client dyads, evaluations of the service have suggested that women attended by independent midwives felt empowered and actively involved in all decision-making throughout the duration of the relationship. In one evaluation (Scotney 1992), this was particularly emphasised in relation to midwives who practised caseload midwifery. Women in Scotney's evaluation appeared to be less satisfied with the concept of team midwifery. Subsequent to the publication of Scotney's report, the practice concerned moved from a team to a caseload approach. In all parts of New Zealand, committees consisting of consumers and midwives now meet regularly to review individual independent midwives' performances. Such reviews consist of a discussion of caseloads, the midwife being held accountable first to her clients and then to her profession.

## Political and financial developments

Independent midwives initially often provided a service that complemented that of the GP or obstetrician, the woman choosing to have her prenatal care shared between midwives and doctors. With the system of the maternity benefit paid to *each* practitioner, the arrangement was generally financially satisfactory for practitioners, although midwives argued that the payment they received was finally value for their professional expertise.

The increase of 100 per cent to maternity benefits payment was, however, declared to be costly for the country, and two years later the cost analysis began in earnest. Early in 1992, newspaper articles were being written claiming that independent midwives were 'blowing the budget'. The publicity succeeded in forcing the Minister of Health to convene a Tribunal to consider the whole issue of maternity benefits.

This Tribunal sat in November 1992 and considered evidence from the New Zealand Medical Association, the New Zealand College of Midwives and the Department of Health. In presenting their evidence to the Tribunal, the New Zealand Medical Association argued for separate schedules of payment to doctors and midwives, claiming that doctors had superior knowledge that had to be recognised. The New Zealand College of Midwives, conversely, argued for one schedule of payments, maintaining that midwives were the experts in normal childbirth. The New Zealand College of Midwives also successfully argued that the issue of the assessment of women by medical practitioners was beyond the scope of the Tribunal's terms of reference.

By May 1993, the Minister of Health's decision was made public, and the New Zealand College of Midwives claimed victory. A single schedule of payments was to be retained and a reasonable increase in attendance fees awarded. Most midwives were pleased with the results, although the decrease in mileage allowance has negatively affected rural midwives. This Tribunal, however, started the erosion of midwives' remuneration (Calvert S 1998) as the hourly attendance fee that was claimed by most midwives was substantially reduced, while the attendance at birth fee, claimed by all medical practitioners, was substantially increased.

This Tribunal was, however, only the first of many reassessments of the payment schedule of maternity benefits, and since then there have been many changes. The present system of payments, introduced in 1996 and revised in 1998, calls for one lead maternity carer who controls a budget for normal pregnancy and must pay associate carers from this. In many instances, this lead maternity carer is a midwife, in others, it is a GP or obstetrician.

Midwives are now looking to alternative forms of creative practice outside hospitals. Some midwives are forming partnerships with health centres operated by trade unions. The union claims the maternity benefit and pays the midwives a salary and holiday pay, as well as providing the equipment. Other similar organisations of independent practitioners were also formed to allow groups of midwives to work together and gain contacts as lead maternity carers. This idea has, however, had only limited success, this being most apparent in Wellington.

## Partnership revisited in independent midwifery practice

In the above discussion, it is clear that while campaigning for legislation to change, there was considerable focus on the partnership of midwife and woman, not only at the level of individual midwife–client dyads, but also at a much more political level. In all the subsequent changes to practice, particularly with the financial changes thrust upon midwives at an ever-increasing rate, it is perhaps easy to think that the ideals so readily espoused pre-1990 have since become invisible. As Tully *et al.* (1998) say, putting the professional–client partnership into practice has been a convoluted process that has involved considerable consultation and negotiation. It is through partnership that these authors claim that midwifery is able to establish its territory with regard to birthing.

These claims suggest that the midwife is the expert in normal birth and that, as such, her professional identity differs from that of nurses and doctors. In making such claims, these authors are at risk of excluding the voices of the women with whom they claim to be in partnership. The authors, however, dispute that the notion of partnership with clients is in jeopardy:

> Making the partnership model of practice a reality involves reworking understandings and relations associated with professional 'expertise'. Most importantly, it involves constituting midwifery practice as autonomous in relation to competing health professions but not autonomous with respect to clients/consumers. (Tully *et al.* 1998:248)

Yet the model of partnership alluded to by these authors was devised solely by midwives (Guilliland and Pairman 1994) and takes the form of a prescription for practice. Further criticisms have been levelled by Fleming (1998), who suggests that this model is not conducive to autonomous midwifery practice.

Surtees (1998) has critiqued this midwifery model of partnership, suggesting that any discourse that counters the dominant medical model of childbirth is limited by the requirements of the law. The core of medical discourse still exists and is maintained by the emphasis on surveillance and monitoring that covertly suggests that the midwifery emphasis on normal pregnancy cannot be safe. Surtees further suggests that partnership is something that has maintained the professionalism of midwives and that, while it may be ideal to challenge the dominant discourse of obstetrics, little attention has been given in New Zealand to the meaning of partnership for either women or midwives.

The partnership model assumes that normal birth is something for which all women should strive and that midwives only function as midwives in such an environment. As such, it is self-limiting and exclusionist. Tully *et al.* acknowledge this limitation, suggesting that some midwives may regard the partnership between midwives and consumers as 'representing only the interests of women with a particular orientation to birthing' (1998:251).

Such criticisms were voiced by Rose (1995), who suggested that many midwives were not working independently and that those midwives who worked in hospitals had much to offer in developing partnerships with women. The next section of this chapter considers some of the developments that have taken place in hospitals.

## Hospital-based midwifery practice from 1990

Despite the immediate readiness of some midwives to enter independent practice, and the subsequent initial increase in the number of midwives practising independently since the 1990 Nurses Amendment Act, the majority of midwives in New Zealand still practise in hospitals. Most midwives in larger hospitals initially practised within a medical model of childbirth as the institutions were fragmented into pre- and postnatal wards, and labour and delivery suites.

In 1991, however, a 'Know your midwife' scheme was introduced in one large organisation, as outlined by Flint and Poulengris (1987). All the women who used the hospital's facilities, unless under the care of an independent midwife, had the opportunity for continuity of care from a team of hospital midwives. Such a change involved the use of innovative rosters and the willingness of midwives to move away from the concept of eight-hour shifts. While successful from the point of view of the clients involved, practising in this way has been undesirable for some midwives as it has proved too disruptive to their off-duty life.

Most midwives, however, responded positively to the challenge, and several obstetric hospitals soon developed similar schemes. In Wellington, for example, all primary care is provided by independent midwives, while the hospital provides secondary services that fall outside the maternity benefits schedule (Calvert S 1998). In most other major centres in New Zealand, midwives now offer patterns of care designed to suit the needs of their client groups, the notion of the 'eight-hour shift' generally being consigned to history. However, the funding debates, which have influenced independent midwives, have also affected hospital care, and just as individual practitioners must take on the role of lead maternity carer, so too must midwives in hospitals that are going to assume that role.

Despite the funding debate, which now dominates, it was in small hospitals and birthing units that midwives employed by the health service were best able to offer continuity of care. As hospital stays became shorter, one Area Health Board began, under an experimental scheme, to offer continuity of care with hospital midwives following their clients into the community for as long as required (Fleming

1988). This was later extended to schemes in which midwives in small hospitals frequently assumed primary responsibility for a group of clients throughout their pregnancy, labour and postnatal period, generally in co-operation with local GPs.

## A personal perspective

At the time of the change in the law, I was the midwife employed to run the country's first birthing unit in Turangi in the centre of the North Island. Here I enjoyed the opportunity of undertaking both home and domino births. The area in which I practised was fairly isolated and the clients generally Maori women belonging to the Tuwharetoa tribe and their *whanau* (extended family). Until August 1990, the law required that I work with one of the town's GPs, with whom I had a good relationship, carrying out prenatal care together in his surgery or in women's homes. While he would attend births, he remained in the background. This situation came to a halt when he announced that he was leaving the area, and as no other GP held an obstetric qualification, all women would be required to move out of the area to give birth.

Fortunately, the law changed the same week, and with the support of my employers I was immediately plunged into independent practice and given an access agreement to use the birthing unit. Such a rapid move was somewhat daunting but had the support of the town's *kaumatua* (Maori leaders), who represented the townspeople. It was here that I experienced partnership of a different nature from that in which I had been involved as a college member. The people of the town were firmly in support of maintaining maternity services locally because of its isolation from major centres and its low socioeconomic status. Although I am not Maori, the support given to me was overwhelming, and I felt that I was able to call on their leaders at any time for assistance. One of the first joint projects that we undertook was to hold a *hui* (workshop) on birthing traditions on the local *marae* (meeting place).

About 40 Maori women gathered for this occasion and, with much singing, laughter, food and reminiscing, we discussed the traditional beliefs and values of the local Maori tribe and the fears and expectations that these women held regarding pregnancy, birthing and parenting. The values of the traditional customs were hotly debated among the women while I mainly observed. On the second day, I was

invited to speak on what I could offer. Given the help and understanding of these women, I felt that I could offer myself as a support
person and guide to women with normal pregnancies but that I would
also participate in the care of those who exceed the boundaries of
normal. I also emphasised what I considered to be normal, and the
meeting was in agreement with the parameters I set myself.

Following this meeting, I was the sole health care provider for most
of the local women, although I occasionally shared the prenatal care
with one of the town's general medical practitioners who did not attend
the births. Women who experienced complications in the prenatal
period were referred to the nearest obstetrician and, on the very rare
occasions when complications occurred in labour, were transferred to
one of two base hospitals by ambulance or helicopter. The arrangements in this town appeared to be satisfactory to most clients, the GPs
and myself. During my four years of practice in the area, I enjoyed a
collegial relationship with the latter, and we often shared informal
discussions on topics relevant to clients in my care; in addition, if a
second opinion was needed, this was generally willingly given.

Such a gathering of women as we had experienced at *Tokaanu
marae* had not previously been possible in the history of the town of
Turangi, which had only come into existence in the 1960s, at which
time the medical model of birth was firmly in control. It set the scene
for Maori women to return to their *whanau* when pregnant with the
firm knowledge that their cultural traditions would be respected. Individual women began to come forward, initially making tentative
suggestions with regard to their own birth, but very soon a support
network began to emerge, and I would often find a woman who had
given birth appearing as a support person for her friend or cousin
some weeks later.

Working in such self-created structures did indeed work well for
the majority of the women in the Turangi area and for me as a
midwife. The partnership between the local Maori people and myself
was strong and mutually supportive. However, being a sole practitioner for much of the time led to burn out and the need eventually to
work regular hours. When relinquishing my position as the sole
midwife in the area, I was replaced by a group of three midwives who
worked together to provide cover for the women while allowing
themselves some time off. I remained a member of this group for
some time.

In my practice and other similar practices, the partnership issues
have, however, become blurred. While many midwives state that they

practise in such a way, we have all had to address many issues to protect our survival. Working with a powerful group such as the Tuwharetoa tribe has been richly rewarding, but practitioners themselves must ultimately each be responsible for their own professional practice. It is difficult to link such notions of professional accountability with the notion of partnership. These are issues that need debating in the future to ensure the survival of midwifery.

## Conclusion

The developments in midwifery in New Zealand have shown how a profession almost at the brink of extinction can be resurrected and forge itself new opportunities. This has been achieved through the partnership of midwives and clients. In this chapter, partnership has been explored at a local as well as at a political level. It has, however, been shown that this notion has become somewhat hackneyed and needs to be revalidated in order to ensure that decisions are taken jointly and that midwives continue to work in the best interest of their clients. The time has perhaps come to reassess the nature of partnerships within the profession as we look towards its future.

## References

Calvert I (1998) *Birth in Focus: Midwifery in Aotearoa/New Zealand*. Palmerston North: Dunsmore Press.

Calvert S (1998) Making decisions: focusing on my baby's wellbeing. MPhil thesis, Massey University, New Zealand.

Clark H (1990) To independence. Opening address at First National College of Midwives Conference, Dunedin.

Department of Health (1990) *Nurses Amendment Act, 1990. Information for Health Care Providers*. Wellington: Government Printer.

Donley J (1992) *Herstory of New Zealand Homebirth Association*. Wellington: Domiciliary Midwives' Society of New Zealand.

Fleming V (1988) *Community Midwifery Care*. Unpublished research report for the Chief Nurse, Auckland Area Health Board.

Fleming V (1998) Autonomous or automatons? An exploration through history of the concept of autonomy in midwifery in Scotland and New Zealand. *Nursing Ethics* 5(1): 43–51.

Flint C (1986) *Sensitive Midwifery*. London: Heinemann.

Flint C and Poulengris P (1987) *The 'Know Your Midwife' Report*. Privately published by the authors.

Gordon D (1957) *Backblocks Baby Doctor*. London: Faber.

Guilliland K and Pairman S (1994) The midwifery partnership. *New Zealand College of Midwives Journal* **11**: 5–9.

Maternity Services Committee (1979) *Obstetrics and the Winds of Change*. Wellington: Government Printer.

Mein-Smith P (1986) *Maternity in Dispute: New Zealand 1920–1939*. Wellington: Government Printer.

New Zealand College of Midwives (1990) *Constitution*. Unpublished.

Rose E (1995) Letter to the Editor. *New Zealand College of Midwives Journal* **12**: 5.

Scotney T (1992) The Wellington Domino Midwifery Service. Proceedings of the New Zealand College of Midwives Second National Conference. Wellington.

Surtees R (1998) Power, Professionalisation and Midwifery: The 'Midwifer-ication' of Childbirth. Paper written as part of a MA degree in Feminist Studies, Canterbury University.

Tully L, Daellenbach R and Guilliland K (1998) Feminism, Partnership and Midwifery. In: du Plessis R and Alice L (eds) *Feminist Thought in Aotearoa/New Zealand*. Auckland: Oxford University Press.

World Health Organization (1966) *Definition of a Midwife*. Geneva: WHO.

# Chapter 10

# Women-centred Midwifery: Partnerships or Professional Friendships?

*Sally Pairman*

## Introduction

In 1995, Karen Guilliland and I published a monograph, *The Midwifery Partnership: A Model for Practice* (Guilliland and Pairman 1995). This monograph explored the development of the concept of midwifery as a partnership in New Zealand and presented a theoretical model to describe it. The model arose from reflection on our personal experiences and practice as midwives, and our observations of, and discussions with, many other midwives and women. In 1996, I commenced a research study for a Master's thesis and decided to explore further the nature of the relationship between midwives and women, this time using the experiences and perceptions of a small group of midwives and women. In this paper, I will briefly discuss the methodology and methods used for the study and summarise the findings. I will then focus in greater depth on the notions of partnership, friendship and professional friendship.

## Overview of the study

This study was designed to explore both the nature of the relationship that midwives and women enjoy together during pregnancy, labour and birth and the postnatal period, and the understanding that women and midwives have of this relationship. The outcomes of this study were then used to refine the theoretical model of midwifery as a partnership (Guilliland and Pairman 1995).

The design for this qualitative exploratory study was underpinned by a feminist philosophy. In particular, it drew upon the work of Patti Lather (1986, 1991), integrating her notions of reciprocity and dialogical theory-building into the methodology of the study and thus allowing the theoretical model (Guilliland and Pairman 1995) to provide the *a priori* theoretical framework for the study without predetermining the outcome.

Six independent midwives and six of their clients explored their experiences of the midwife–woman relationship through individual semi-structured interviews and then through two focus group meetings of participants. Participants were actively involved in the analysis of the data and the identification of the emerging themes. On completion of this process, the model of midwifery practice previously developed (Guilliland and Pairman 1995) was shared with the participants, who collectively explored areas for refinement in light of the findings of the study.

The midwife participants were all self-employed midwives working independently who volunteered to take part. The criteria were that the midwife provided continuity of care throughout the childbirth experience; that at least 70 per cent of her practice in the previous year was total midwifery care; and that she provided both home and hospital services. The women were clients of these midwives. The women volunteered in response to information given to them on my behalf by the midwives. One woman from each midwife's caseload was chosen by ballot. The criteria for the women were that they had given birth between six weeks and four months previously and that the woman and baby were both well at the time of the study.

The final group consisted of six midwives aged from 33 to 43 years with 4–19 years' midwifery experience, 1–5 of these in independent practice. Five midwives identified as Pakeha (New Zealanders who are of non-Maori origin) and one as Maori/Pakeha. Two midwives worked in mainly homebirth settings, two had rural practices, and two had urban-based practices. There were six women participants, ranging in age from 27 to 34 years. Three had just had their first child, two had had their second, and one had had her fifth. All the women identified as Pakeha. Two women had had a homebirth and four a hospital birth, two of these being in small rural maternity units, one in a secondary care maternity facility, and one in a city-based primary care maternity facility.

As the participants are representative neither of all midwives nor of the wider birthing population, the results are not generalisable to all midwife–woman relationships. The study deliberately chose participants who were engaged in midwife–woman relationships based on continuity of care and independent midwifery practice. These factors were identified by Guilliland and Pairman (1995) as being essential to the practice of partnership, and it was anticipated that this study would examine this partnership in more depth, from a practice base, and then if necessary enable a refinement of the midwifery model of partnership. Thus, while the findings are not generalisable to all midwife–women relationships, they do provide a valuable insight into the practice of partnership. In so doing, they have confirmed the literature, practice and experiences that were the basis of our development of the midwifery partnership model and have enabled a refinement of the midwifery model of partnership.

This study does not set out to explore the relationship of midwives and women working within a 'shared care' model with another practitioner. Some shared care will occur within an independent midwifery model as midwives must involve obstetricians when women's needs move beyond the midwifery scope of practice. This type of shared care relies on equal status, an equal involvement in decision-making with the woman, equal responsibility and good communication. Other shared care models place the midwife in a dependent position, with medicine as the primary decision-maker. There has been no research to date examining the relationship between midwives and women in these kinds of arrangement, or exploring whether or not there are any features of midwifery partnership in these relationships.

Guilliland's (1998) associated study has identified that the clients of midwives working independently and with continuity of care have significantly better outcomes than those of midwives working in shared care. Another future study could examine whether or not it is the practice of midwifery as a partnership between the woman and the midwife that is the critical element in achieving these positive outcomes for women.

## Summary of the findings

The data that emerged through this research confirmed and supported Guilliland and Pairman's (1995) model of midwifery as a partnership between the woman and the midwife. The findings

provided richness and depth to the discussion of the midwife–
woman relationship and enabled some refinement of the original
model (Pairman 1998).

The midwife and the woman contribute equally to the relationship
and value what each brings to it. The woman, with her knowledge of
self and family, also brings an expectation of trust, equality, respect
and openness to the professional care she seeks from the midwife.
The woman brings a willingness to participate actively in her care,
sharing responsibility for her decisions and assuming control over
her experience. The midwife, from her foundation of professional
standards and ethics, brings her ability to be 'with woman'. In this,
she utilises her knowledge, skills and 'self' in practice and is accessible and supportive to the woman. The midwife also brings her
ability to practise independently and to develop practice wisdom.
Both the woman and the midwife bring themselves as women to the
relationship, and the shared experience of being female contributes
to the nature of the relationship (Pairman 1998).

The midwife and the woman work together in a particular way that
integrates the notions of 'being equal', 'sharing common interests',
'involving the family', 'building trust', 'reciprocity', 'taking time'
and 'sharing power and control'. Through the relationship, both the
midwife and the woman are empowered in their own lives. The relationship also has emancipatory outcomes as a new knowledge of
childbirth and midwifery is generated. This new kind of professional
relationship challenges the dominant medical model of childbirth
(Pairman 1998).

Underpinning the relationship are philosophical beliefs that must be
held by the midwife and may also be held by the woman. These
beliefs are: that pregnancy and childbirth are normal life events; that
midwifery is an independent profession; that midwifery provides
continuity of care-giver; and that midwifery is women centred. These
beliefs underpin the midwifery partnership because they direct the
practice of midwifery (Guilliland and Pairman 1995).

The study teases out 'midwifery partnership' as meaning 'professional friendship'. It advances an understanding of the relationship
between midwives and women, including its significance at a
personal, professional and political level. I will turn now to look at
one aspect of the findings, that is, the identification by the participants
of the midwifery partnership as being this 'professional friendship'.

## The nature of the relationship: friendship or partnership?

In the study, the women and the midwives use the terms 'friendship' and 'partnership' to describe their relationship, each initially appearing to have a different meaning. When these are examined more closely, however, it is apparent that the women and the midwives are describing a relationship with the same characteristics. The different terminology, therefore, stems from the different contexts within which they operate. The midwives work within a professional context in which a partnership relationship is seen as an important aim and the notion of partnership underpins the professional guidelines that direct their practice. The women are not constrained by professional dictates and describe the relationship as they experience it, as a friendship. They too, however, recognise the professional focus of the relationship and its time-limited nature. For both groups, the use of the term 'professional friend' captures the unique nature of the midwife–woman relationship.

All the women described their relationship with the midwife as being one of friendship. Implicit in these descriptions of friendship are characteristics inherent in the midwife–woman relationship, including knowing each other, women with women, equality and trust. It is the presence of these characteristics in the midwife–woman relationship that led the women to describe the relationship as a friendship. The women clearly do not expect these characteristics in their relationships with other health professionals:

> She was more of a friend than a nurse, that's what I liked about her... I felt like we were friends, not nurse–patient relationship. She was just good to talk to, we got on well, we were just like two good friends. And she was supportive. (Amy, AA 1. 1–8)

> You felt more like you were talking to a big sister, or a really close friend rather than a doctor. (Sarah, SC 1.2)

A survey on women's friendships among nurses carried out by Chinn *et al.* (1988) in America found that respondents believed that their close friendships with women gave them the freedom to develop as whole and autonomous individuals. Respondents agreed that, with women friends, they can talk openly and freely, do not need to explain themselves, are not judged and gain a sense of self-worth. Friendships provide opportunities for mutual nurturing and sharing (Chinn *et al.* 1988).

For the women in this study, the shared experience of being women contributed to the development of the relationship. The women felt more at ease sharing the intimacy of pregnancy and birth with another woman who understood how it was to live in a female body. As Dianne said:

> I thought I'd feel more at ease with a female, because it's a female thing and the midwife was female. (Diane, DMcD 1.2)

Women think and learn differently from men, and their communication is characterised by connectedness and emotional joining (Noddings 1984, Belenky *et al.* 1986). As Bizz points out:

> I suppose I feel that men don't know what it's all about. That might be totally wrong. I'm sure they do their best to try, but generally I find women are better at listening certainly, and tend to be a lot more equal with each other. Often I find men tend to put themselves above you. (Bizz, BF 1.6)

The personal characteristics of the midwife and the way in which she used her 'self' in practice enabled the midwife and the woman to get to know each other easily. The women described attributes in the midwife such as 'acceptance', 'supportive', 'human', 'a good listener', 'warm', 'approachable', 'responsive' and 'positive' that contributed to their sense of ease with the midwife. These aspects of the midwife's personality were just as important as the perception that she was 'informed', 'knowledgeable', 'competent' and 'professional':

> I just had so much confidence in her. She was so knowledgeable and yet also very professional and approachable, very real – it wasn't clinical at all – very human... She was a very good listener... She always explained what was happening and I never felt stupid asking what I thought were the silliest, trivial little things. (Bizz, BF 1.2–3)

> She listened; regardless of whether I sounded stupid or not, she listened. Whereas you know what doctors are like – 'oh no, that never happens', or 'I've never heard of that'. MW would say 'what makes you think that?' ...I always felt totally in control. And she would always ask me if it was all right to visit on such and such. She never just took it for granted that I was a patient and I was going to do what I was told. (Amy, AA 1.4)

Chris, one of the midwives, recognised how important her communication skills were to her ability to develop a relationship with women and practise midwifery:

> I think the physical midwifery is probably only about 5 per cent of the job. I think probably 90+ per cent of it is actually counselling type work where there's a lot of listening and reflecting and maybe floating some ideas around and helping a woman sort out what she wants to do... The physical care – it's almost the easier part of it. (Chris, CS 1.2–5)

The midwife visiting in the woman's own environment or the woman visiting the midwife enhances this personal knowing of each other. Seeing a woman in her own home allows the midwife to get to know the family better and see the woman within the context of her home life:

> Especially doing home visits and being involved in the homebirth setting you get to know their neighbours and their dog and their children (not in that order) and their partners and you get to know a little bit about their lives as well; it's the whole family. (Juliet, JT 1.2)

> Most women I find that you end up getting quite close to and there's a strong bond between you... often its not only the woman herself either, you get involved with the children and often the partners as well... some partners take time off around the time of the birth and you obviously get to know some a lot more than others. Often extending to friends and grandparents, and you find you get introduced as 'this is my midwife' and that you seem to end up taking a special part in their family. (Heather, HA 1.2)

A further characteristic of the midwife–woman relationship is its women-centred nature. This, too, links with the notion of friendship between two women. Linda describes how much she looked forward to the midwife's visits because, for that period of time each visit, she felt 'special', the midwife's attention and concern being focused on her as a person rather than on her as a pregnant woman:

> It's nice to actually sit down and have some attention paid to you. I mean you do from work colleagues and family and that, but it's nice to be able to talk to somebody other than that... I used to write in my diary for two or three days before she'd come 'MW's coming on Friday' and then I'd have it in my diary at work 'MW's coming, meet her at 1.30' or whatever, and

I'd really look forward to her coming. Really look forward to it, it was great... She made me feel special... That's another thing I didn't expect MW to be... I thought she was there for the baby and not for me, and that if I was feeling depressed I couldn't talk to her about it because it was me and not the baby – but I could. (Linda, LF 1. 4–13)

Bizz and Sarah reiterate this feeling of being seen as an individual with the midwife's attention being on them alone:

Every antenatal meeting she always asked initially how I felt and what I'd been doing. And even after the baby was born it was how I felt and how are you, which was really good. Yes, she was very concerned about what I wanted. It was very important. (Bizz, BF 1.4)

It was more the confidence, that they were so friendly, and that they were interested solely in you when they came for that hour, hour and a half, or half an hour. No matter what time it was they just made you feel that you were the only one on their books. Nothing was a problem in that you could deal with it together. (Sarah, SC 1.7)

Most women, with busy lives and many roles such as wife, mother, sister and worker, find themselves focusing their concern on others and trying to juggle the needs of their children, partners and families. The only time that they may have to focus on themselves may be that which they spend with close friends. For the women in this study, it seems as if the time they spend with the midwife is unique in that they are seen as themselves and their concerns are validated. Thus, their relationship with the midwife shares characteristics of other friendships that they may have in their lives.

The midwives themselves are conscious of the woman-centred nature of their relationship with the women for whom they care. Chris made the distinction between a pregnant woman and a woman who is pregnant. The subtle difference in language carries much deeper meaning and shows that the midwives see themselves primarily in relation to another woman for whom pregnancy is only one part of what is happening in her life:

You're caring for a woman who's pregnant, not a pregnant woman, and although it's a very subtle difference, to me that really is the essence of it. So you're actually working with the woman and it's almost as if the preg-

nancy's a small part of it. It's really her and her life you become involved
with and be a sounding board for. (Chris, CS 1.4)

This understanding of a relationship between two women brings
with it a recognition that these two women are also equal and that
both contribute to the relationship:

> I found that I learned things about MW as she learned things about me. She
> didn't expect me to do all the talking about me and my life and how things
> were going here – she'd tell me how Matthew [her son] was doing and he
> came with her on a couple of visits. So I got an insight into the midwife
> and her family as well. (Sarah, SC 1.2–9–10)

> She was there to do her job and not be bossy and I was there to do a job and
> not push her around. We just cooperated I suppose. (Amy, AA 1.4)

The women-centred nature of the relationship did not exclude the
partner and other family. Instead, the woman decided how she wanted
her family to be involved. It was important to the women that their
families felt part of the process and felt at ease with the midwife:

> She made him feel involved at the delivery so that was really good. He
> washed and gave Nicholas his bath and things like that while I went for a
> shower. She helped him to do that. He felt at ease and confident with MW.
> I think he was surprised at how relaxed it all was. (Sarah, SC 1.8)

Juliet believes that, because of the intimate nature of the
midwife–woman relationship, it is essential that the woman and
midwife feel comfortable with each other. The midwife inevitably
becomes emotionally involved with the woman, and this also
contributes to the notion of the relationship as being one of friendship:

> I find a lot of women want quite a close relationship, want to build up a
> relationship where you get to know each other really well, where there's
> maybe more than being a midwife, where there's actually being a really
> good friend… it's hard to cut off where your role as a midwife stops and
> where your role as a friend… where they cross over. But I think they need
> to cross over… especially being involved in such an intimate time in a
> woman's life there's got to be a close relationship, you've got to feel good
> about each other. She's got to feel okay about you being there at that time
> in her life and you are emotionally involved. (Juliet, JT 1.2)

Chris describes the relationship that she has with women as one of partnership. For her, the relationship develops over time and is characterised by a sense of equality between the two 'partners', both of whom make different but equally important contributions to the relationship:

> Well I guess it develops. The initial visit is often at the very beginning not quite formal but, as the session or visit progresses, becomes a lot more relaxed and I guess that it's almost like a friendship developing really... like a working partnership with women. I see them very much as my equal and think that they feel the same, and certainly a lot of them would consider it a friendship. Partnership's a really good description to me, but it sort of gets a bit used and so I'm trying to think how to describe it in a way that's not sort of quite so hackneyed I suppose. The women know themselves better than anyone else and they need to share themselves with me for me to get to know them and I share what professional knowledge I've got with them, so it's sort of a round in a circle sort of link and I certainly don't see it as an up–down relationship... Sometimes maybe it's a tiered sort of relationship but that levels out as the relationship grows really. (Chris, CS 1.2)

The relationship is underpinned by continuity of care. Time was an important theme in this study and is intrinsic to the relationship as it takes time for the relationship to develop and for trust to build between the midwife and the woman. The midwives were always accessible to the women and would spend a significant time with them at each visit. The timespan of pregnancy and childbirth meant that, over the 9–10 month period of the relationship, trust developed, the relationship deepened and there was time for informed decision-making and time to work on issues such as self-responsibility, control and power:

> It does take a while to get to know someone. And you're inviting them to partake in something that's going to happen only once or twice in your lifetime. So you want to be sure that the person who's attending is going to respect your wishes and is going to be on the same wavelength as you. (Dianne, DMcD 1.6)

> You see it time and time again, massive changes that women make during that time, and I'm sure that if they didn't have the continuity of care that would just never happen. It happens because they do talk with you about the issues that are there for them and they work out some options and give it a go, and they're supported to do that. (Chris, CS 1.5)

The reason the midwife and the woman get to know each other is only because the woman is pregnant and seeks professional care from the midwife. As Heather describes, the relationship forms for the specific purpose of ensuring midwifery care during pregnancy and childbirth that will lead to a healthy mother and a healthy baby through a positive birth experience:

> We're a partnership working towards an end really, a healthy mother and a healthy baby. That's what the mother has brought you in for, to ensure that happens, to give them a good experience. (Heather, HA 1.2)

Because of its specific nature, the relationship is time limited. It lasts only as long as the pregnancy and birth, and through to about six weeks postpartum. Once the shared need for the relationship has passed, it is over. The relationship may continue for some midwives and some women, but it continues on a different basis and for other reasons:

> It's not an ongoing thing which is quite sad. But you can't expect it to be. You've got to realise it's not going to be like that. (Linda, LF 1.9)

As Juliet says, it would be unrealistic for her as a midwife to try to maintain an ongoing relationship with all women:

> I have had situations where it's been really difficult to let go of that relationship at the end... where woman have expected the visits to keep on going because we are friends. And having to say 'I'd really like to see everybody all the time, I'd love to be able to come to the christening of your baby, I'd love to come to all the birthday parties and all those things', but if you did it for everyone you wouldn't be doing anything else. It's really hard, it's hard for the woman and it's hard for me as well. (Juliet, JT 1.2)

As was agreed by all participants at the second group interview, most do not want the relationship to continue. Once the focus of the pregnancy and birth is past and the midwife has fulfilled her professional function, the relationship naturally changes. Some may continue a different relationship, but for most it is over until the next pregnancy, and this is appropriate:

> I think because it was such an intimate relationship, having been here for the birth and I put so much faith in her. It was like she was part of the family... She was born when Claudia was born sort of thing... In a way it

was sad to see her go, but it was good, because it was the beginning of something new again. Suddenly I was there to bring up the baby, and I had got what I needed from MW and I was confident and she left me I a really good situation… When she actually left it wasn't sad – I thought it would be but it wasn't. It was like 'thank you very much, you've been wonderful, from now on I feel great about carrying on' – just another phase really. (Bizz, BF 1.12)

Oh I missed her. I missed her heaps. Because you get used to it, it goes on for months… I didn't feel like I needed her, but it was just good to yack to someone who understood what you were saying. (Amy, AA1.13)

Linda discovered that the relationship differed from friendship when she tried to buy a gift for the midwife and realised that she did not know her as well as she thought. While she and the midwife shared the intimate experience of childbirth together, they focused on this rather than the personal life and tastes of the midwife. Thus, the personal knowledge the woman has of the midwife does not necessarily extend into all aspects of her life:

I never felt like a client… It's quite funny because I wanted to get MW a gift and I went shopping and I thought 'I don't want to get her a box of chocolates, I don't want to buy her a bottle of wine or anything like that', I wanted to get her something that she can keep because just to show her how much I really did appreciate her. And I went out and looked, I spent a good two days trying to find something because I didn't know… I had never been to her house and I don't know what her taste was, and that I felt really strange. I said to my partner 'It's really weird you know, she knows me intimately and we've known each other now for a good six or seven months (six months I suppose) and I still wouldn't have a clue what to get her', and I did find that very weird. I ended up getting her some moisturiser – a special thing from one of these authentic, alternative places which she did like, well I think she did. But you know you've got to pick out something that I'd like myself. That was the funny thing. It sort of honed in on me that I don't know MW that well – as well as I thought I probably did. (Linda, LF 1.8)

## Friendship

Harlene Caroline (1993), a psychiatric nurse, used concept analysis to explore the characteristics of close adult friendship and its distinguishing features. The most distinctive feature of friendship is that it is voluntary and that friends choose the extent to which they will accommodate each other. In addition, friendship is primary in that it is broad and involves significantly large parts of a person's life. Friendships are possible at any age, unlike other social relationships such as spouse, worker or parent, which tend to be limited by age. There is always a quality of exchange between friends, and this reciprocal exchange includes intimacy and love. Close friendships are enduring, with a sense of history (Caroline 1993).

Friendship is preceded by certain conditions. These are proximity, the developmental capacity for friendship, which includes being trustworthy and able to share information about themselves, the current ability to commit resources to the friendship, a feeling of liking or attraction and a 'getting to know you' transition (Caroline 1993). Being involved in friendships has a variety of consequences for the participants, which include feeling loved, being connected, enhanced self-esteem and empowerment. Friendships also help to meet cognitive needs, provide companionship and social support, and provide a frame of reference for social behaviour and the judgement of one's own abilities (Caroline 1993).

Caroline (1993) uses illustrative cases to further explicate the concept of friendship. A model case is one that has all the attributes of the concept, whereas contrary cases have none of these. Borderline cases have some of the attributes but are different in at least one way. A related case shows a concept similar to that of the one analysed but without the essential attributes, and an illegitimate case example is one in which the concept as it has been defined is used inappropriately.

The midwife–woman relationship fits the category of a borderline case. The relationship has intensity, mutuality and meaningfulness, but the bond between the woman and the midwife is their shared experience of childbirth. Once this need for the relationship is over, the individuals do not have the bond of affection or commitment to each other necessary for the relationship to endure. An example of a related case is acquaintanceship, which is superficial and casual and lacks the intensity of friendship. Caroline (1993) believes that the nurse–patient relationship represents a contrary case, as the majority of nurse–client relationships are neither voluntary, chosen nor enduring. The relationship does not occupy a primary part in either the nurse or the patient's life, and it is founded on the legal and moral responsibilities of the nurse to the client.

The notion of friendship as an inappropriate description of health professional relationships is supported by Bignold *et al.* (1995) in their exploration of the relationship between specialist paediatric oncology nurses and the families for whom they care. While recognising that the relationship between these nurses and the families with whom they work often contains elements of friendship such as affective involvement and committed concern, it is not voluntary, having been entered into because of the family's need for the nurse's professional care and support.

Bignold *et al.* (1995) suggest instead that the relationship is one of 'befriending'. Befriending, by their definition, entails the affective and concerned involvement of the professional in the lives of the patient and family, but does not necessarily involve the client entering substantially into the life-world of the professional. In other words, befriending is a predominantly 'one-way' relational process that in no way diminishes the authenticity and genuineness of the relationship (Bignold *et al.* 1995). Befriending involves 'emotional labour' requiring skills such as 'listening, being there, talking and waiting, mixed with giving direction, advice or actively making plans' (Bignold *et al.* 1995:178). It involves emotional as well as physical presence, involved concern, warmth and empathy.

Bignold *et al.* (1995) suggest that friendship is not an appropriate description of most nurse–patient relationships but that befriending may describe some specific nurse–patient relationships. Such relationships occur when there is long-term involvement and extended contact, including time in the patient's home. In particular, these authors believe that befriending relationships are based on a 'real partnership' in which both partners work together mutually acknowledging their respective expertise and responsibility (Bignold *et al.* 1995). For New Zealand midwifery, however, the notion of partnership does not fit with the idea of a 'one-way' relational process. Instead, partnership involves equality, reciprocity and mutuality.

The midwives and the women in this study use different words – friendship and partnership – to describe the same relationship. It is the same relationship but from a different perspective. Both the midwives and the women describe the equality, trust, intimacy, reciprocity and personal knowing of each other that develop over time. The different words used, however, carry a different meaning and reflect the different perspectives of the midwives and the women.

## Partnership

For midwives in New Zealand, the term 'partnership' is very much part of the midwifery culture. 'Partnership' as a concept underpins the New Zealand College of Midwives philosophy, code of ethics and standards for practice, as well as the relationship between the woman and the midwife (New Zealand College of Midwives 1993). In our model of midwifery as a partnership, Karen Guilliland and I define partnership as:

> A relationship of 'sharing' between the woman and the midwife, involving trust, shared control and responsibility and shared meaning through mutual understanding. (Guilliland and Pairman 1995:7)

Partnership is increasingly being seen as the ideal relationship for midwives and women because of the inherent power-sharing that must occur in a partnership relationship (Gooch 1989, Page 1993, Davis 1994, Hancock 1996, Parratt 1996, Young 1996). Partnership is a concept that is also beginning to be widely used in other health professional literature as a way of describing health professional–client relationships that are more egalitarian and less hierarchical (Lowenberg 1994, Powell-Cope 1994, Casey 1995). In partnership relationships, the patient has more authority and control than in the traditional allopathic model, and interaction is reciprocal, as between two adults of comparable status (Lowenberg 1994).

Powell-Cope (1994) has identified partnership as the basic interpersonal relationship between the health care providers and family care-givers of people with AIDS. Partnership involved negotiating or 'working out' care for the good of the person with AIDS. Subcategories of partnership included 'conveying information', 'knowing', 'being accessible' and 'maintaining belief'. Information flowed reciprocally between the health care provider and the family care-givers. In order for the partnership to be successful, the family care-givers had to feel that health care providers valued their input. Partnership rested on knowing, which for this population referred specifically to the desire to be recognised as a significant person in the patient's life. Being accessible was a key component in negotiating partnership. This meant not only the health care provider being accessible and following through on actions, but also the family care-giver having access to the person with AIDS. Maintaining belief was sustaining faith in the family care-giver's capacity to get through specific events, thus facilitating partnership by assisting family members to continue to provide care for the person with AIDS (Powell-Cope 1994).

Powell-Cope (1994) suggests that the concept of partnership may be in opposition to Swanson's (1991) definition of caring, which sees caring as a process that arises from the nurse without the obligation for the client to reciprocate. Partnership in this study emerges as a more interactive process congruent with reciprocity and mutual empowerment (Powell-Cope 1994). Reciprocity and sharing information are both concepts that are mentioned by the midwives in their above description of partnership. Maintaining belief appears to be a similar concept to 'being with', while the concepts of knowing and accessibility are defined differently in the midwife–woman relationship.

Partnership may be an ideal that is more difficult for nursing than midwifery to enact. In her study into partnership between paediatric nurses and the parents of children in hospital, Casey (1995) found that traditional attitudes and routine practices continued to prevent progress towards equal decision-making and sharing of expertise, even in units that purported to work in a partnership model. In order for partnership to occur, both participants have to be prepared for an equal interaction and be willing and able to share their knowledge and expertise. The balance of power is fundamental and may only begin to shift when the patient is at home and the nurse is the stranger (Casey 1995).

A New Zealand nurse theorist, Judith Christensen, has developed a theory of nursing partnership (Christensen 1990). Christensen argues that 'partnership' is an appropriate term for nursing because it implies an alliance between two or more people involved in a shared venture. Both participants are active, both recognise their rights and obligations, and each has a role to play to achieve a negotiated outcome (Christensen 1990). Christensen's notion of partnership does not require power-sharing; instead she focuses on the collaborative and unidirectional nature of the partnership.

Christensen describes the patient–client experience of nursing as a passage, the giving and receiving of nursing enabling the person to make optimal progress through a significant health-related experience, such as surgery. Passage involves three stages – the beginning, entering the nursing partnership and leaving the nursing partnership. Co-existing with these stages and supporting the work that occurs in them is the phase of negotiating the nursing partnership. Christensen (1990) identifies mutual work for the nurse and patient at each phase, which is interactional and essential to the outcome of the patient's passage.

Underpinning the nursing partnership are specific contextual determinants that arise from the patient, the nurse, the community and the partnership, which influence the nature of the partnership as it is experienced by both patient and nurse. Specific to the context of the partnership are the concepts of episodic continuity, anonymous intimacy and mutual benevolence. It is these underpinning concepts which highlight the greatest difference between Christensen's (1990) nursing partnership and the partnership relationship being described by the midwives and women in this study.

Episodic continuity refers to the way in which separate nursing episodes are integrated into an overall experience that reflects the continuity of 'being nursed'. The patient is nursed by many different nurses in individual episodes, but both patients and nurses view nursing as a continuous phenomenon (Christensen 1990). In the midwife–woman relationship being described in this study, continuity comes from one or two midwives working with one woman throughout the period of the childbirth experience. While contact may be episodic during the antenatal and postnatal phases, the midwives provide care that is consistent and integrated. Each episode of care is as long as necessary. The women and the midwives view the experience as a relationship rather than 'having midwifery care'.

Anonymous intimacy refers to the opportunity that nurses have to develop close relationships with their clients. Many nurses contribute to a single patient's passage, and one nurse has contact with many patients. The nature of nurses' work, however, gives them access to closeness with patients (Christensen 1990). This intimacy is anonymous rather than based on a personal knowing of each other. In the midwife–woman relationship, the midwife and the woman do know each other very well. They have an intimate relationship based on personal knowing, as well as a physical intimacy related to the nature of childbirth and the work of the midwife.

Mutual benevolence is reciprocal goodwill between nursing and its recipients. Nursing is an altruistically motivated profession, and nurses offer compassion as well as specialised knowledge and skill. This is valued by patients, and nurses are regarded by them with kindness and gratitude (Christensen 1990). In the midwife–woman relationship, the mutual regard that the woman and the midwife have for each other goes deeper than benevolence. By characterising the relationship as a friendship, the women and the midwives indicate the depth of personal feeling that they have for each other. There is a

genuine liking that comes from their shared experiences and opportunities really to get to know each other.

Another essential difference between Christensen's (1990) use of
partnership and that of the women and midwives in this study lies in
the power balance of the relationship. In discussing the work of the
patient in the partnership, Christensen talks of becoming a client,
managing self, surviving the ordeal, affiliating with experts and inter-
preting the experience. She uses terms such as 'acquiescing to expertise', 'fitting in' and 'tolerating uncertainty', all of which imply that
the client is expected to adjust to the environment. As the client gets
ready to leave the nursing partnership, Christensen talks of the client
'resuming control'. This is a very different partnership from the one
described in this study, in which the women and the midwives work
together, sharing power and control to enable the woman to define her
own environment and experience.

It can be argued that the midwife–woman relationship is characterised by elements of both friendship and partnership. It is an
intense, meaningful and shared relationship involving an emotional
and physical presence, concern, warmth and trust. It is a reciprocal
relationship between two equal participants that is mutually empowering. It is also a relationship that forms for a purpose and ends once
that purpose has been achieved. The meanings of these two
concepts – friendship and partnership – were discussed by the participants at the second group interview. All agreed that Bizz's use of the
term 'professional friend' encompassed what they felt about the relationship they had together:

> I think we had a really good relationship actually. It was more of a friend
> relationship, but a friend you could trust in – a professional friend you
> could rely on. (Bizz, BF 1.3)

'Friendship' and 'partnership' are terms used by both the women and
the midwives in this study to describe the midwife–woman relationship. An examination of the concepts of friendship and partnership
shows that the midwife–woman relationship does indeed have characteristics of both. The relationship is not a friendship because it is not
voluntarily entered into; instead, the relationship forms for the specific
purpose of giving and receiving midwifery care through the childbirth
experience. Once this shared purpose has been achieved, the relationship is not sustained. Despite this limitation, the midwife–woman
relationship has many elements in common with the notion of friend-

ship. These include reciprocal love and intimacy, trust, warmth and genuine concern.

The midwife–woman relationship, as experienced by the participants in this study, fits with most definitions of partnership, although it is clearly different from the nursing partnership described by Christensen (1990). The midwife–woman relationship is between two participants who have equal status and share power and control. Following discussion with the participants in this study, the term 'professional friend' was felt to capture the intensity and intimacy of the midwife–woman relationship. For the participants, the relationship was most like friendship, but they recognised the time-limited and focused nature of the relationship and thus added 'professional' to 'friend' in acknowledgement of this.

## Note

This chapter is a slightly modified version of a paper presented at the 1998 Australian College of Midwives ACT Branch Conference, 'Birth Among Friends', 17–18 September, Canberra. That paper was subsequently published in the *New Zealand College of Midwives Journal* **19**: 5–10.

## References

Belenky M, Clinchy B, Goldberger N and Tarule J (1986) *Women's Ways of Knowing*. New York: Basic Books.

Bignold S, Cribb A and Ball S (1995) Befriending the family: an exploration of the nurse–client relationship. *Health and Social Care in the Community* **3**: 173–80.

Caroline H (1993) Explorations of close friendship: a concept analysis. *Archives of Psychiatric Nursing* **7**(4): 236–43.

Casey A (1995) Partnership nursing: influences on involvement of informal carers. *Journal of Advanced Nursing* **22**: 1058–62.

Chinn P, Wheeler C, Roy A, Berrey E and Madson C (1988) Friends on friendship. *American Journal of Nursing* August: 1094–96.

Christensen J (1990) *Nursing Partnership: A Model for Nursing Practice*. Wellington: Daphne Brassell Associates Press.

Davis K (1994) Responsibilities of choice. *Nursing Standard* **8**(44): 20–1.

Gooch S (1989) Power to women in partnership. *Nursing Times* **85**(25): 45.

Guilliland K (1998) A Demographic Profile of the Self-employed (Independent) Midwife in New Zealand. Unpublished Master's thesis, Victoria University of Wellington, New Zealand.

Guilliland K and Pairman S (1995) *The Midwifery Partnership: A Model for Practice*. Monograph series 95/1. Wellington: Department of Nursing and Midwifery, Victoria University of Wellington.

Hancock H (1996) Women and birth. Triumph or travesty. *Birth Issues* **5**(2): 5–10.

Lather P (1986) Research as praxis. *Harvard Educational Review* **56**(3): 257–77.

Lather P (1991) *Getting Smart*. London: Routledge.

Lowenberg J (1994) The nurse–patient relationship reconsidered: an expanded research agenda. *Scholarly Inquiry for Nursing Practice: An International Journal* **8**(2): 167–90.

New Zealand College of Midwives (1993) *Midwives Handbook for Practice*. Dunedin: New Zealand College of Midwives.

Noddings N (1984) *Caring: A Feminine Approach to Ethics and Moral Education*. London: University of California Press.

Page L (1993) Redefining the midwife's role: changes needed in practice. *British Journal of Midwifery* **1**(1:) 21–4.

Pairman S (1998) The Midwifery Partnership: An Exploration of the Midwife–Woman Relationship. Unpublished Master's thesis, Victoria University of Wellington, New Zealand.

Parratt J (1996) Practising midwifery independently: for the majority of midwives? *Australian College of Midwives Incorporated Journal* September: 23–8.

Powell-Cope G (1994) Family caregivers of people with AIDS: negotiating partnerships with professional healthcare providers. *Nursing Research* **43**(6): 324–30.

Swanson K (1991) Empirical development of a middle range theory of caring. *Nursing Research* **40**(3): 161–6.

Young D (1996) The midwifery revolution in New Zealand. What can we learn? *Birth* **23**(3): 125–7.

# Chapter 11

# How Can We Relate?

*Mavis Kirkham*

## The purpose of the relationship

There seem to be two views on the purpose of the midwife–mother relationship. These are not the separate views of mothers and midwives but views that spring from the very different discourses of organisations and of women.

Sheer scale means that organisations must generalise. From the organisational viewpoint, the midwife–mother relationship is the medium through which the service is provided. The service works best where the relationship works well, but the aims are generalised, laid down, and hopefully audited, to cover all service users and all eventualities. Thus, a service experienced as fragmented by individual women may be seen as organisationally efficient in terms of staff deployment, even though it does not permit individual relationships to develop.

For the service user, the relationship is about feeling safe and able. Many midwives, similarly, seek to enable their clients to feel safe, to 'take up their power' (see Chapter 1) and see themselves as 'women who can' (see Chapter 3). Midwives also want to feel safe and able in their work.

This dichotomy may be seen, slightly differently, as that of the technocratic or medicalised view and the holistic view (Davis-Floyd 1992). In this analysis also, the technocratic view is concerned with generalisation and treating all women 'as if' they are not able to give birth using their own powers; the professional role is emphasised as one of decision-making. The holistic view trusts, and thereby usually enhances, the woman's ability to give birth; the active role is hers. These viewpoints are demonstrated in Chapter 4 as 'risk versus potential'.

227

The boundaries between these approaches are far from absolute. Organisational and medical aims should include the achievement of individual aims, yet there is inevitably a tension between the individual and the general.

## My journey

### *The tensions of practice*

I have experienced considerable tension between what I was taught and what I have observed as a midwife. My midwifery training, in 1971, inevitably centred on skills and knowledge that were largely medically defined. Previous work as a social scientist in Africa had equipped me to observe as an outsider and to recognise patterns of oppression. It was probably this experience which ensured that much of my socialisation as a midwife did not 'take'. I was taught how midwives and mothers should behave on a consultant unit labour ward. I observed how differently midwives and labouring women behaved in the GP unit and at home, as well as the contrast between day and night on the consultant unit. I saw the many covert tactics that midwives used to protect women, such as the phenomenal number of occasions on which a vaginal examination revealed an anterior lip of cervix in the presence of a time limit on the second stage, and the frequency with which otherwise adept midwives dropped sterile scissors when delivering those women whose consultants insisted upon an episiotomy. Midwives did not contest the rules; instead, they made covert efforts to create some leeway for women in very tightly defined situations.

I compared midwives in the way in which they treated parents and students, especially when they were nervous. When I was treated as useless, I shrank and became more nervous and incompetent; when treated as useful, I bloomed and could help. So it was with parents. I was known to be a graduate, rare then among student midwives, I pondered how different midwives responded to me and how they treated those whom they perceived as different, deviant or possibly threatening.

Women taught me the ignorance that was implicit in the knowledge I had gained as a student. For example, my training had left me with the assumption that labour somehow made a woman incapable of using her legs. I had only seen women labour and deliver in bed, have a bedbath and be taken to the ward on a trolley. Then I came to see women walk in labour. One day, I delivered a woman who chose to stand, unsupported, for the birth. Her baby was taken to the resuscitaire, and she followed and stood beside the resuscitaire, with the cord and clamp between her knees, anxiously watching her baby. My ignorant assumptions dissolved. I have had so many similar experiences of my ignorance with regard to women, and families, who knew and did what was right for them. I have managed to carry out homebirths most years since I qualified, and that too has increased my education.

I have had excellent role models and the privilege of working in small units, with midwives and mothers who chose to be there rather than experience the 'conveyor belt' obstetrics of the local large units. I have thus seen women being heard and respected, as well as their immensely able response to the, often unaccustomed, experience of being heard. I remember the Sister who admitted a young woman to a labour ward with no fetal movements, who held her while she sobbed, did not deny the woman's experience and continued to hold her while organising a panoply of medical tests and a police search for her husband. Much later, she passed her into the arms of the woman's quaking husband with the words, 'She's been so brave but you're the one she needs.' That teenage husband visibly grew into his responsibility and his bereavement; their subsequent care was provided as a couple.

I remember the community midwife who took personal on-call for the poverty-stricken single mother of a large family whose baby was booked for adoption. The woman laboured while her children were at school. The midwife disturbed nothing in the bedroom. The woman looked away when the baby was delivered, and the baby was then dressed by a neighbour in the kitchen and collected by the social services. The midwife, and every trace of the delivery, was gone when the children returned from school. Excellent postnatal care was conducted within school hours. That woman had categorically refused to go to hospital; I wonder what would have happened had she not felt able to approach 'her' midwife.

I remember the many women who were heard by midwives and the way in which they, in turn, supported their midwives. They showed me that my role, as parentcraft Sister, was to help individuals to make their path through and round our system. They came back to talk to future classes about how they did just that. I saw women bring about small changes and other women build on those changes.

So I learnt about my ignorance and gained a knowledge of what could be done. It became important to enable that knowledge to be shared and to create circumstances in which it could be used. Like Nicky Leap (Chapter 1), I took a more facilitative role because I learnt what women and families could do.

## The tensions of research

I moved into midwifery research because I had so many questions and because I was a researcher before I was a midwife. Research is being used to challenge some areas of technological ritual in obstetrics, can unite midwives and mothers and can serve as a rallying cry:

> The best weapons childbirth practitioners have in the battle to improve maternity care is that the data are all on our side. (Goer 1997:27)

Publications such as *Effective Care in Pregnancy and Childbirth* (Chalmers *et al.* 1989) and the Cochrane Database of Systematic Reviews make such 'weapons' available to midwives. Publications such as *Obstetric Myths versus Research Realities* (Goer 1995) and efforts to help childbearing women gain the skills critically to appraise research reports (CASP 1997) all serve to aid midwives and women to work together in partnership.

Reviewing the evaluations of recent innovative midwifery projects, Lesley Page highlights the advantages of providing continuity of carer and concludes:

> The message which is coming through from the research is that what is best for mothers may also be best for midwives. (Page 1997:652)

Given the nature of much of the evidence, the coming of evidence-based care gave cause for hope. Yet the evidence-based practice concept assumes an expert practice that is done to a 'patient'. It may not fit a natural process (Bogdan-Lovis 1999) in which the midwife seeks to 'minimise disturbance', 'maximise potential', trust the woman's expertise and 'shift power towards the woman' (see Chapter 1). The recognition of a hierarchical authority of expert knowledge can also create vulnerability in the face of the authority of economic interpretations. Many schemes, based on excellent evidence, have still been closed for economic reasons.

The introduction of informed choice held some hope for moving power towards the woman. Each of the MIDIRS Informed Choice leaflets for women carries the heading, 'This leaflet is based on research to help you make your own choice' (MIDIRS 1996), yet evidence-based client choice is a complex issue to introduce into hierarchically organised practice. (We are currently researching this in evaluating the MIDIRS Informed Choice leaflets.) Informed choice is an intellectual activity, very different from 'feeling safe enough to let go' (Chapter 5). It involves a degree of choice and weighing of options that many women do not exercise in the rest of their lives. The 'skittering', 'water-boatman' style of attending of the deprived women described by Jean Davies in Chapter 6 is utterly different from that envisaged in the informed choice literature. As Nicky Leap states in Chapter 1:

> There is a fragile element within the notion we call 'informed choice'. Apart from the potential for decision-making that is biased by the person who is doing the informing, there are many situations in which no amount of information will clarify the decision process for women... I have found that, in many situations, raising the notion of 'uncertainty' has led to more fruitful discussion than has pursuing the idea of 'informed choice'. Embracing uncertainty sometimes brings a sense of calm, a sense that what will be, will be. This is not about engendering a passive fatalism but more about enabling women to learn to trust that they will cope whatever comes their way. Working through these issues is particularly important in a culture that privileges notions of 'choice' and 'control'.

This is important for two reasons. First, midwifery has embraced evidence-based practice, clinical guidelines and quality standards. There was little option, and much good is contained therein. However, this was done without examining the language and inherent values, yet another embodiment of male culturally coded values to which we will have to adjust our care. Second, the issue of uncertainty is important. The glorious thing about research is that it 'fosters a sense of uncertainty' (Chalmers 1983:152). Midwifery is about living with uncertainty and helping women to do so, yet all the guidelines of evidence-based medicine and standards of quality management tend to foster rule-based behaviour and the illusion that we can control childbearing and overcome uncertainty:

> Guidelines come to be interpreted as 'rules', and any non-compliance has to be defended. The institutional structures do not allow midwives to use a sound theoretical basis on which flexibly to use their clinical judgement in response to each woman's unique circumstances. (Taylor 1999:5)

It is possible for clinical guidelines to be written and owned by midwives and to reflect the realities of midwifery practice. The creation of the clinical guidelines for the midwives unit at Edgware in London is an excellent example of this process (Jones 2000). It is also possible for midwives to create guidelines for midwifery-based care, even in large consultant units (see, for example, Central Sheffield University Hospitals 1998, Leicester Royal Infirmary NHS Trust 1996), that challenge the many routine practices which are not evidence based and which go on to influence practice more widely. This is nevertheless not an easy process, and it tends to be achieved on a small scale, in small midwifery units or in midwife-led care within larger units. The problems of the monolith remain.

## Hierarchies and midwives: the containment of opposing values?

The midwife is traditionally 'with woman' in the singular, but for many years now she has worked within hierarchical organisations. The centralisation of maternity care into hospital-based organisations has brought benefits, but has also required much adjustment from midwives. Many of the problems in this adjustment sprang from the tensions between organisational viewpoints and those of individual women. Ironically, the viewpoint of public health, which might bridge this gap, has been largely lost in NHS maternity care in the UK since it was based in hospitals in the late 1970s.

There are clear parallels between the needs of midwives and mothers, and the skills they need in those roles: support, facilitation, transmitting confidence and bringing out the abilities of others. The negative side of these parallels comes into play with attempts to meet the needs of only one side of the midwife–mother partnership. There is thus a fundamental problem where midwives are required to facilitate clients in exercising skills that they have not had the opportunity to develop themselves. Midwives cannot empower women where they themselves are disempowered (Jamieson 1994, see also Chapter 1), and 'disempowered midwives disempower women' (see Chapter 4). Yet midwives are expected to support women in exercising choice and control (Department of Health 1993), even though they may not have had the opportunity to exercise choice and control in their work and thereby to have developed the necessary skills or experienced such facilitation.

Health care organisations aim to be efficient, achieving the maximum health gain with the minimum use of resources. I feel that maternity care fits oddly into this formula since most childbearing women are, and remain, healthy, the prevention of ill health is almost impossible to measure, and health can be impaired by childbearing. Nevertheless resources, including midwives, must be controlled and used flexibly in organisational terms. When the service is seen in such industrial terms, care becomes fragmented and conveyor belt-like, and little attention is given to developing relationships between midwives and mothers. Continuity of care is difficult to achieve in these circumstances as institutional values rarely acknowledge relationships. Nevertheless, brave attempts are being made by individuals and it is possible, by legislation, to superimpose a system of case-holding midwifery upon a hospital system, as has happened in New Zealand (see Chapters 9 and 10).

## Midwives' adaptation to power structures

### An oppressed group

Working within institutions as employees has meant that midwives have received orders from their employers and given orders to their 'patients'. As Mary Cronk (Chapter 2) and Tricia Anderson (Chapter 5) describe, such a situation led midwives to treat women as children, This was not surprising as that was the treatment they were themselves receiving. We have all been referred to by senior obstetricians as 'my midwives' or 'my girls'; even 'my nurses' has been known to pass uncorrected.

Within hierarchical systems, the dominance of midwifery earlier in the twentieth century by medicine and more recently by general management has led midwives to cope by internalising the values of the power-holders. This is the behaviour of an oppressed group (Freire 1972), whose leaders respond to external power-holders rather than to the traditions and values of their own group (Roberts 1983, Heagarty 1996). In such circumstances, there is much pressure to internalise oppressive values and act them out upon colleagues and clients (Leap 1997, Stapleton *et al.* 1998). All of these factors have contributed to a culture of midwifery within organisations in which power lies with the professionals, relationships are not valued, and midwives feel undervalued as both women and carers (Kirkham 1999a).

This is not to say that good care cannot be achieved within such organisations. Maternity services are totally dependent upon midwives making the best that they can of their, usually brief, relationships with childbearing women. Yet such organisations embody values that do not acknowledge the fundamental importance of care and of relationships. Celia Davies (1995) describes this as the cultural coding of organisations and professions, built upon values that are coded as male, for example control, measurement, mastery and hierarchy. Midwifery springs from values coded as female: support, caring and enabling women to feel safe and able. 'The work that women do, after all, is noticed when it is not there, and taken for granted when it is' (Davies 1995:165); it does not carry status. Midwives striving to give good care, as valued by individual women, therefore, live with the stress of working against the organisational grain and having little value placed upon their efforts.

## *Professionalisation*

In a situation of relative powerlessness, midwifery leaders chose the path of professionalisation. Such a path offered respectability, a degree of status and the power of acknowledged expertise. The expert knows best. In England, it was a leadership committed to professionalisation with due deference to medicine, which worked to achieve the 1902 Midwives Act. It has been demonstrated in many settings that the legal regulation of midwifery and its educational provision is likely to ensure professionalisation (De Vries 1985, Mason 1990). In recent years, the professionalisation of so many occupations around health care has meant that midwives had to continue along this path or be disadvantaged.

The professionalisation of midwifery, with its emphasis on expert knowledge has, however, also emphasised professional power over that of clients (Kirkham 1996, 1998). Ruth Wilkins (Chapter 3) sees professions as being grounded in those same, masculine values that are organisationally oppressive. She examines 'the paucity of the professional paradigm', which she sees as alienating midwives and mothers from their own experience and encouraging 'an object-orientated perception of clients or patients' (see Chapter 3). Within a professional paradigm, there are many contradictions in the call to woman-centred midwifery practice.

## Changing or avoiding hierarchies in favour of relationships

Hierarchical structures such as those which exist in the NHS tend to distort the midwife–mother relationship. Efforts have been made, within the NHS, to improve those relationships. *Changing Childbirth* (Department of Health 1993) is an excellent example of this, as are the many efforts to implement it. I hesitate, and deliberately do not use the past tense here. Although many of those innovations no longer exist, something of the spirit remains. Nevertheless, there are problems when efforts to humanise a service reach midwives as orders through a hierarchical system, or equally when midwives want to change and management does not respond.

In some places, recent changes have flattened the management hierarchy within midwifery, although midwives have often experienced this as the removal of midwifery leadership. General management control has, however, grown. Recent quality moves work in the same direction. Evidence-based practice and local and national clinical guidelines all provide external pressures to render practice uniform. Given the problems inherent in midwifery in hierarchical settings, it is not surprising that many chapters in this book choose to examine the midwife–mother relationship where the hierarchy is less present: in the community, in the client's home or in independent practice. These are also the settings where women are cared for in their own social context.

## Support

In recent years, as research has developed and become increasingly important in the maternity services, the value of supportive relationships has been demonstrated. This has been thoroughly researched with regard to support in labour where it is acknowledged that:

> The constant presence of a supportive birth companion is one of the most effective forms of care in childbirth. (MIDIRS 1996:1)

Antenatal support from known midwives also has long-term, health-promoting effects for mothers and children (see Chapter 6 and Oakley *et al.* 1996).

It is interesting that, while we have research knowledge that is clearer here than in most areas of maternity care, it is often not acted upon. Midwives frequently care for more than one woman in labour, and the number of antenatal and postnatal visits is reduced. Such moves are clearly a response to economic imperatives.

The actual giving of support appropriate to an individual, with whom they have fleeting contact, is often stressful for midwives, who must constantly balance the client's wishes against their continuing relationships with their colleagues (Levy 1998, 1999). We thus have a dichotomy in our knowledge and practice. Support is known to be effective, yet the values of the system in which we work prevent this knowledge being put to best use. In the tensions that occur between research-based knowledge and authoritative knowledge (Jordan 1993, Davis-Floyd and Sargent 1997), the latter carries weight. Thus, midwives are blocked from acting upon both their traditional knowledge and research-based evidence even when the two reinforce each other.

Nevertheless, when support is seen as an important factor in maternity care, the issue of the relationships through which support is given needs to come to the fore, as must the development of those relationships over time.

## Continuity of care

Relationships between individuals can only develop where those concerned continue to meet. Independent midwifery is founded upon this principle, and efforts have been made to create continuity of care projects within the NHS, with a good outcome (Flint 1993, Page 1995, McCourt and Page 1996, Allen *et al.* 1997, Green *et al.* 1998). Yet institutional values have often overridden those of continuity of care and led to the end of such schemes, even when successful. There is, therefore, much that can be learnt from countries with a system of independent case-holding midwifery within mainstream maternity services.

It is not surprising that many of the chapters of this book are concerned with settings where there is continuity of care. Indeed, Nicky Leap and Sally Pairman have played an important part in establishing and developing such a model of care, Nicky in London and Sally in the much more receptive context of New Zealand.

## Mothers and continuity of care

Where women experience continuity of care, they speak of it as being very important; this is demonstrated in many places in this book and in evaluations of care (McCourt and Page 1996, Sims and Kirkham 1999). In these circumstances, with the development of the relationship between midwife and woman, and the growth of trust, it is possible for the woman's agenda to be addressed. The active agent in maternity care can then become the childbearing woman.

## Midwives and continuity of care

The development of continuing relationships between individual midwives and mothers can change midwives, moving their primary loyalty towards their clients and team of colleagues, rather than their employer or profession (Brodie 1996a, 1996b). An appropriate response to individuals then becomes the primary purpose of care and of relationships. The discourse becomes that of women rather than of generalisation. Women respond to this positively (McCourt and Page 1996, Allen *et al.* 1997), and trust can develop.

In settings with continuity of carer, midwives can both give and facilitate better support for mothers (see Chapter 1). It is significant that, in such settings, midwives also build better support systems for themselves (Allen *et al.* 1997, Stapleton *et al.* 1998). This may well be because they are outside, or sheltered from, disempowering hierarchical pressures.

While continuing responsibility for the care of individual women can bring clear benefits for midwives in terms of autonomy, support and job satisfaction, it can also be experienced as a threat. Midwives contemplating such care from within existing systems fear sacrificing what they have within the *status quo*. Thus, midwifery managers fear the loss of managerial control (Wraight *et al.* 1993), and midwives working shifts fear the loss of their accustomed working patterns (Henderson 1997, Sims and Kirkham 1999). The threat to established defence reactions often leads midwives to say either 'It can't work' or 'Women don't really want it.'

Evaluating a team midwifery scheme in Doncaster (Sims and Kirkham 1999), I interviewed midwives working on the labour ward before and after the one-year project. In the initial interviews, many midwives working adjacent to the project perceived it as a threat. After the project, when it was known that the new patterns of working would not continue or change their working lives, they were remarkably honest about its positive affects on both mothers and team members.

After generations of adjustment to working within hierarchies, and the constant organisational change of recent years, it is scarcely surprising that midwives do not all seize with enthusiasm the prospect of further profound change and adjustment, particularly when they have little choice in its introduction. This has frequently been demonstrated in relation to attempts in recent years to give choice and control to women with regard to their maternity care. It is problematic to expect midwives to give what they do not themselves have. While some midwives have been keen to implement innovations, many pilot projects have been surrounded by resistance to change among midwives adjacent to the innovation (see, for example, McCourt and Page 1996, Henderson 1997).

## Trust

One theme running throughout this book is the importance of trust between mothers and midwives. Trust is defined as a 'reliance upon or confidence in a person or thing' (*Collins Dictionary* 1987).

I can envisage a continuum in terms of women's engagement with the maternity services (Figure 11.1). At the negative end of the continuum, the service is unknown and cannot be discovered; this must be the experience of women who lack a common language with their carers and know no-one who has used the service. Beyond this comes predictability. This may be negative: one can rely on the fact that, or be confident that, a person or service will be uniform and predictable, even if not as one would wish. Thus, women can observe midwives attending to prescribed physical 'checks' and avoiding communication relating to their clients' concerns, or behaving in a way that leads women to predict that their midwives' lack of ease with homebirth will lead them to find a reason to transfer the woman to hospital (see Chapter 4). Predictability may be lacking in personal engagement but involving some trust, as in commercial 'brand loyalty'. Some women may value the NHS and see midwives as a good thing even though they do not form relationships with actual midwives. There are many levels between mere predictability and trust (see Chapter 4), extending up to the midpoint of the continuum.

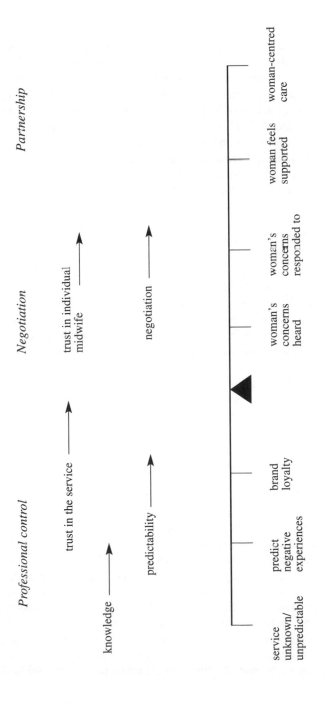

**Figure 11.1** Continuum of a woman's possible engagement with the maternity services

Up until this point, the professional has control, but the midpoint is the fulcrum where the power balance starts to move towards the woman. Beyond this point, relationships with individual midwives develop and negotiation becomes possible. The next stage occurs when the woman finds that her concerns are heard, and then that her concerns are responded to. Where this response is effective, she feels supported and enabled. This end of the continuum is woman-centred care, power being shared and partnership being possible.

Within relationships, trust must rest upon common values. This is not to say that it is essential for the midwife and mother to have a common viewpoint, but the midwife must be aware of, and able to offer respect for and support within, the mother's values and priorities. In this situation, the mother feels that she is acknowledged and valued; she feels safe in the relationship. The midwife can then make a woman 'feel special' (see Chapters 3 and 10). She can also 'give' (see Chapter 1) what the woman seeks and defines, rather than what the midwife defines as being best for her.

Trust, like all aspects of relationship, is two way. Midwives have their own continuum and the more secure end of the woman's continuum may contain threats to the midwife's sense of security. For midwives, relationships with women are maintained in the context of many working relationships. To protect her relationships with colleagues and power-holders, the midwife seeks to ensure that clients' behaviour does not threaten these. Valerie Levy demonstrates midwives balancing many relationships; indeed, she pictures this as being achieved upon a tightrope. Thus, hospital midwives in antenatal clinics are in a relational impasse in which a woman, referred from the community staff for hospital booking, reveals that she really wants a homebirth (Levy 1998). Doubtless the midwives involved with the women in Nadine Edwards' study (see Chapter 4) were very aware of institutional norms and managers' attitudes, as well as limitations in their own confidence with regard to homebirth.

In such situations, the midwife, if she trusts the mother, becomes involved with attitudes and values that are deeply threatening in the context of her relationships as a professional and an employee. In such circumstances, relationships are negotiated and renegotiated, and trust has to be reconstituted (Levy 1998) or replaced by mistrust.

I have tried to find a way of relating the woman's continuum of engagement with the service to the midwife's continuum of engagement with childbearing women. The fulcrum is, in a sense, in the same place in each case. As the woman takes power, the midwife's power lessens, which can create tension in the midwife's relationships with her colleagues and employers. Yet each continuum is highly influenced by context and how individuals choose to behave in their context. My attempts to picture a relationship between continua can only relate to the start of a child's game of Pickupstixs, where the slightest movement in one of a heap of sticks upsets the balance of several others.

Midwives so often seek to make mothers' behaviour predictable in terms that are organisationally acceptable, and they exhibit more trust in mothers whose behaviour can be predicted to fit these norms. My own research, some years ago (Kirkham 1989), showed midwives policing mothers' behaviour in labour to fit what they perceived to be the acceptable norms of the labour ward and giving information more readily to women who demonstrated compliance. Therein lie the roots of the inverse care law (Tudor Hart 1971, Arnold 1987, Brown and Lumley 1993, Walker *et al.* 1995) – the inequities in our service that lead to a lower standard of care for those who, for reasons of culture, class or language, cannot demonstrate such compliance. Even where innovations are offered to improve continuity of carer, the sad pattern continues. White women and women whose first language is English have been reported as being more likely to be cared for within team midwifery schemes (Hemingway *et al.* 1994, Hirst 1999).

It is not useful to blame midwives, even though they experience and expect blame (Kirkham 1999a). Indeed, it is important to examine the ways in which the conflicting pressures upon midwives undermine their trust in themselves. It is important too to examine the negative parallels in the relationships of midwives and of mothers within the NHS maternity services. It is exceedingly difficult for midwives to demonstrate trust in women when the culture of the NHS does not lead them to feel that they are trusted or trustworthy in their key working relationships. If care is to improve, the culture within the NHS must be addressed. 'A culture within midwifery which can be hierarchical, competitive and punitive, towards both midwives and mothers' (Taylor 1996:216) has a corrosive influence upon midwives' ability to relate in a confident and trusting manner.

Midwives seek to be acceptable and trustworthy within a complex mesh of relationships that includes those with clients. Chris Bewley (Chapter 8) examines one: how midwives without children present themselves as credible to childbearing clients. Margaret Chesney (Chapter 7) examines a further area of complexity, that of midwives' relationships with interpreters and their relationships with clients through interpreters. When an interpreter, seeking to help a woman to relate to the NHS as she sees it, orders her to 'speak when she is spoken to', the midwife is made very aware of the values underpinning her practice and their lack of fit with much that is around them. It is a real challenge to respond in a way that shifts power towards non-English speaking mothers and treats interpreters with respect. It would help if this challenge were more widely acknowledged and supported.

## Trust and safety

Feeling safe enables us to achieve our maximum potential, either as mothers or as midwives. Where there is threat (the opposite of trust), we are inevitably defensive, rigid, unable to give and clinging to the power we have.

Safety is so often seen as a medical judgement or a management issue, as in risk management. Thus, the power to judge what is safe becomes a professional issue, with consequent disempowerment for the woman. The adult–child parallels are clear in the assumptions of who 'knows best'. If we accept safety as being entirely a matter for professional judgement, the mother must place herself entirely in the hands of the expert. She may then feel safe, but it is the safety of dependence. She cannot, in such dependency, feel able. To say this is not to deny professional knowledge but to place it in the context of many other ways of knowing.

*Changing Childbirth* contains a statement relating to this:

> Safety is not an absolute concept. It is part of a greater picture encompassing all aspects of health and wellbeing. (Department of Health 1993:10)

This is a profoundly important, but little debated, part of that key government report. We continue to define safety in narrow clinical or managerial terms, deciding as experts what constitutes an unacceptable level of risk. Such decisions often involve the perceived safety–security of the health professional rather than that of the mother. Where control is the dominant language, it is difficult to raise issues of potential and growth, which, as every parent knows, are inevitably linked to risk.

There are important issues of client control, as against professional dominance. Women's perceived control of care and carers has been linked with a range of positive outcomes (Green *et al.* 1988), yet the language of control, while important in countering the control of others, is less than adequate in childbearing. Trust seems to be the key. Tricia Anderson's title for her study of relationships in the second stage of labour (Chapter 5) seems to highlight the central issue. 'Feeling safe enough to let go' demonstrates this relationship between safety and trust.

Whatever the clinical outcome, trust is enabling. Nadine Edwards, in Chapter 4, concludes:

> However the birth process unfolded, where trust was the foundation of the relationship between the woman and her midwife, the woman interpreted her experience in terms of growth and change. This was usually related to a general increase in confidence but could have wider implications.

## Skills for relationships

Midwives need key skills in order to sustain relationships that help women to feel safe and able. One central example is midwives' belief in women, which enhances women's belief in themselves and is the key issue in trust, with all its positive effects. Yet this belief can only be sustained where midwives believe in themselves and the effectiveness of their skills.

Differing aspects of midwifery skill will be called for at different stages in the relationship. If the second stage of labour is about letting go, the postnatal period is one of taking up. Fundamental midwifery skills continue, including the need for the midwife to convey the belief that the mother is capable, and to facilitate support.

### *Being with and standing back*

Presence, being with women, is very little valued within a professional culture that values action and measurable skill, yet the importance of the midwife's presence runs through this book. The continued calm presence of the midwife, particularly during labour, demonstrates to the woman that her experience is normal. The midwife conveys by her unruffled presence that what she witnesses is to be expected and can be coped with, and that all is well. She provides a safe anchor (see Chapter 5). Confidence is infectious and very easily transmitted. When this is achieved, there is a real skill in withdrawing to allow the woman and those who love her to build upon that confidence in private. The skill of withdrawal is exercised briefly at many points, as well as at the end of midwifery care.

There is, of course, a reverse side to such a managed, positive presence or withdrawal. Apprehension and panic are even more easily transmitted than confidence, with damaging affects. It is easy, with a primary, professional focus on monitoring for abnormality, to fail to transmit confidence, to be 'absently present' (Berg *et al.* 1996), or worse.

### Emotional labour

Much of a midwife's work is concerned with 'dealing with other people's feelings' (James 1989). Such emotional labour involves the management of emotion in a number of respects, such as helping women to cope with distress and pain, giving and facilitating support through a major life transition with all its relationship changes, and conveying confidence and calm. It is also important to recognise 'when to be still or withdraw' (Chapter 1). Many aspects of this work are described in this book, yet relatively little has been written on such skills in midwifery, and I borrow the term 'emotional labour' from sociology (Hochschild 1983) and from nursing (James 1989, Smith 1992, Staden 1998). Since such work is not recorded, is scarcely described and is unlikely to be formally taught, it is transmitted from midwife to midwife orally and by observation. Such transmission is, however, inhibited by the many pressures upon the midwife, which are seen as being more important.

It is often assumed that midwives have skills in the management of emotions that are gained in normal life, especially as women. While this may be true, it means that such skills are likely to be learnt from a position of deference and being taken for granted. These circumstances may be conducive to the construction of defence mechanisms or gaining skill in the suppression of emotions rather than to their management.

## Women's skills, women's knowledge?

At a number of points in this book, common experiences, as women or mothers, are mentioned as enhancing the understanding between midwives and their clients.

Chris Bewley (Chapter 8) examines the experience of midwives without children who work in hospital and therefore do not have relationships with women that have developed over time. They reported that clients frequently asked whether they had children. The midwives saw this as a search for kindness and sympathy as well as an enquiry into whether they were 'suitably qualified' to care for the women during their rite of passage to parenthood. These childless midwives developed a range of strategies for appearing 'normal' in the eyes of their clients and, as a result, 'the midwives retained control of the conversation and thereby the relationship'. This 'experiential disadvantage' was thus likely to lead to an increased emphasis on professional knowledge and expertise; a professional power advantage.

In the absence of an existing relationship, the client's question is likely to pose a threat to the equilibrium of the one meeting between midwife and mother, although that meeting could last a whole shift during a labour. Midwives are likely to invest more of their selves in longer relationships. From the midwife's point of view, it is not worth uncomfortable personal preliminaries if a relationship is not going to develop, yet the mother seeks to establish some basis for trust with her carer, especially in labour. Chris Bewley's ongoing larger study of midwives without children will, hopefully, examine how midwives manage this aspect of self-identity where they provide continuity of care in a community setting.

I learnt a great deal from Ann Garner, a Sheffield community midwife who could not have children (Aspinall *et al.* 1997). Most women who were booked with her knew women whom she had delivered so it was known that Ann did not have children but kept Labradors. The general reaction was that her childlessness was her loss, but her generous availability as a midwife was the local community's gain. I doubt if she was often asked whether she had children. She had decided to manage such questions with reference to the Labradors long before I met her.

There are nevertheless 'sweeping statements' in the literature that 'imply that midwives who do not have children are somehow lacking' (Chapter 8), and these value judgements merit examination. The issue of how to be a 'mother figure' or a 'surrogate mum' (Chapter 5) is much wider than that of whether or not the midwife has given birth. The nurturing and mothering of an adult becoming a mother herself is a very special skill. To learn such skill, it is useful to have experienced such nurturing. It is also useful to have thought about it and learnt from those for whom one cares. It is important that midwives have the skills to develop strategies for learning from women and using the self in ways that are nurturing rather than draining. Opportunities to learn such skills are not always available to students or midwives, nor are we always sustained with the confidence to take such opportunities. Ann Garner taught me much as she allowed mothers and student midwives to take up their power (Aspinall *et al.* 1997).

Apart from the knowledge acquired in giving birth, there is the issue of what, and how, women know as women. While women are not an homogenous group, there are some common experiences and reactions to the female lot. Sally Pairman states that 'Both the woman and the midwife bring themselves as women to the relationship, and the shared experience of being female contributes to the nature of the relationship' (Chapter 10). Much of this shared experience springs from the division of labour, particularly the division of emotional labour in our society. We could learn from the literature here.

*Women's Ways of Knowing* (Belenky *et al.* 1986) broke important conceptual ground on how knowledge is produced, comprehended and ultimately internalised. Not surprisingly, although this is often undocumented, women go about these processes differently from men. The variations lie not in the biological differences between women and men but in the division of labour and the value attached to those divisions in our society (Hurtado 1996).

The considerable literature on 'women's ways of knowing' (Belenky *et al.* 1986, 1997, Goldberger *et al.* 1996) must stimulate us to examine this issue. Women's knowing may be seen as examples of 'subjugated knowledge', as described by Foucault (Gordon 1986). In midwifery knowledge, two sorts of subjugation may be seen. First, there is the subjugation of traditional and experiential midwifery knowledge by the authoritative knowledge of medicine and, to a lesser extent, of research. Second, there is the subjugation of the experiential knowledge of childbearing women by midwives in their professional capacity. Midwives can both experience exclusion and exclude (Kirkham 1999b) in this and other ways. Parallel experiences of oppression do not necessarily create a bond between women and midwives, yet subjugated knowledge is essential for criticism and for change (Gordon 1986). United, the knowledge of midwives and mothers could achieve much to change dominant modes of knowing. There remains, however, the question of how to unite.

Belenky *et al.* (1986) examine five ways of knowing or strategies for knowing (Goldberger *et al.* 1996): silence (knowing in action), received knowing, subjective knowing, procedural knowing and constructed knowing. Such a classification can, at the very least, help us to acknowledge and respond to mothers' ways of knowing, which may be very different from the professional paradigm with its emphasis on intellectual knowledge.

## Bridging cultural divides

Without an understanding of other ways of knowing, we tend to respond only to those who ask, yet so many research reports quote women as saying, 'If I'd asked she might have told me, but you don't like to ask.' Many women feel they cannot ask because midwives exude business. For many women, such as those with whom Jean Davies (Chapter 6) worked, 'skittering' patterns of speech and 'water-boatman', ever-moving consciousness demonstrates coping mechanisms within which such questions are unlikely to be formulated. Where an interpreter is needed, there are further factors ensuring that a woman's concerns are not raised.

The need for 'cultural brokerage' (Chapter 7) arises wherever there is cultural difference. There is much of relevance here in the New Zealand concept of 'cultural safety' and the way in which that concept has been taken up throughout education. 'Cultural safety requires that all human beings be nursed *regardful of all that makes them unique*' (Nursing Council of New Zealand 1996:3, emphasis original). This education is based upon the belief that 'a nurse or midwife who understands their own culture and the theory of power relations can be culturally safe in any context' (ibid:4). The objects of cultural safety in the education of New Zealand midwives are 'designed to help create self-knowledge and lead to practice wisdom' and to 'produce... midwives who are culturally safe to practice, *as defined by the people they serve*' (Ramsden 1995:6, emphasis added). This is an explicit statement of intention to move power to women, and it has immense political implications.

## *Listening and drawing out*

Before we can relate appropriately, we must listen and learn who the woman is to whom we seek to relate. This includes a host of skills included in Nicky Leap's word 'cluefullness': picking up 'the overt and covert clues from women and their worlds' (Chapter 1). Several chapters in this book demonstrate women's skill in picking up cues from midwives regarding their world and its expectations of clients. Professional pressures often prevent midwives, who have these skills in other contexts, from being 'cluefull'.

Supportive listening leads us to ask the right questions, which can 'encourage women's awareness and sense of independence and responsibility' (Chapter 1). This is the question-posing technique of the mother who seeks to develop her child. While it was also the technique of Socrates, it has a very long tradition as the skill of drawing out the potential of others in which women excel (Belenky *et al.* 1986). Such questioning is an immensely powerful technique, widely used by women in many roles, to reveal the power and potential of the person questioned. '[The] time they spend with the midwife is unique in that they are seen as themselves and their concerns are validated' (Chapter 10), yet the protective privacy in which this skilled and powerful technique is exercised makes it invisible and little acclaimed. In midwifery, the use of such skills for empowerment restores our practice to a motherly, developmental tradition established long before our present culture of practice. In the present day, however, we have a duty to research, develop and render visible such vital skills.

In the public view, support is fundamental to the practice of midwifery. This is beautifully demonstrated in a wider community development setting in which those who listen and facilitate collaborative working to 'draw out and empower' become known as 'midwife teachers' because they embody the spirit of support and empowerment which is intrinsic to midwifery; 'they enable the community to give birth to fledgling ideas and nurture the ideas along until they become powerful ways of knowing' (Belenky *et al.* 1997:14). The challenge is to be 'midwife teachers' to our own skills as midwives.

## The place of the self

Chris Bewley's infertile respondent said 'when they ask me about children they're asking my person, not my profession, my Being'

(Chapter 8). This was clearly experienced as being intrusive and painful. Such experience must be respected, yet it is not without irony in the context of the midwife's license to intrude into the body and being of her client.

Ruth Wilkins (Chapter 3) reports women as wanting 'a close personal relationship' with their community midwife, and Sally Pairman (Chapter 10) speaks of 'professional friendship'. In both contexts, women see these relationships as closer and different from those with other health professionals. Yet, even within friendship, choices are made on the presentation of self. Where the language and concepts of professionalism alienate both midwives and mothers from their own experience (Chapter 3), we are likely to respond from feelings of threat and discomfort rather than weighing the use and the protection of self. Midwives have many defence reactions that have been developed for good reasons. Only when midwives work in ways that help us build trust in ourselves and in each other will we feel safe enough to use our selves to best affect.

## Taking power

This book demonstrates both what is possible and what is needed in relationships between midwives and mothers. It also leaves me very aware of where the potential of this relationship is not being realised and needs go unrecognised.

There are striking parallels between the experiences and the needs of midwives and mothers, yet so often they meet in settings where both lack power and midwives' fear and professional allegiance do not allow them to identify with women. It is my hope that naming the issues creates the possibility for debate. Describing what is being done creates the possibility that more *can* be done. Thus we continue to nibble at the monolith of hierarchical organisations and the professional paradigm.

The problem lies in our reluctance as midwives to take up our power and form relationships and alliances, and in our fears of moving the power towards women despite the benefits described by midwives who do this. We may be able to learn from the New Zealand experience of 'partnership on a political level' (Chapter 9). Val Fleming describes the role of the consumer within midwifery in New Zealand, for example in membership and board membership of the New Zealand College of Midwives. That college also developed the

Midwifery Standards Review Process, whereby two midwife peers and two consumer representatives conduct an annual review of each midwife's practice (Skinner 1998, Stewart 1999). These are examples of political moves of power towards women in organisational terms, which are likely to reflect and increase the power of women at the level of individual relationships with midwives. In England, such moves involve token consumer representatives on committees where they tend to feel swamped and outnumbered. There is a long way to go. This political partnership has, however, not been without problems for its advocates in New Zealand:

> When New Zealand domiciliary midwives were seen to be taking the side of women in support of the midwifery model, we were criticised as being unprofessional. We were publicly accused of lowering the standards of the profession. At a midwives' seminar one midwife argued that a midwife's first loyalty was to her profession, while I maintained that it was to the women we attended.

> These different concepts of loyalty are really about power relations.
> (Donley 1997:45)

These issues went on to be debated locally and internationally. An International Confederation of Midwives meeting in 1996:

> Recognised as a major issue the need to strengthen partnership of women and midwives. It also acknowledged the need to raise the political consciousness of midwives.

> The latter need was obvious because internationally the majority of midwives was not quite ready to let go of its professional status and power which is dependent on a captive clientele within a bureaucracy (Donley 1997:46).

How *do* we relate more bravely with ourselves in order to relate with women?

## References

Allen I, Dowling SB and Williams S (1997) *A Leading Role for Midwives? Evaluation of Midwifery Group Practice Development Projects*. London: Policy Studies Institute.

Arnold M (1987) The cycle of maternal deprivation. *Midwife, Health Visitor and Community Nurse* **23**(12:) 539–42.

Aspinall K, Nelson B, Patterson T and Sims A (1997) *An Extraordinary Ordinary Woman: The Story of Ann Garner, a Sheffield Midwife.* Sheffield: Ann's Trust Fund.

Belenky MF, Clinchy BMc, Goldberger NR and Tarule JM (1986) *Women's Ways of Knowing: The Development of Self, Voice and Mind.* New York: Basic Books.

Belenky MF, Bond LA, and Weinstock JS (1997) *A Tradition that Has no Name: Nurturing the Development of People, Families and Communities.* New York: Basic Books.

Berg M, Lundgren I, Hermansson E and Wahlberg V (1996) Women's encounter with the midwife during childbirth. *Midwifery* **12**: 11–15.

Bogdan-Lovis L (1999) Personal communication and seminar given at the University of Sheffield.

Brodie P (1996a) Australian team midwives in transition. International Confederation of Midwives, 24th Triennial Conference, Oslo.

Brodie P (1996b) Being with Women: The Experience of Australian Team Midwives. Unpublished Master's thesis, University of Technology, Sydney, Australia.

Brown S and Lumley J (1993) Antenatal care: a case of the inverse care law? *Australian Journal of Public Health* **17**(2): 95–103.

CASP (Critical Appraisal Skills Programme) (1997) *CASP for MSLCs. A Project Enabling Maternity Service Liaison Committees to Develop an Evidence-based Approach to Changing Childbirth.* London: CASP.

Central Sheffield University Hospitals (1998) *Evidence-based Guidelines for Midwifery Led Care in Labour.* Sheffield: Central Sheffield University Hospitals.

Chalmers I (1983) Scientific enquiry and authoritarianism in prenatal care and education. *Birth* **10**: 151–6.

Chalmers I, Enkin M and Keirse MJNC (eds) (1989) *Effective Care in Pregnancy and Childbirth.* Oxford: Oxford University Press.

Davies C (1995) *Gender and the Professional Predicament in Nursing.* Buckingham: Open University Press.

Davis-Floyd RE (1992) *Birth as an American Rite of Passage.* Berkeley, CA: University of California Press.

Davis-Floyd RE and Sargent CF (1997) *Childbirth and Authoritative Knowledge.* Berkeley, CA: University of California Press.

Department of Health (1993) *Changing Childbirth: The Report on the Expert Maternity Group.* London: HMSO.

DeVries R (1985) *Regulating Birth: Midwives, Medicine and the Law.* Philadelphia: Temple University Press.

Donley J (1997) Reclaiming partnership in birth. *Midwifery Today* **43**: 45–69.

Flint C (1993) *Midwifery: Teams and Caseloads.* London: Butterworth Heinemann.

Freire P (1972) *The Pedagogy of the Oppressed.* Harmondsworth: Penguin.

Goer H (1995) *Obstetric Myths versus Research Realities. A Guide to the Medical Literature*. Westport, CT: Bergin & Garvey.

Goer H (1997) How to use the medical literature for fun and profit. *Midwifery Today* **43**: 27.

Goldberger N, Tarule J, Clinchy B and Belenky M (eds) (1996) *Knowledge, Difference and Power: Essays Inspired by* Women's Ways of Knowing. New York: Basic Books.

Gordon C (1986) *Michael Foucault: Power/Knowledge. Selected Interviews and Other Writings 1972–77 by Michael Foucault*. Brighton: Harvester.

Green JM, Coupland V and Kitzinger JV (1988) *Great Expectations: A Prospective Study of Women's Expectations and Experiences of Childbirth*. Cambridge: Child Care and Development Group, University of Cambridge.

Green JM, Curtis P, Price H and Renfrew M (1998) *Continuing to Care. The Organisation of Midwifery Services in the UK: A Structured Review of the Evidence*. Hale, Cheshire: Books for Midwives Press.

Hart J Tudor (1971) The Inverse Care Law. *Lancet* 27 February: 405–12.

Heagarty BV (1996) Reassessing the Guilty: The Midwives Act and the Control of English Midwives in the Early 20th Century. In: Kirkham M (ed.) *Supervision of Midwives*. Hale, Cheshire: Books for Midwives Press.

Hemingway H, Saunders D and Parsons L (1994) *Women's Experiences of Maternity Services in East London: An Evaluation*. London: East London and City Health Authority.

Henderson C (1997) *'Changing Childbirth' and the West Midlands Region 1995–1996*. London: Royal College of Midwives.

Hirst J (1999) Women's Perspective of the Quality of their Maternity Care: A Comparison of Pakistani and Indigenous 'White' Women. Unpublished PhD thesis, University of Leeds.

Hochschild AR (1983) *The Managed Heart: Commercialisation of Human Feeling*. Berkeley, CA: University of California Press.

Hurtado A (1996) Strategic Suspensions: Feminists of Colour Theorise the Production of Knowledge. In: Goldberger N, Tarule J, Clinchy B and Belenky M (eds) *Knowledge, Difference and Power: Essays Inspired by* Women's Ways of Knowing. New York: Basic Books.

James N (1989) Emotional labour, skills and work in the social regulation of feeling. *Sociological Review* **37**: 15–42.

Jamieson L (1994) Midwifery empowerment through education. *British Journal of Midwifery* **2**(2): 47–8.

Jones O (2000) An Example of Innovation: Supervision in a New Midwives' Unit. In: Kirkham M (ed.) *Developments in the Supervision of Midwives*. Hale, Cheshire: Books for Midwives Press.

Jordan B (1993) *Birth in Four Cultures,* 4th edn. Prospect Heights, IL: Waveland Press.

Kirkham MJ (1989) Midwives and Information-giving During Labour. In: Robinson S and Thompson AM (eds) *Midwives, Research and Childbirth*, Volume 1. London: Chapman & Hall.

Kirkham MJ (1996) Professionalisation Past and Present: With Women or With the Powers that Be? In: Kroll D (ed.) *Midwifery Care for the Future.* London: Baillière Tindall.

Kirkham MJ (1998) Professionalisation: Dilemmas for Midwifery. In: Abbott P and Meerabeau L (eds) *The Sociology of the Caring Professions,* 2nd edn. London: UCL Press.

Kirkham MJ (1999a) The culture of midwifery in the NHS in England. *Journal of Advanced Nursing* **30**(3): 732–9.

Kirkham MJ (1999b) Exclusion in Maternity Care: Midwives and Mothers. In: Purdy M and Banks D (eds) *Health and Exclusion.* London: Routledge.

Leap N (1997) Making sense of 'horizontal violence' in midwifery. *British Journal of Midwifery* **5**(11): 689.

Leicester Royal Infirmary NHS Trust (1996) *Handbook of Evidence-based Guidelines for Midwife-led Care in Labour.* Leicester: Obstetrics and Gynaecology Directorate, Leicester Royal Infirmary NHS Trust.

Levy V (1998) Facilitating and Making Informed Choices During Pregnancy: A Study of Midwives and Pregnant Women. Unpublished PhD thesis, University of Sheffield.

Levy V (1999) Protective steering: a grounded theory study of the processes by which midwives facilitate informed choices during pregnancy. *Journal of Advanced Nursing* **29**(1): 104–12.

McCourt C and Page L (1996) *Report on the Evaluation of One-to-one Midwifery.* London: Thames Valley University/Hammersmith Hospital.

Mason J (1990) The trouble with licensing midwives. *Midwifery Today* **14**: 24–42.

MIDIRS (1996) *Support in Labour.* Informed Choice Leaflet No 1. Bristol/York: MIDIRS/NHS Centre for Reviews and Dissemination.

Nursing Council of New Zealand (1996) *Draft Guidelines for the Cultural Safety Component in Nursing and Midwifery Education.* Wellington: Nursing Council of New Zealand.

Oakley A, Hickey D, Rajan L and Rigby AS (1996) Social support in pregnancy: does it have long-term effects? *Journal of Reproductive and Infant Psychology* **14**: 7–22.

Page L (ed.) (1995) *Effective Group Practice in Midwifery.* Oxford: Blackwell.

Page L (1997) Misplaced values: in fear of excellence. *British Journal of Midwifery* **5**(11): 652–4.

Ramsden J (1995) Cultural safety: implementing the concept. *New Zealand College of Midwives Journal* October: 6–9.

Roberts SJ (1983) Oppressed group behaviour: implications for nursing. *Advances in Nursing Science* July: 21–30.

Sims A and Kirkham M (1999) *Report of the Evaluation of the Community Midwifery Pilot Project, Locality 6.* Doncaster: Doncaster Health Authority.

Skinner J (1998) The Jewel in the Crown: A Case Study of the New Zealand College of Midwives Standards Review Process in Wellington. Unpublished MA thesis, Victoria University, Wellington, New Zealand.

Smith P (1992) *The Emotional Labour of Nursing*. London: Macmillan.

Staden H (1998) Alertness to the needs of others: a study of the emotional labour of caring. *Journal of Advanced Nursing* **27**: 147–56.

Stapleton H, Duerden J and Kirkham M (1998) *Evaluation of the Impact of the Supervision of Midwives on Professional Practice and the Quality of Midwifery Care*. London: ENB.

Stewart SM (1999) Midwifery standards review in New Zealand: a personal view. *British Journal of Midwifery* **7**(8): 511–14.

Taylor M (1996) An Ex-midwife's Reflections on Supervision from a Psychotherapeutic Viewpoint. In: Kirkham MJ (ed.) *Supervision of Midwives*. Hale, Cheshire: Books for Midwives Press.

Taylor M (1999) The death of midwifery? *AIMS Journal* **11**(1): 4–6.

Walker JM, Hall S and Thomas M (1995) The experience of labour: a perspective from those receiving care in a midwife-led unit. *Midwifery* **11**: 120–9.

White J (1996) Midwifery: the balance of intuition and research. Paper presented at the New Zealand College of Midwives 1996 Conference, Christchurch.

Wraight A, Ball J, Seccombe I and Stock J (1993) *Mapping Team Midwifery*. Brighton: Institute of Manpower Studies, University of Sussex.

# Index